JU$T
REWARDS

JU$T
REWARDS

*The Case for Ethical
Reform in Business*

David Olive

KEY PORTER BOOKS

Canadian Cataloguing in Publication Data
    Olive, David
        Just rewards

    Includes index.
    ISBN 1-55013-053-6

    1. Business ethics.   2. Corporations — Corrupt
    practices.   I. Title.

HF5387.058   1987   174'.4   C87-094121-6

Key Porter Books Limited
70 The Esplanade
Toronto, Ontario
Canada M5E 1R2

Jacket Design: *David Montle*
Typesetting: *Vellum Print and Graphic Services Inc.*
Printing and Binding: *John Deyell Company*
Printed and bound in Canada

87   88   89   90   6   5   4   3   2   1

CONTENTS

For Margaret Anne

High instincts before which our mortal nature
Did tremble like a guilty thing surprised.
—William Wordsworth

PREFACE

I like business.

After several years of writing about it, I am still awed by people working to transform a mere idea into a thriving commercial enterprise — and in the process creating jobs, useful products and services, and a heightened level of prosperity in the community as a whole. Business nurtures extraordinary qualities in people. The men and women who succeed at it are audacious and self-directed; they have unbounded faith in themselves and their goals and a remarkable ability to stare down the most daunting risks.

The current crisis in business ethics is a betrayal of those qualities and the people who exhibit them. For no matter how isolated, every corporate crime undermines the image of all businesses. Today, these crimes are taking place on an unprecedented scale.

Of course, the history of business, like that of most human endeavours, has been marred by periods of ethical vacuity. But none has been so widespread as the current ethical crisis, which extends beyond the stock market and affects every industry and every profession — such as law and accounting — that serves business. And never before has business possessed so much potential as a destructive force: today, a single decision by one company can lead to a plant explosion that kills thousands of people in India, the manufacture of a medical product that injures tens of thousands of people in America, and the failure of one bank that precipitates a string of bank collapses across an entire country.

The recent proliferation of media accounts of corporate wrongdoing encourages the belief that a conspiracy of evil must be at work in the business world. Yet there is no sinister design behind the insider-trading abuses, the airline-safety violations, the heartless "downsizing" of workforces, the dangerous products, and the toxic spills. In most cases it is simple greed that has led so many companies and individuals astray. And this preoccupation with getting ahead while paying little heed to the consequences is jeopardizing the health of business and of the society in which it operates.

"The pursuit of individual self-aggrandizement, individual gratification, and individual pleasure has led more and more of us into the scramble for wealth and power," says Arthur Schafer, director of the Centre for Professional and Applied Ethics at the University of Manitoba. "Business civilization regards work solely as a means to profit, income, consumption. Creative work ceases to be viewed as an end in itself. The cash nexus replaces the spirit of work; the real value of work is lost." Sadly, cash itself can eventually become something of a malady for its possessor — or such is the assertion of psychiatrists who have noticed that sudden wealth often brings on feelings of isolation, boredom, guilt, and lack of motivation. This condition has become so prevalent doctors have coined a word for it: affluenza.

Immoral behaviour is bad for business. Like an infectious disease, it starts small and spreads until the contagion either is destroyed or has undermined whole companies and entire industries. High corporate crimes such as the sale of dangerous products and wilful abuse of the environment often have their origin in the petty felonies lower down the corporate ladder that continually threaten to sap the moral strength of the average business. Common street crime — muggings and the like — costs the United States about $4 billion a year; white-collar crime exacts a higher toll, in the neighbourhood of $200 billion per year.

White-collar crimes have a highly leveraged impact on the corporate victim. The errant loan officer at a bank who accepts under-the-table payments totalling only a few thousand dollars may imperil the bank by vetting millions of dollars' worth of loans that are sure to go sour. And while payoffs such as free meals, tickets to sporting events, and airfares to exotic locales are easily rationalized as venial indulgences by employees who accept them, the cumulative effect is to make individual companies less efficient and the economy as a whole more vulnerable to competition from abroad. And when moral laxity overtakes an entire industry — as has happened in construction and defence contracting, for instance — that inefficiency is passed on to consumers in the form of high prices. Indeed, sometimes every taxpayer is hit with the cost of cleaning up after rogue businesspeople.

Consider the damage from a single outbreak of irresponsible corporate conduct. When Edmonton's Canadian Commercial Bank and the Northland Bank of Calgary collapsed in the fall of 1985, they were not the only victims of their carelessness. Canadian taxpayers absorbed the multibillion-dollar cost of bailing out the banks' depositors. Fearing that the imprudent lending policies of the CCB and the Northland were widespread among smaller, so-called "second-tier" banks, skittish depositors withdrew their funds from these institutions. This action precipitated the rapid decline of Toronto's Continental Bank of Canada and the Mercantile Bank of Canada and Vancouver's Bank of British Columbia and Morguard Bank of Canada, all of which were forcibly merged out of existence. Shareholders in the banks lost millions of dollars, and the operations of thousands of bank borrowers were disrupted. Chastened by the bank collapses, and the failure of eleven trust companies in recent years, federal policymakers delayed and in some cases abandoned plans to remove legislative restraints that all financial institutions had sought.

Calamities of that sort are transforming what should have been a golden era of business into an era of government crackdowns. Beginning in the late 1970s, pro-business governments in the United States, Canada, Great Britain, and West Germany have given business every opportunity to display, free of constraints, the economic curative powers it has long claimed to possess; even the Soviet Union and China are flirting with primitive forms of capitalism. But the unshackling of chains that limited business's movements has coincided with its seeming inability to tell right from wrong and to act accordingly. The current outbreak of immoral corporate conduct, and the public outcry for reform that it has ignited, have forced these same pro-business governments to turn on the business community that worked so hard to install them in power.

Such is the reluctance of industrial polluters to respect the environment that the U.S. Environmental Protection Agency's inspectors have begun to tote guns. EPA prosecutors now argue in court that the miscreants they have brought to justice are guilty of violent crimes, since pollution shortens victims' lives. In the spring of 1987, the Canadian government introduced a tough environmental-protection bill to replace the cumbersome and ineffectual Environmental Contaminants Act. The new legislation makes pollution a "crime against the environment". It provides for fines of up to $1 million per day and jail terms of up to five years for corporate executives guilty of major pollution offences.

Congress has ordered the U.S. Sentencing Commission to draft uniform guidelines for punishing businesses convicted of a federal crime, a move designed to give judges throughout the country more power to dictate how companies are to become morally straight. The Sentencing Commission's model is the remedy designed by the Securities and Exchange Commission, whose own sanctions against companies found guilty of making improper payments to officials of foreign governments include demanding that the offending company hire outside accountants and lawyers to probe how far the wrongdoing has gone, draw up a corporate code of ethics, and implement training programs to make sure employees know what kind of conduct is lawful and what is not. Within the next few years, the judiciary will have a strong hand in determining how companies that get caught are run.

In 1987 alone, the federal government in Canada will put more than eight hundred new regulations onto the books, including rules governing the transport of dangerous goods, the handling of environmental contaminants, a workplace hazardous-material information system, and a standard national form for reporting insider trading on stock markets. The Ontario government, which oversees Canada's biggest share-trading arena, has reacted to the insider-trading scandals on Wall Street by boosting the fine for insider trading from $25,000 to $1 million and doubling the possible jail term to two years. More prosaic criminal venues are not escaping notice either. The Ontario government has drafted legislation designed to protect consumers from funeral-home operators who declare bankruptcy or abscond with money paid them for prearranged funerals.

Complying with government regulations already costs business $100 billion per year in the United States, and this amount will rise steeply as new regulations hit the books. The amount paid in fines is also soaring as those responsible for enforcement become more vigilant and judges more condemning. If only to mount a holding action against legislators bent on reforming business through more restrictive laws, business must quickly clean house. "Unless the corporation is in fact and perception more accountable to a wider representation of interests beyond that of its own management of the day," says Toronto corporate-ethics consultant J. Richard Finlay, "government will be forced to move in again and ensure a check on business power."

Governments will not be alone in subjecting business to more scrutiny in the next few years. Business now gets unprecedented coverage in television programs, periodicals, and books which are increasingly going beyond rags-to-riches storytelling in order to probe its inner workings. A result of this intense coverage is that topics such as the release of toxic chemicals into the air over Bhopal, the insider-trading scandals, and the distribution of un-safe products like the Dalkon Shield regularly become part of the everyday conversation of millions of people.

Corporate wrongdoers are subject to more public exposure than ever before, and the fallout can be devastating. In July 1987, a federal grand jury accused Chrysler Corp. of systematically replacing or disconnecting the odometers of more than 60,000 cars and trucks that were then driven by company managers for up to 640 km and later sold as new. The revelation threatened to erase the goodwill Chrysler had assiduously cultivated since its brush with bankruptcy almost a decade earlier. Chrysler chairman Lee Iacocca admitted the practice was "unforgivable and we've got nobody but ourselves to blame". While insisting the practice was not illegal, Iacocca promptly unveiled a "goodwill" program of extended warranties to the vehicle-buyers affected. "The only law we broke was the law of common sense," said Iacocca. "[But] this is the court of public opinion and that's what ultimately counts. Life is a matter of perceptions...." Iacocca said a survey taken soon after Chrysler was indicted showed that 69 per cent of the U.S. adult population knew about the indictment within two days of its being issued.

Corporations have for the past few decades been learning about the trouble irate consumers are capable of stirring up. But today even shareholders, who once were the most docile of the average corporation's potential critics, are clamoring for reform. Woodrow Wilson once observed, "The way to stop financial 'joy-riding' is to arrest the chauffeur, not the automobile." Now share-holders, unhappy that their investments suffer while executives who lead their companies into troubled waters go unpunished, are increasingly seeking redress from corporate wrongdoers by hauling executives into court. This situation makes finding people willing to serve as corporate directors onerous, sometimes impossible. A 1986 survey by the accounting firm Touche Ross found that one-third of the 1,126 corporate directors in the United States had been driven by the increased danger of being held liable in lawsuits to consider relinquishing one or more of their board seats. Recruiting the brightest lights on campus isn't easy, either, for a firm making headlines for staying in South Africa or destroying a river. Books such as *In Search of Excellence* and annual lists of best and worst employers in publications as diverse as *Fortune* and *Mother Jones* now steer MBA grads to corporations that promise to deliver the best futures.

The greatest force for reform, though, may be pension funds, which own a huge chunk of corporate North America. Inspired in part by the advent of ethical mutual funds, which entrust individual investors' money to companies deemed to be on the ethical straight and narrow, pension-fund managers are responding to a perception that their own clients are becoming more socially conscious. Hundreds of funds managed on behalf of governments, universities, and labour unions have been forced to withdraw money from companies that invest in South Africa, have been implicated in toxic-waste dumping, have bad labour relations, or refuse to implement affirmative-action programs. "Increasing agitation on the part of shareholders is clearly emerging as a major challenge to North American boardrooms," says Finlay. "The power of such a movement will be all the greater if the sleeping giants of capitalism — including professional and union-run retirement and pension funds — join in the march."[1]

---

1 Fund managers who withdraw their investments from "unethical firms aren't reacting only to their own and their clients' moral qualms. There is cold hard cash at stake, as well. Most studies into the relative profitability of companies that set high moral standards versus those that don't give the former an edge in historical rates of profitability. One of the most interesting studies of this kind was conducted by Mark Pastin, director of the Center for Ethics at Arizona State University. In his 1986 book, *The Hard Problems of Management*, Pastin shows that a list of leading U.S. corporations that have paid dividends during the past one hundred years — one of Pastin's measures of stability and success — roughly coincides with those that have given ethics a high priority. Pastin's study of twenty-five multinationals based in the United States, Great Britain, France, and West Germany reveals a winning formula in which companies such as Motorola, Siemens, Cadbury Schweppes, and 3M enjoy a higher level of profitability than the norm by showing more care for their shareholders than most companies; paying inordinate attention to suppliers, customers, and others they depend on; and encouraging candour among employees.

Of course, the ultimate penalty for immoral conduct is to be put out of business. Bankruptcy has recently claimed many victims of dubious morals: A.H. Robins Co., the maker of the Dalkon Shield; Manville Corp., which for more than a generation deceived consumers and its own factory workers about the dangers of handling asbestos; and Texaco Inc., which is alleged to have illegally pursued its takeover of Getty Oil Co. Hundreds of once-proud banks in the United States that fell victim to the malfeasance of unscrupulous executives are either bankrupt or have been merged out of existence. Faced with hundreds of millions of dollars in Bhopal-related legal claims, Union Carbide Corp., like many companies whose irresponsibility has caught up with them, became vulnerable to stock-market poachers and has had to sell off the most lucrative parts of its business to save its independence.

The last great period of ethical soul-searching in business took place in the early 1970s, in the wake of revelations that multinationals such as Lockheed, ITT, and Gulf Oil had made improper political payments to officials of foreign governments. At the time, management guru Peter Drucker was skeptical that the supposed heightened awareness of ethical concerns by businesspeople would result in lasting change for the better. He wondered if there was "more to 'business ethics' than the revivalist preacher's call to the sinner to repent.... Altogether, 'business ethics' might well be called 'ethical chic' rather than ethics — and indeed might be considered more a media event than philosophy or morals."

Drucker's doubts more than a decade ago were well-advised, given the shaky commitment of that era's business leaders to ethical reform, a concept they did not fully understand and were reluctant to adopt. Today, however, wrongdoing is more widespread, and is no longer just an issue among hulking multinationals. Now it's businesspeople themselves as often as government officials and other outside observers who are pressing for meaningful reforms. "Those who break the law must be punished; institutions should be reformed," says Felix Rohatyn, a leading New York investment banker with more than thirty years' experience. Calling on his peers to co-operate with Congress in shaping new laws to curb corrupt practices, Rohatyn says, "If they do [co-operate], our financial market system will emerge stronger and cleaner from its inevitable torment; if they do not, the resulting legislation could be so punitive as to result in damage to us all." Certainly the pressure for tougher regulations is mounting. U.S. attorney Ralph Giuliani, who spearheaded the drive to round up Wall Street brokers guilty of illegal insider trading in the mid-1980s, disagrees with stock-market officials who insist the market is capable of regulating itself. "I think those people...completely discount human nature and the fact there has to be a certain number of restraints on human behavior in order to create freedom. ... There is a tendency in human nature, when you acquire power, to misuse that power."

This book is concerned with the ethical dimension of corporate power. The first half traces the evolution of business morality from ancient times to the present and explores the factors giving rise to the current moral malaise afflicting the corporate community. The remaining chapters are devoted to an examination of methods by which corporations are attempting to forge lasting internal ethical reforms; the inculcation of moral values in MBA students — the next generation of business leaders; and profiles of consumer advocates, pension-fund managers, and other critics outside the business mainstream who are agitating for corporate ethical reform. The final chapter reveals the innovative means by which many progressive companies and managers are going beyond a strict definition of business's social responsibilities in order to promote the general welfare of the communities in which they operate.

This book would not have been possible without the tireless assistance of the staff of Key Porter Books. I am also grateful to my editor, Charis Wahl, for her enthusiasm and diligence. I wish to acknowledge the generosity of *The Globe and Mail* in granting me a leave of absence in which to complete the book, and to thank Margaret Wente, Peter Cook, and Timothy Pritchard of the *Globe's Report on Business* for their continuing support while it was in progress. I owe special thanks to my parents, and to Ken Tancock, Kenneth Mucha, Don Laing, and Joann Webb, whose inspiration and guidance have for many years been an invaluable touchstone. More recently, it has been the strength I have drawn from friends that has seen me through this project, and my gratitude to them I cannot begin to express.

Every day that I have worked on this book I have been reminded that there are no moral absolutes. It is a frustrating task to discern the black and white of ethical issues when usually neither extreme is visible and one is forced to chart an uncertain course through the dull haze between them. Having made the voyage countless times in an effort to understand what gives rise to ethical quandaries, I admire the businesspeople who make that trip every day. And who can face themselves in the mirror each morning in the knowledge that the means by which they attained their rewards were just.

PART ONE

Prisoners of Mammon

CHAPTER ONE
THE UGLY CAPITALIST

"Wealth accumulates, and men decay." — Oliver Goldsmith

Annals of Avarice: The Dalkon Shield Case

A. H. Robins Co. is no fly-by-night outfit. From its nineteenth century origins as a drugstore in Richmond, Virginia, the company became a thriving, respected multinational enterprise. In 1983, it sold $563 million worth of prescription drugs and such brand-name products as Robitussin cough syrups, Chap Stick lip balm, Dimetapp cold remedy, and Sergeant's pet supplies. That year it turned a record profit of $58 million.

Robins's chairman, E. Claiborne Robins Sr., grandson of company founder Albert Hartley Robins, was as well known to the philanthropic community of Virginia as his firm's products were to druggists throughout the United States and Canada. In 1969, Robins Sr. donated $50 million to the University of Richmond, at the time the largest gift made by a living person to a university or college. The Robins family extended its charity to a multitude of other educational and cultural institutions and causes; in 1983, *Town & Country* magazine placed Robins Sr. among the top five on its list of "The Most Generous Americans". By most accounts, A.H. Robins was a model corporate citizen: It had been active in Richmond Renaissance, a two-year-old effort to revitalize the downtown district of its hometown; and had helped organize "Businesses Who Care", a coalition of Richmond companies that encouraged local businesses to give more generously to charitable activities. And in more than a century of doing business, since it was founded as an apothecary shop soon after the Civil War, A.H. Robins was not known to have attracted even one product-liability lawsuit — a rare accomplishment among major drug firms.

Between 1971 and 1975, the A.H. Robins Co. sold approximately 4.5 million Dalkon Shields in more than eighty countries. The Shield, one of the most aggressively marketed medical products in history, was a crab-shaped intra-uterine device made of plastic with a slender, multifilament "tail string" attached. For a time it was the most widely used IUD in the world.

Being of simple design and materials, the Shield was destined to be a lucrative product under any circumstances. Still, in order to keep production costs low (25¢ per Shield, versus a $4.35 selling price) Robins made the Shields at its Chap Stick plant in Lynchburg, Virginia, where labour and overhead costs were 40 per cent lower than at its main plant in Richmond.

Attached to the Shield was a tail string, which had no medical function but served two purposes: to enable the wearer to make sure the device was in place and to help a medical clinician to remove it. Since the 1960s, the strings on almost all IUDs were monofilaments — that is, a single strand impervious to bacterial invasion. The Shield's tail, by comparison, was a cylindrical sheath containing between 200 and 450 monofilaments separated by spaces. Neither end of this string was sealed. In 1970, just seventeen days after Robins bought the manufacturing rights for the Shield from its inventors, the product-management co-ordinator of Robins's pharmaceutical division warned in an internal memo to thirty-nine top executives that such multifilament strings were reported to exhibit a "wicking" tendency — meaning any bacteria that got into the spaces between the filaments would be protected from the body's natural bacteria-fighting agents as they travelled, or "wicked", their way up the string from the vagina into the uterus to the base of the Shield, to which the string was knotted. One year later, the quality-control supervisor at the Chap Stick plant complained of a lack of quality-control procedures in the Shield's manufacturing process, and also alerted his superiors to the wicking problem, suggesting the simple precaution of using heat to seal the open string ends. To date, at least, there is no evidence the first, 1970, warning was acted upon by Robins. As for the Chap Stick inspector, he testified years later in a Shield-related trial that his warnings were deemed "insubordination" by his immediate boss, who warned the inspector that "my conscience didn't pay my salary." In 1978, the forty-one-year-old inspector, who had raised questions about the quality of several Robins products with his superiors, was forced out of Chap Stick and given six months' severance pay. Officially, he was being let go, the inspector later recalled, because of a "departmental reorganization based on economic motives or something to that effect".

Robins executives in time became vaguely aware that the string was being cited by many doctors and other health professionals as a conduit of bacteria into the uterus, and they gave some thought to replacing the existing tail with a non-wicking version. "Robins searched for an alternative string, but it wasn't a very energetic search," says *Washington Post* investigative reporter Morton Mintz, who wrote a compelling book about the Shield's development, *At Any Cost*, in 1985. Ultimately, the search was abandoned without an alternative string being substituted.

Since it was a device, not a drug, the Shield did not require Food and Drug Administration approval in order to be introduced to the public. Robins did not begin to receive results from its own field tests of the Shield until sales were underway. Long after these tests revealed disturbing efficacy and health problems, Robins continued to promote the Shield as a contraceptive marvel. Doctors and family-planning clinicians derived their assessment of the Shield from promotional material provided by Robins, which in turn based its claims for the Shield's superior effectiveness and safety on questionable data compiled in the late 1960s. The promotional material also did not draw doctors' attention to the fact that, almost alone among IUDs, the Shield employed a multifilament tail string.

The string, as it happened, often snapped. Doctors who broke the tail in attempting to remove the Shield sometimes had to resort to surgery. Further complicating the removal procedure was the Shield's unique design. As a means of strengthening its grip in the uterus, the Shield's badge-like matrix was equipped with four or five spinicules, or fins, protruding from both sides. These "vicious spikes", as a female OB-GYN in Pennsylvania who refused to prescribe the Shield called them, were effective in preventing involuntary expulsion of the IUD. However, they also made the planned removal of the device a painful ordeal for many Shield wearers. Robins had known from the beginning that painkillers would be advisable for many women, but for the first two years it kept that knowledge to itself.

The most obvious problem with the Shield was that it proved five times more likely to fail as a contraceptive than Robins's marketing department had promised: about 110,000 wearers of the device, some 5 per cent of Shield users, became pregnant. But there were more insidious drawbacks which, thanks to the chronically typical misdiagnosis of female ailments by medical practitioners, were not immediately identified as being related to the Shield. Thousands of Shield wearers around the world suffered internal bleeding, pelvic infections, and spontaneous abortions. Many women became sterile. The Food and Drug Administration has recorded fifteen cases in which American women wearing the Shield died from complications following septic spontaneous abortions, a previously rare type of miscarriage. At a 1985 press conference, Robins itself revealed that a study by an outside consultant indicated the Shield may have injured 87,000 to 88,000 of the 2.2 million women in the U.S. who wore it. In certain Third World countries where hygiene and health-care methods are primitive, improperly treated infections caused by the Shield have almost certainly taken a proportionately greater toll among Shield users.

Robins denies the tail of its Shield acted as a conduit of bacteria. In 1974, it withdrew the product from distribution in the U.S. during the course of an interminable debate within the FDA as to whether Robins should be ordered to do so; years later, Robins would cite its voluntary action in asserting that it had acted responsibly.

On February 29, 1984, three senior Robins executives — president Claiborne Robins Jr., great-grandson of the founder; Carl D. Lunsford, senior vice-president for research and development; and William A. Forrest Jr., vice-president and general counsel — appeared in the Minneapolis courtroom of Judge Miles W. Lord. For a decade Robins's lawyers had been vociferously disputing Shield-related claims against the company; they had also quietly made many out-of-court settlements with the proviso that the lawyers representing women who succeeded in their claims against Robins would agree neither to take on other Shield cases nor to share their evidence and courtroom strategies with other lawyers pursuing claims against Robins. In approving a $4.6 million settlement of seven of the then nine thousand Shield-related claims against Robins, Lord expressed his frustration with the company's attitude:

"Today as you sit here attempting once more to extricate your-selves from the legal consequences of your acts, none of you has faced up to the fact that more than nine thousand women claim they gave up part of their womanhood so that your company might prosper. It has been alleged that others gave up their lives so that you might prosper . . . ."

"Yet your company, without warning to women, invaded their bodies by the millions and caused them injuries by the thou-sands. And when the time came for these women to make their claims against your company, you . . . inquired into their sexual practices and into the identity of their sex partners. You ruined families and reputations and careers in order to intimidate those who would raise their voices against you. You introduced issues that had no relationship to the fact that you had planted in the bodies of these women instruments of death, of mutilation, of disease . . . .

"The only conceivable reasons that you have not recalled this product are that it would hurt your balance sheet and alert women who have already been harmed that you may be liable for their injuries . . . .

"If this court had the authority, I would order your company to make an effort to locate each and every woman who still wears this device and recall your product. But this court does not. I must therefore resort to moral persuasion . . . .

"Please, in the name of humanity, lift your eyes above the bot-tom line."

The Robins executives responded by lodging a complaint against Judge Lord. He had, they said, "methodically destroyed their personal and professional reputations" and "grossly abused his office". And so Judge Lord, sixty-four, was like so many Dalkon Shield victims before him, hauled before the bench, and made to listen as Robins's lawyers raised questions about his character.

Not until November 1984, a decade after the Shield was with-drawn from the U.S. market, did Robins launch a global media campaign to alert women to the possible dangers of its IUD and offer to pay the medical costs of removal. In the same month, Robins directors voted to increase the dividend on company shares — 42 per cent of which were owned by the Robins family — to a record 19 cents, three times the 1975 level. Robins was only a few months away from declaring a catastrophic $462 million loss for the year 1984, due mostly to the high payout to IUD claimants. And it was only nine months away from outright bankruptcy: In August 1985, when the crush of IUD claims became too oppressive, Robins took refuge from its creditors by filing for voluntary reorganization, a form of bankruptcy. (By the middle of 1987, the number of Shield-related claims against the company had reached about 320,000, and claimants' lawyers said the $1.85 billion set aside by Robins to satisfy the claims would probably not be sufficient.)

Under the provisions of the bankruptcy, Robins Jr. and his top managers continued to run the company with the court's supervision. Despite the firm's difficulties, they ordered the improper payment out of the Robins treasury of $1.8 million in "deferred bonuses" to 18 present and former executives. Robins Jr. gave his father a raise, more than doubling his annual consulting fee to $100,000. In the fall of 1986, the judge overseeing Robins's bankruptcy froze most of the bonuses, cut Robins Sr.'s fee to $1, and demanded the company helicopter be sold. (Robins Jr. had made substantial personal use of the helicopter to shuttle to golf courses and his country home; he reimbursed the company only for fuel and pilot time.)

In all the above proceedings, no charges were laid against Robins or its executives. The company continues to deny responsibility for injuries alleged to have been caused by the Shield. To this day, it is not clear if the men who run Robins comprehend the severity of the physical and emotional pain inflicted by their product.

"You certainly knew, when you started marketing this device, that pelvic inflammatory disease [PID, an ailment commonly linked to Shield use] was a life-threatening disease, did you not?" a plaintiff's lawyer asked Robins Sr. in a formal deposition in 1984.

"I don't know that," Robins said. "I have never thought of it as life-threatening."

Robins was asked if he knew PID could cause sterility.

"Maybe I should, but I don't know that," Robins said. "I have heard that. I am not sure where."

Certainly the Shield victims now have an intimate knowledge of PID. If the company's protestations of ignorance are true, they wonder how it is that the people who run a major pharmaceutical concern can fail to know what their products are capable of doing to a person's body. They wonder why Reagan-era economic libertarians, deeming the FDA an obstruction to free enterprise, would want to do away with it when the FDA and the accumulation of three generations' worth of consumer-protection legislation had presented no obstacle to the Shield's being put on the market.

But mostly they wonder why Robins at this late stage still considers itself in the throes of a financial and not an ethical crisis. As one victim who chose not to endure a court trial said, "Money's fine, but were they going to give me my ovaries back? Are you going to give me a boy child and a girl child? Maybe for that I would have waited for trial."

A Moral Siesta

> "The meek shall inherit the earth,
> but not the mineral rights."
> —J. Paul Getty

There are times when business appears to be the triumph of money over morals. This is one of them.

History is pockmarked with periods of selfish grasping and material excess, of course. But the 1980s should not have become one of these. The unbridled strivings of the Gilded Age's robber barons and the manic speculations of Roaring Twenties plungers gave rise to legislative reforms expressly designed to protect society from those who would peddle shoddy goods, manipulate the stock market, or swindle depositors out of their life savings. These advances, most of them forged during the Great Depression, were bolstered in the decades that followed. During the 1950s, when professional managers succeeded autocratic proprietors at the head of major business enterprises, companies instituted reforms to become more responsive to social issues and to the rights of their shareholders. They became still more responsible during the 1960s and 70s, when governments imposed strict new rules against polluters, companies that made improper political payoffs at home and abroad, and those that discriminated against women and minorities in their hiring practices.

And yet, so soon after the enlightenment and soul-searching of the 1960s and early 1970s, and despite unprecedented numbers of legal safeguards, business today is in a moral crisis of epidemic proportions. Scores of banks and other financial institutions across North America are collapsing, and in about two-thirds of cases criminal activity by executives is to blame. Other banks stand accused of not helping law-enforcement officials stem the laundering of $100 billion through banks each year even though the practice is the lifeblood of organized crime. Millions of gallons of toxic wastes are dumped indiscriminantly into lakes, rivers, and municipal sewer systems. Thousands of products known by their makers to be faulty or even dangerous are sold to an unsuspecting public. In unsafe Canadian workplaces one worker is injured every twelve seconds; and defence contractors in the United States steal their government blind. Ottawa extends a helping hand to fledgling entrepreneurs with a Scientific Research Tax Credit program; while many firms taking advantage of the program operate legitimate businesses, hundreds of scam artists forsake any thought of science and instead conduct research into clever new ways to defraud the government, collectively bilking the SRTC program of about $1 billion.

Nowhere is the malaise more evident than on Wall Street, where there is a bull market in scandals. Unfairly advantaged traders use inside information to pile up multimillion-dollar fortunes in an afternoon and rogue informants spread false news in order to manipulate stock prices. One venerable and respected brokerage house steals from its bankers while another trades cocaine for secret information. Corporate "raiders" extort huge sums from publicly traded companies by demanding that their own small stock holdings in a targeted company be bought back at an outrageous premium — a threat entrenched managements submit to in order to keep their jobs.

But the maladies of the market are only symptomatic of a business world in which nothing is quite what it appears — where counterfeit goods account for 3 per cent of world trade, and only 16 per cent of products billed as "new and improved" are more than cosmetically altered. And while much of the banditry is concocted in boardrooms, companies are undermined by internal theft — bribes, kickbacks, and expense-account cheating. Indeed, underlying the high corporate crimes that attract media attention is an individual moral laxity that leads ordinary people to "forget" to declare income for tax purposes or to sell a car to a stranger rather than a friend because they know the transmission is about to fall out.

Sadly, the current amorality owes largely to a narcissism that has sprung from the ruins of 1960s liberalism. The young champions of the 60s causes — civil rights, urban renewal, the war on poverty at home and abroad, environmental protection, U.S. withdrawal from Vietnam — lost most of their battles and felt betrayed by the political leadership of the times. Eventually, the flower children hung up their beads and, promising they would someday return to the battlefields of social reform, signed up as lawyers, accountants, and investment bankers. Business-school enrolments soared throughout North America. The shift in goals is most starkly evident in Quebec, which had always trained its children to be clerics, academics, and solicitors; Quebec now leads Canadian provinces in the production of business graduates.

Comfortably ensconced in their office-tower aeries, many of the biz grads and lawyers who have chosen corporate life out of a sense of self-preservation imagine that business is all about creating jobs, useful products, and a better standard of living for us all. Certainly that is what corporate recruiters, delighted that finally business is respectable on campus again, have been telling them. Unfortunately, when the new recruits are exposed to the underside of business life, most choose not to agitate for reform but to look out for Number One. The first priority, when faced with the pressing responsibilities of living in the right neighbourhoods, driving the right cars, and frequenting the right vacation retreats, is to make the imperfect and unseemly system work for oneself. Former student protester Jerry Rubin, who now runs a chain of "business networking" salons and claims to have invented the term "Yuppie" (for young urban professional), insists his generation is still a force for social reform. "We haven't sold out," he says. "We're taking over!" Indeed they are, but Rubin's fellow 60s barricade-basher Abbie Hoffman thinks their priorities are skewed. "Of course the Yuppies worry about nuclear war," Hoffman says. "It would interfere with their career plans."

Shorn of its many disguises, business is properly viewed not as a system for creating jobs, improving the quality of life, enfranchising black South Africans, or making possible "Masterpiece Theatre" and touring art exhibitions. These things may accompany, but are always incidental to, making a profit. The noted Chicago economist Milton Friedman said it first in 1964, and his oft-repeated thesis holds today with most corporate managers:

"Few trends could so thoroughly undermine the very foundation of our free society as the acceptance of a social responsibility [for companies] other than to make as much money for their stockholders as possible. This is a fundamentally subversive doctrine."

This concern with profits need not, in itself, lead to unethical conduct. Indeed, most companies set out to make a *moral* profit. "The first responsibility of any business," says corporate ethics consultant J. Richard Finlay, "is to not knowingly do harm — and to make certain that it knows no harm is being done."

Yet, inherent in capitalism is the inevitability that harm *will* be done. For while the pursuit of profits does create better products, increased employment and tax revenues for needy communities, it is a lot like sports and war. In order for a company to win — and it must keep winning or it will wither and die — somebody else generally loses. Just as the automobile put the buggy-whip-makers out of business, so the modern corporate struggle to wrest market share from rivals threatens the very existence of every industry's weakest players. In the capitalistic system, which economist Joseph Schumpeter calls "creative destruction", the goal of every capable manager is ultimately to prevail over his rivals — putting them out of business before they annihilate him.

All too often, what distinguishes the weak from the strong is not innovative products, efficient production, and competitive pricing but a willingness to cut corners on quality, workplace safety, careful husbandry of the environment, and a wilful abridgment of the Old Testament proscriptions against lying, cheating, and stealing. The only meaningful standard becomes profitability. Profits are not only a way of keeping score; they provide a war-chest to fund new skirmishes.

Once, many arbitrary, autocratic company founders, for all their faults, worried as much about their firms' images and the quality of their products — their legacy to their children — as about the daily profit-and-loss figures. By contrast, today's senior executives, running companies owned by thousands of anonymous shareholders, look often only on the stock market — not on their clients, workers, or their own progeny — as their jury. They assess their performance according to the profit and revenue increases they are able to coax from a company during a, say, six-year tour of duty. Meanwhile, middle managers often are not overly concerned with winning the respect and approval of a CEO unlikely to be around long enough to notice or promote them. Like free agents in sports, many rising young stars in business angle for advancement in firms they do not yet work for: since salary increases are highest when one trades up to a better job at a different company, the temptation is to shine brightly in a job—without consideration of the long-term adverse consequences of one's actions—until the headhunters appear.

Executives have another powerful incentive to boost short-term performance. Just as the nuclear era tends to make one live for today because there may not be too many tomorrows, the average corporate manager is faced with a clear and present danger. His or her failure to produce successive quarter-by-quarter profit increases and maintain high stock prices leaves the company vulnerable to corporate takeover artists stalking Bay and Wall streets—and a takeover could cost a senior manager his or her job. It is this performance paranoia, coupled with the instant gratification of bonuses tied to profit results, that makes corporations so uninterested in the long-term consequences of dubious activities. The pressure to perform isolates most executives from the concerns of the outside world. At a Toronto cocktail party in the summer of 1986, a senior Royal Bank of Canada money-market trader described the frantic pace of his work. When it was suggested that his job required the skills of an air-traffic controller, the banker was indignant. "You don't understand," he bellowed. "An air-traffic controller is only dealing with lives. We're talking about *money.*"

Not so long ago, business people, particularly in Canada, were loathe to reveal greed as a motive. Only mavericks such as Toronto developer Joseph Burnett provided glimpses into the greed ethic. "Homo sapiens is a selfish, self-centred being who does everything for his or her own benefit," Burnett told the now-defunct *Quest* magazine in 1972. "It may help someone else, but that is incidental." But in the 1980s, greed is openly acknowledged, and respectable. At a conference on Native Canadian business enterprises in 1986, Barbara McDougall, then minister of state for finance, celebrated the rise of Native-owned businesses. "There's one underlying motive in business shared by all—it's greed," said McDougall, who once worked in the securities industry. "We support it wherever it happens." Joe Burnett now has blue-chip company. "Greed," Toronto financier

Conrad Black told Peter Newman, "has been severely under-estimated and denigrated. There is nothing wrong with avarice as a motive, as long as it doesn't lead to anti-social conduct."

But greed does bring out the worst in people — and in corporations. At the best of times, it encourages expediency. Forty years ago, Hooker Chemical Co. determined that the cheapest means of disposing of waste from its chemical plant at Niagara Falls, N.Y., was to dump it in an abandoned nineteenth-century canal. In the late 1970s, this deadly chemical brew, which included dioxin, the most toxic substance ever synthesized by man, began to leak through the crumbling walls of the canal. The residents of some five hundred nearby homes experienced abnormally high rates of miscarriages, birth defects, and other health disorders. Love Canal became the archetype of industrial poisoning of the environment.

Greed also encourages an unfathomable insensitivity. The manufacturers of Thalidomide and of the Dalkon Shield, which inflicted irreparable injury and caused innumerable deaths, sold their products in spite of warnings by their own scientific advisers. In the 1970s, the Ford Motor Co. distributed Pintos long after reports were filed that in accidents in which Pintos were struck from behind, the gas tank exploded, incinerating the car's occupants. According to an internal document leaked to the press, Ford executives used National Highway Traffic Safety Administration figures to estimate the relative financial merits of recalling the car for repairs versus leaving the cars on the road compensating the likely number of complainants for burn injuries and deaths:

Cost to Ford of settlements:
180 burn injuries @ \$67,000 = \$12,100,000 ⎫
180 burn deaths @ \$200,000 = \$36,000,000 ⎭ \$48,100,000

Pinto repair cost:
12,454,545 cars @ \$11 = \$137,000,000

The arithmetic was compelling: the Pinto was not recalled.

Not every company is so much a captive of its bottom line, of course. In the early 1960s, when J.C. Penney Co. received a few insurance claims on radios sold in its stores that had caught fire in its purchasers' homes, Penney tested the radio at its in-house product-quality centre. Although fewer than 1 percent of the radios tested were defective, Penney stopped selling the line, alerted the manufacturer, placed national ads informing customers of the potential hazard, and offered immediate refunds.

Similarly, Hewlett-Packard, the large computer manufacturer, wasted no time in recalling a slightly flawed version of its 1290-A blood-pressure transducer, a vital piece of equipment used in hospital operating rooms. A large number of units were being returned for repair from two hospitals, where improper cleaning methods had caused the machine to give inaccurate blood-pressure readings. There had been no reports of machines that had been properly cleaned giving inaccurate readings, and there was every reason to expect that operating-room personnel would immediately detect false readings from an impaired 1290-A. An FDA-supervised recall would be embarrassing and might damage H-P's reputation. However, prompted by even the slimmest possibility that someone under the knife in an operating room somewhere in the world might die or suffer severe injury because one of its products malfunctioned, H-P recalled all 50,000 units from around the world—at a cost in the millions of dollars.

Johnson & Johnson of New Jersey made the same calculation in 1982 when it learned a psychopath had contaminated some of its Tylenol analgesic capsules with cyanide. Tylenol accounted for the largest single share of J&J's profits. In a highly publicized campaign, however, J&J recalled $100 million worth of the product from supermarket and drugstore shelves.

Possibly J&J had followed the only possible course of action, but its response struck most Americans as heroic. *The Washington Post* lauded J&J for being "a company willing to do what's right regardless of cost" and J&J's chief executive was publicly congratulated by Phil Donahue and his audience.

The sad lesson of Tylenol may be the fact that so many people were surprised that J&J did "the right thing", given the extent of corporate wrongdoing often perpetrated by the most respected and venerable of companies. In 1986, Exxon Corp., the world's largest oil company, was fined $2.1 billion for overcharging customers on oil deliveries from a Texas oilfield between 1975 and 1980. Toronto-based Suncor Inc., an oil firm 25 per cent-owned by the government of Ontario, was fined $200,000—the largest fine of its kind—for breaching anti-combines legislation in attempting to control gasoline prices by forbidding one of its dealers to slash prices (in other words, for behaving as if there was a free-enterprise environment).

These days, whole industries appear to have taken a holiday from ethics. Deregulation of the U.S. airline industry quickly led to cutthroat competition among established carriers and dozens of upstart operators. This was accompanied by cost-paring drives which, in part, were responsible for a tremendous surge in safety violations. Alarmed by a sudden increase in air-traffic deaths to a level not seen for almost a decade, the U.S. Federal Aviation Administration made a sweeping inspection of airline maintenance programs in 1985 and 1986, uncovering tens of thousands of safety infractions. The agency imposed fines of millions of dollars on almost every major U.S. carrier, including Eastern Air Lines Inc. (accused of 78,000 safety violations), Pan American World Airways Inc., American Airlines Inc., Western Airlines Inc., and Continental Airlines Corp.

Defence contractors have similarly been overcome by a collective moral lapse. With $320 billion a year to spend on new toys and repairs to old ones, perhaps it's no surprise the Pentagon has been suckered into buying $500 hammers and $7,200 coffee-makers. In 1985, the U.S. Air Force asked General Electric Co. and United Technologies Inc. to pay back $208 million in alleged overbillings. Altogether, some four hundred suppliers have been suspended or permanently barred from defense contracts lately; in 1986, nine of the Pentagon's top ten private-sector contractors were under criminal investigation for alleged kickbacks and other fraud. The probes have resulted in convictions against several firms including General Electric, Litton Industries Inc., and Sperry Corp. (now Unisys Corp.).

In some cases, questionable behaviour has taken the form of a concerted effort to make the public pay for an industry's mistakes. Many insurance companies, for example, deceived the public in the mid-1980s. In a reckless drive to steal market share from one another in the early 1980s, property and casualty insurers slashed their premium rates. All the insurers had to show for their efforts after a few years was a sea of red ink. Determined to get back into the black, insurers posted shocking premium hikes and denied coverage to entire industries. For a time, they hid their rank mismanagement by blaming the exorbitant premiums and debilitating insurance shortage on skyrocketing court awards—a bid for self-absolution which, on closer inspection, proved only that the insurers were adept at publicizing a few cases of staggering court awards to their own considerable advantage. The industry is healthier now, and its outrageous past conduct is matched only by its audacity in trying to win back business—and goodwill—in the aftermath of the "crisis". When school boards in Ontario, which had suffered premium hikes of up to 600 per cent and even denial of coverage, attempted to establish a joint self-insurance scheme, the Insurance Brokers Association of Ontario cried foul, claiming that the school boards "tried to raise a spectre of fear and uncertainty that liability insurance for school boards may not be available in the future, or that its costs would be prohibitive." Well, who first gave them a reason to be fearful and uncertain?

Alarmingly, greed has attacked the very nerve centre of business—the financial-services industry. In 1985, Canada had fourteen Canadian-owned chartered banks. In 1986, it had eight. The most devastating collapses were those of the Canadian Commercial Bank of Edmonton and the Northland Bank of Calgary in the fall of 1985, the first bank failures in Canada since 1923. The managers of the banks argued that the weakened Western Canadian economy had crippled the ability of their lending clients to pay interest on their loans. However, most of the bad loans, the chief federally appointed investigator of the CCB disaster declared, were "bad the day they were written". In his haste to transform the young CCB into a major lending power, founding president G. Howard Eaton had engaged in imprudent lending. His successor, Gerald McLaughlan, simply reconditioned the bad loans—that is, wrote new loans that incorporated the old ones plus unpaid interest—and gave fresh loans to dubious credit risks in order to bolster CCB's dwindling asset base.

The most galling aspect of this levitation act, however, was the way all the fees generated by so much indiscriminate lending activity enabled the CCB, and to a lesser extent, the Northland, to report relatively healthy earnings even as they teetered on the precipice of ruin. On that basis, investors continued to buy shares in CCB and Northland, and the banks were able to satisfy regulators as to their solvency. When it was too late—federal authorities were forced to close the two banks in September 1985—Canadian taxpayers footed the bill for reimbursing the banks' depositors, and shareholders saw their investment wiped out.

Imprudent, and sometimes illegal, practices led to the downfall of many other Canadian financial institutions during the 1980s: Astra Trust Co., Re-Mor Investment Management, Argosy Financial Group of Canada, Crown Trust Co., Greymac Trust Co., Seaway Trust Co., and Fidelity Trust Co. The chief executive officer of Argosy, which went into receivership in 1980, was sentenced in 1985 to six and a half years in jail after being found guilty with three colleagues of bilking about a thousand small investors out of $24 million in savings. The victims included the CEO's father, who lost $300,000 as a result of Argosy mismanagement. One last-ditch attempt to save the firm involved gambling away $11,000 in a day at the race track. Alas, Argosy investors didn't get out of the gate.

What factors have given rise to this corporate crime wave? For starters, unlike the perpetrator of a mugging or assault, the white-collar criminal seldom confronts his or her victim. The insider-trading scandal, for instance, was spurred on by the lack of readily identifiable "victims". Suppose, for example, an investor decides to unload shares in ABC Corp., not knowing the firm is about to be taken over by another company at a generous premium. Does it matter that the person buying those shares from the investor has been tipped off about the looming takeover? The seller wants to sell anyway; the buyer hasn't pressured the seller into dumping the shares. Besides, if the person with inside information doesn't buy the stock, someone else will. There are even a few respected academics who argue that insider trading is essential—it ensures that stock prices immediately reflect all available information.

You'll notice, though, that the people who hold to this view are not rallying to have the insider-trading or other meddlesome laws changed. If a law is holding them back, they just go ahead and break it. And in this practice corporate miscreants are hardly alone. General lawlessness has taken hold among those in the front lines of social reform as well. Agitators on both sides of the abortion debate, for instance, regularly break the law, as do animal-rights activists and newspaper editors testing publication restrictions on search warrants.

In fact, business people often consider themselves caught up in righteous causes when impatience drives them to ignore laws they do not like. In October 1986, supermarket giant Loblaws Ltd. decided to strike a blow against Ontario's prudish liquor-vending laws by advertising that it would deliver cases of wine to any home in Toronto, Ottawa, and London that requested this service. The scheme was promptly shut down by the Liquor Control Board of Ontario, which branded it "simply unlawful".

The Bank of Nova Scotia, possibly the most conservatively run of Canada's Big Six banks, set up a full-scale investment-banking operation in Quebec. The audacious move, legal in Quebec but a challenge to regulations in other provinces and to federal banking law, enabled Scotiabank to get a jump on its banking rivals. In the fall of 1986, retailers across Canada mounted a determined assault on Sunday closing laws, hoping that by staying open en masse they would force provinces to scrap venerable restrictions on Sunday shopping. (In December 1986, a Supreme Court of Canada decision upheld the Sunday closing laws.)

Laws don't seem to carry much authority in part because of the light-handed punishment meted out to those who break them, and which punishment serves to perpetuate wrongdoing — indeed, almost to sanctify it.

If ordinary citizens had the awesome resources of corporate criminals the prison population would shrink considerably. Executives rarely feel the sting of judicial rebuke; usually companies, not the people who run them, are hauled into court. While XYZ Co. may collect a fistful of judicial and regulatory censures for ripping off its shareholders, committing unspeakable acts against the environment or making products that kill or maim people, XYZ executives continue to walk the streets without fear of being run out of town on a rail. They are not responsible, the company is. Besides determining and assigning blame within a multibillion-dollar enterprise with tens of thousands of bureaucrats is not easy.

Corporate crimes are tough to prosecute. Usually there are no witnesses, and intent is often impossible to prove. There are no board meetings at which the president says, "Let's whip up some deceptive ads" or "Keep pumping dioxin into the river — no one swims in it anyway." Evidence of this sort, the prosecutors' so-called "smoking gun", is rare. Instead, muckrakers and prosecutors must sift through countless corporate decisions that merely hint at impropriety, and assign blame for acts that no single executive is responsible for. Within corporations, projects of dubious legality may be given code names. Motives for illegal acts may be hidden behind vague euphemisms and outright misnomers. Schemes to circumvent pollution-abatement laws, for instance, may be described in company documents as "Environmental Compliance Procedures"; and a strategy to unload shoddy products may be buried in an "Enhanced Product Safety Guidelines" manual.

The most effective shield for corporate wrongdoers, however, is the "line of command" at most major companies. Communication is usually "top-down". This means line managers get their orders, and are not invited to discuss the implications of those orders with the senior managers who issued them. Indeed, they risk being labelled troublemakers if they do—and troublemakers have stunted careers, which explains why, when problems erupt, the trouble often can be traced to overzealous managers and division chiefs who have complied with head office's orders for higher profits and lower costs, often by latching onto the most obvious—and illegal—option.

Because corporate crimes are so difficult to prove, prosecutors indulge in various forms of plea-bargaining in order to obtain a conviction or at least a fine. In many cases involving serious corporate crimes, defendants are convicted on pleas of *nolo contendre* (no contest), which are tantamount to guilty pleas but do not carry the same stigma. Another weak-kneed but prevalent device is the consent decree, in which companies and executives neither affirm nor deny past delinquencies, but affirm they will not commit said offences in the future. In 1986, household products distributor Amway Corp. of Michigan was fined $100,000 in settlement of federal-government charges that its nationwide newspaper ad campaign exaggerated the earnings potential of an Amway distributorship. Typically, Amway was not required to admit guilt. Can a bank robber pay a modest fine, admit no guilt, and promise to not rob any more banks?

Fines seldom reflect either the magnitude of the crime or the ability of a company to pay. Indeed, the court costs in such cases often exceed the fine with the result that many firms prefer to pay fines rather than curb their unlawful activities. Delaware governor Pierre S. Du Pont IV said as much in accusing a company that bears his name, leading Delaware employer E.I. du Pont de Nemours, of preferring to pay a $500-a-day fine than stop its pollution of state waterways. Governor Du Pont recommended the fine be raised to $10,000 or $20,000 a day. In Louis Auchincloss' bestselling 1986 novel, *Diary of a Yuppie*, Robert Service, a young corporate lawyer, defines what passes for corporate morality in the 1980s: "There is no particular moral opprobrium in incurring a penalty," Service says, "any more than there is in being offside in football. . . . You break the rules, pay the penalty and go back to the game."

In a late 1970s crackdown on insider trading, the Securities & Exchange Commission, the U.S. stock-market watchdog, accepted *nolo* pleas from most of the malefactors it brought into court — and, surprise, insider trading became an even bigger scandal in the mid-1980s. There have been few insider-trading convictions in Canada. After failing for several years to assemble enough proof to bring an insider-trading case, the Ontario Securities Commission won a case in 1983. Come Carbonneau, while chief executive of Corporation Falconbridge Copper of Toronto, bought shares of the company just before it issued a press release on a favourable assay on one of the firm's test holes. Carbonneau made a profit of $3,125 on the 1981 transaction. Two years later he was fined $150. A few months later, a former executive of insurer Scottish & York Holdings Ltd. of Toronto pleaded guilty to charges of failing to report insider trades and was fined $3,900.

Even with tougher laws on the books and more severe punishments handed down though, many entrepreneurs could probably still be counted on to resort to the petty larcenies that are sometimes an unavoidable part of getting a new business off the ground. Firms in their start-up phase are characterized by a struggle for survival, in which ethical considerations are not a high priority. Japan's Sony Corporation, long cited as an avatar of astute Far Eastern management worthy of North American emulation, came out with its first "pocketable" transistor radio in 1957. Alas, the item was just a bit too big to fit into a man's standard shirt pocket. So Sony outfitted its salespeople with slightly larger-than-normal shirt pockets — just big enough to slip the pocketable radio into. Deception of a different sort saved McDonald's Corp. from a trip to the business boneyard. From the beginning, in the late 1950s, founder Ray Kroc was intent on putting a McDonald's stand in every town in America. But in order to attract financing to build all those restaurants, McDonald's needed a healthy income statement with which to overcome the skepticism of bankers, who were certain fast food was a passing fad. Unfortunately, McDonald's didn't have any profits. So it essentially made them up. "We fully disclosed everything in the footnotes," McDonald's then accountant, Gerry Newman, told John Love in *McDonald's: Behind the Arches*. Basically, McDonald's calculated its expected future earnings — on the basis that all would go *well*, of course — and displayed these optimistic projections so prominently as to ensure they would be mistaken for actual earnings. "Our numbers were funny numbers, but without them we never would have gotten the loans to expand," says Newman, "because we didn't have real profits."

A similar cash shortage plagued Richard Branson, thirty-five, founder of Great Britain's dynamic conglomerate Virgin Group, whose record arm boasts such artists as Phil Collins. In one of his early ventures, a mail-order discount-record operation, a scarcity of funds drove Branson to make ends meet by using a variety of tricks. "We would post the top three [record] packages and hope the postman wouldn't notice that the other five hundred underneath weren't stamped," Branson says. "Then we'd go to different post offices when we got caught." But after narrowly avoiding a jail term in 1970 for an attempt to evade taxes, Branson was cured. "A rap on one's knuckles at a young age ensures that you never get tempted again."

Unfortunately, this is hardly a universal truism. Even if it were, when business people succumb to the siren song of illicit profit, once can be too often.

Annals of Avarice: The Saga of Jeffrey Levitt

Jeffrey Alan Levitt looted the Old Court Savings & Loan Association of Baltimore City, Maryland. Unfortunately, the damage didn't stop there.

Called to the Maryland bar in 1970 at the age of twenty-eight, Levitt worked for several years as a real-estate-settlement attorney. By 1978, he had become secretary, general counsel, and settlement attorney for First Progressive Savings & Loan Association Inc., where he repeatedly breached his fiduciary responsibility by withholding funds due to First Progressive. Levitt also arranged loans to himself; the interest payments on these loans were typically in arrears. In early 1982, Levitt and an associate bought control of First Progressive, and in September of the same year—using funds stolen from First Progressive—bought a majority interest in the much larger Old Court Savings & Loan.

As president of Old Court between 1982 and 1985, Levitt systematically embezzled the thrift institution, in part by charging it sky-high management fees for consulting services he often did not provide. In order to fatten up Old Court's deposit base, Levitt launched a nationwide advertising campaign that promised interest rates among the highest in the land. The new deposit money flooded in during 1984 and early 1985, even though Old Court's finances were precarious. The depositors could not have known this, however, since by 1984 the glossy financial statements of Old Court were works of fiction, falsified in order to mask the thrift's true financial condition to both clients and regulators.

In total, Levitt stole and misappropriated $14.7 million from Old Court before the spring of 1985, when the fragile institution finally disintegrated. Responding to charges arising from Old Court's insolvency, Levitt pleaded guilty to twelve counts of grand theft and thirteen counts of breach of fiduciary responsibility. He drew a sentence of thirty years' imprisonment. It was the biggest case of white-collar crime in Maryland history, and one of the stiffest sentences ever imposed on a white-collar outlaw.

In happier times, Levitt and his wife, Karol, had spent and spent and spent. There were two condos, seventeen luxury cars, a stable of racehorses, a Rolls-Royce golf cart with a TV and stereo tapedeck in the dash. Outside one house was an $18,000 putting green. Inside another, fifteen sterling creamers and thirty-three sterling trays. ("Who did they think would come over for dinner," the *Washington Post Magazine* wondered. "The Sixth Fleet?") The Levitts joined a few country clubs. Then they bought one.

During his two-and-a-half-year tenure as Old Court president, Levitt had erased some of the stigma of an earlier career as a slum landlord notorious for housing-code violations (a tenant once shot at him). He was influential, and his bid for respectability through the donation of Old Court funds to charity had begun to pay social dividends.

After being knocked off his Old Court pedestal, however,

Levitt and his wife were subjected to scorn and ridicule. Locals referred to them as "The Couple That Ate Baltimore". There were stories about the time, at Baltimore's Belvedere Hotel, that Jeffrey and Karol, after a full dinner, in front of witnesses, each ate six desserts. There were Levitt jokes: What do you call their water-bed? The Bay of Pigs. How did they get her into her jail cell? Greased the bars and threw in a Twinkie.

On the steamy, grey morning of July 2, 1986, Jeffrey Levitt was led into a cramped Baltimore courtroom. The viewing stands were crowded with curious onlookers, whose emotions ranged from contempt for Levitt's having blown his chance to live out the American Dream to envy at his having come so close. Levitt was not the spectacle of bloated consumerism his audience had expected, however. He had lost a lot of weight during the six months he had already spent in jail on a contempt-of-court charge for having overspent the $1,000-a-week allowance that had already been imposed on him. Levitt had shrunk to about two hundred pounds. His eyes were clouded, lifeless. When he spoke, the old mirth was gone from his voice.

The real surprise, though, was that he was sorry. Sorry that 35,000 Old Court depositors' funds were still frozen. Sorry that the taxpayers of Maryland would have to spend millions of dollars cleaning up his mess and restoring a sense of stability to the savings-and-loan system.

The spending, Levitt said, "became a compulsion . . . it just grows and grows. . . . You get carried away." Levitt had not looked beyond the bottom line. But he had a conscience, after all — if not before being brought to justice, then after six months of solitary introspection. "I accept full responsibility," he told the judge in the hushed Baltimore courtroom. "It was wrong. I did it myself. I did it with other people. . . . There's no denying it."

The judge called Levitt a "disgrace". Then the last president of Old Court Savings & Loan was led away, shuffling awkwardly in his leg irons.

They say Levitt now teaches math to his fellow inmates. State officials have been doing their sums, too. Old Court's collapse triggered a run on Maryland's entire $9 billion savings-and-loan industry, which was curtailed only after the personal intervention of Governor Harry Hughes. In the aftermath, Maryland regulators are calculating how much bailing out Old Court depositors is going to bloat the state deficit. And they wonder, naturally enough, about the implications of deregulating financial institutions — a trend well underway in the United States, Canada, and Britain — when two generations' worth of legislative safeguards did not begin to protect Jeffrey Alan Levitt from the general public or himself.

CHAPTER TWO
THE EVOLUTION OF
BUSINESS MORALITY

Business has always been a force for good and evil. There are obvious virtues of business—in particular, the opportunity it offers people who take it up to strive for self-sufficiency and true independence. Yet it also has few equals as a destructive force, one which through history has crushed the human spirit and made morality its hostage. To chart the progress of business through the ages is to appreciate why the term "business ethics" is often dismissed as oxymoronic, and why business has more commonly been the subject of cynical populist scorn than celebrated, as it also rightly should be, as a liberator of mankind.

Disaffection with commerce started early, with Hammurabi, king of Babylonia. A pluralistic society with a free market thrived in Hammurabi's kingdom between the Tigris and Euphrates rivers, but by 1800 BC wanton thievery among peddlars and contractors had become a serious problem. So serious that in order to curb cutthroat competition among rival builders and grain merchants, Hammurabi was compelled to draft laws against overcharging, shoddy work, and ripping off one's business partners —a precursor of today's agitation for laws to protect minority shareholders. Hammurabi's laws were etched in stone on a black tablet known as the Hammurabi stele, and the King decided it would be a good idea if businesspeople started putting things in writing, too. Four millennia before lawyers became an oppressive fact of business life, Hammurabi insisted—as much to protect businesspeople from one another as to protect the public from businesspeople—that commercial transactions be accompanied by written contracts, signed in front of witnesses. Indeed, Hammurabi took this rather more seriously than is the custom today, to judge from the penalty for failing to comply: "Law 7: If a man has bought silver, gold, manservant or maidservant, ox or sheep or ass or anything whatever from a man's son or slave, without witness or bonds, or has received the same on deposit, that man has acted as a thief, and shall be put to death."

One thousand years later, businesspeople had yet to win the trust and affection of the citizens. The Greek philosopher Plato, whose influence on the study of ethics is as powerful now as when he was alive, was openly contemptuous of business — as one can see in this excerpt from his *Laws*: "There are not many of us who remain sober when they have the opportunity to grow wealthy. The great multitude of men are of a clear contrary temper: what they desire they desire out of all measure; when they have the option of making a reasonable profit, they prefer to make an exorbitant one." What's more, Plato did not foresee a day when businesspeople would redeem themselves, or a time when business would be a calling worthy of the most civilized of men:

> What remedy, then, can be found for the disease [of business] in an intelligent society? Well, the remedy is, in the first place, that the numbers of those employed in trade be kept as low as possible; next, that such occupations be assigned to the sort of men whose corruption will not do great mischief to society; thirdly, some means must be found to prevent the characters of those actually engaged in these callings from readily taking the contagion of complete abandonment and baseness . . .

The anti-business sentiment of Greece spread to classical Rome, where the orator Cicero held most forms of business, and in particular, speculation, in low esteem. "We must also consider mean those who buy from merchants in order to resell immediately," Cicero said, "for they would make no profit without much outright lying." The Romans were more determined even than Hammurabi to bring businesspeople to heel. The Code of Justinian, which began in AD 529, attempted to hold entire industries accountable for the transgressions of any of their members: "Any offence committed by one renders the entire number responsible, which rule has been established to cause them to be more careful in the selection of their members, and exercise supervision over their acts, since the loss sustained by one is felt by all." And brand names, which today trumpet the purportedly superior attributes of one product over another, were imposed by the Justinian Code as a means of keeping track of unscrupulous makers of shoddy goods: "Indelible marks — that is, well-known brands — should be placed upon the arms of apprentices to manufacturers, so that they may easily be recognized, if they should attempt to conceal themselves."

But the Justinian Code, with its 4,652 laws, is not the best-remembered admonition of business dating from Roman times. At a point very early in the days of the Roman Empire, when Israelites over the age of twenty were required to pay a half-shekel into the sacred treasury as an offering to Jehovah, enterprising dealers set up their tables in the temple at Jerusalem and peddled the scarce Hebrew coins for as high a premium as the market would bear. When Jesus cast these money-changers out of the temple, accusing them of turning the holy premises into "a den of thieves", his wrath was directed at all who would seek to profit from trading in the necessities of life.

Long after the Roman Empire had collapsed from successive waves of barbarian invasion, Christ's doctrine endured. It must be said, however, that the profit motive was stifled less for moral reasons than out of sheer practicality. In the millennium after the fall of Rome, European development was characterized by the local market economy of small towns scattered across the continent. The citizens of these walled settlements rarely strayed far from town lest they fall victim to wandering bands of marauding barbarians. Thus cut off from one another, towns strived to be self-sufficient; and individual citizens were preoccupied more with subsistence than with any thought of commercial gain.

The key to attaining such self-reliance was virtually to ban competition as we know it. As a means of protecting the local food supply from rival centres, towns permitted neighbouring peasants to sell food only in their own town marketplace. Most towns applied steep tariffs on goods imported from other settlements and forbade the practice of certain trades in the adjoining countryside so that their own town craftsmen would have work. And the craftsmen themselves formed associations, or "guilds", designed to keep the supply of craftsmen from exceeding demand and to protect their members' reputation by ensuring that their work was of high quality.

Thus the medieval economy shunned risk and speculation. Indeed, the notion of working for a profit was associated almost exclusively — and pejoratively — with the few wealthy merchants
who conducted what little trade existed among towns and
regions. As the influence of towns grew, however, their demand
for food escalated to the point where feudal lords were compelled
to clear and cultivate the tracts of wilderness that separated the
towns. And it was this Agricultural Revolution, not the subsequent Industrial Revolution that could not have proceded
without it, that sparked the next round of antipathy towards
business.

The agricultural upheaval began in the late seventeenth century, when landowners in Britain swept away the old village system of common lands and semi-collective farming. Land became
concentrated in the hands of a few powerful landlords, who were
able to create a vastly more productive regimen of crop production and livestock raising. In the process, though, hundreds of
thousands of poor and custom-bound farmers were dispos-
sessed. They became peripatetic wage-earners hiring themselves
out for the highest pay they could obtain as labourers for the few
remaining substantial farmers or, more commonly, as spinners
and weavers for merchants in the towns.

The industrial or machine age dawned in the 1760s, when British inventor Richard Arkwright built the first cotton "mill",
which brought itinerant workers and new heavy, steam-powered
machinery together under the roof of a single, efficient textile
operation. These mills, or "factories", as Americans would later
call them,[1] were congregated in the dreary, sunless Midlands,
close to the coal and iron needed by the machine age but far from
the south of England, where most Britons had lived. In the drab
new mill towns of Manchester, Leeds, Liverpool, and Glasgow,
people who had been ruthlessly uprooted from pastoral lives
now lived in squalor. The provision of adequate police protection

---

1 In Canadian parlance, a "factory" was a Hudson's Bay Co. trading post,
   which was run by a "factor" — hence, York Factory, Manitoba, one of the
   most important early Bay posts. Eventually the American meaning prevailed
   in the Canadian language.

and water, sewage, and garbage-disposal systems was far out-paced by the rapid growth in population. Housing was hastily built, densely packed, and in short supply: whole families lived in single rooms.

The machine age was not a new dark age. The rural bondage of serfdom from which the new class of wage-labourers had es-caped had not, after all, been such a great bargain. Indeed, the dawn of industrialism marked a titanic positive shift in the human condition. As H.G. Wells wrote in the 1920s, "The power of the old world was human power; everything depended ulti-mately upon the driving power of human muscle, the muscle of ignorant, subjugated men."

Still, for many the emancipation that the machine age ushered in was joyless. The mills had no need of skilled workers, who became destitute or accepted the degradation of a factory job, where they were broken in status from respected craftsmen to anonymous industrial peasants. The mills paid a good wage by the standards of unskilled labour, but one still too low to allow a man to support his family. Thus women, and children as young as six years old—often preferred by the new "cotton lords" because of their small hands and superior agility with a bobbin —were pressed into factory life. Women and children had al-ways worked, of course, but on farms families worked together. Now the unity of families was undermined as the concept of indi-vidual labour took hold; and the dirty, dark, and noisy environ-ment of the mill was a confinement that seemed a cruel exchange for the open fields. The mill owners usually were self-made men under tremendous pressure to keep their "wages bill" low, as they faced severe competition and had accumulated great debt in building a factory and equipping it with expensive machinery.

Still, the Dickensian caricature of the brutish capitalist of the early industrial age is not entirely fair. Most of the cotton lords pushed as close to the limit of the law as possible in their drive for profit, but not beyond it. Many factory owners found the expedi-ent of employing children distasteful and urged that laws be passed forcing all textile operations to abandon the practice. It was a cotton magnate, the elder Robert Peel, who in 1802 intro-duced the first Factory Act in Parliament. Then as now, however, enforcement proved to be nine-tenths of the law: Peel's measures to improve working conditions for mill children were ineffective from the start as they failed to provide for sufficient factory inspectors. It must be noted, though, that the factory life of fourteen-hour workdays and psychologically deadening routine were not much worse than the cottage and small-town sweatshops in which manufacturing had previously been carried on. The new urban agglomerations at least brought the plight of the disadvantaged to the attention of budding philanthropists and reform-minded politicians, and fostered a sense of class interest that would eventually manifest itself in the creation of unions.

What made the ills of early capitalism acceptable was the awesome wealth-generating powers of this new economic system, which for a while transfixed people of all classes. Britain soon was unrivalled in industrial output; London became the world's greatest storehouse of capital; and a new school of thinkers, "political economists", appeared to examine the beast that had made this possible. Impressed by its seemingly mystical powers, Adam Smith, Thomas Malthus, David Ricardo, and other classical economists of the era concluded that the capitalist economy was autonomous and separable from government, and operated according to its own set of "natural laws" — such as the law of supply and demand and the law of diminishing returns.

Smith argued that every person should pursue his own self-interest; that each person knows his own interest better than any other person or government; and that collectively the interests of all individuals translate into the welfare of society as a whole. Malthus theorized that populations tend to increase faster than the supply of goods available for their needs, thus suppressing living standards to subsistence levels. Ricardo, elaborating on Malthus's work, wrote of an "iron law of wages", which ensures that as soon as a worker receives more than a subsistence wage he breeds more children, who consume the excess, thus reducing the worker, and the working class in general, again to subsistence levels.

It was just too bad if one didn't like this "natural" system, for this *was* the system — there were no alternatives. Of course, many of the classical economists' theories have since been discredited. But, for a long time, the tenets of the "dismal science", as the writings of the classical economists were justly known, emboldened the new industrialists in their graspings and dressed poor wages and abysmal working conditions in a veil of respectability. The influence of those times endures: today, even the most sensitive industrialists can be heard to argue that the "system" militates against social reforms in business.

Britain was where capitalism first flourished, but no nation would embrace the promise and individualistic principles of raw capitalism more readily or with as much unquestioning affection as the new nation of the United States. The American Revolution has been romanticized into a story of a frontier people asserting their right to liberty and equality. But it was, in fact, commercial self-interest that inspired the Thirteen Colonies to revolt against their imperial master.

To the extent that they were, after all, colonies, the British settlements that were to rise against the mother country were the subjects of imperialist oppression. But it was, by the standards of the day, a light form of oppression. Distracted by a series of wars with its European neighbours, Britain in fact had not gotten around to exploiting its distant New World colonies. The customs duties Britain finally attempted to impose in the mid-eighteenth century, and which became the colonial propogandists' primary tool in agitating for independence, actually comprised a reduction in existing duties that the colonials in America had been blithely ignoring—just, for that matter, as American merchants had ignored laws prohibiting them from trade in sugar and iron wares of their own manufacture. Indeed, what the American business interests found so odious was a lenient tax regime peaceably accepted by other British subjects, including Britons themselves, and commonplace in most of Europe. Still, the insurrectionists easily aroused antagonism towards Britain among American merchants, shipping magnates, land speculators, and the working population who depended on the business interests. Sooner or later, any colony that suffers imperialist prohibitions against, for instance, trading what it produces, throws off this yoke of oppression. The American colonies did so before the yoke had truly been put in place.

In the decades following its successful rebellion, the United States served as a role model for other peoples wishing to throw off their colonial status—just as Britain's economy, parliamentary system, and even its social mores had been emulated by nations transfixed by the wonders of early industrialization in that country. It is interesting to note, though, that in America's case, only the spirit of self-governance has worn off. France, which was greatly influenced by the American insurrection and revolted against monarchical rule just thirteen years after the United States did, has since evolved into a state with a very high degree of centralized economic planning and government intervention in business. The African, Asian, and South American nations inspired by the American Revolution have mostly opted for socialistic economies or very mixed free-enterprise ones; even Britain has, in this century, come under the sway of—or been "infected" by, as Americans would say—socialist economic principles which Margaret Thatcher is doing her best to undermine.

America, alone among major industrialized nations, has adhered to its vibrant, relatively pure strain of capitalism, in part because of the nation's enduring frontier ethic but also because capitalism and America have grown up together: The Declaration of Independence and Adam Smith's *Wealth of Nations* both appeared in 1776.[2] By contrast, the industrialization of Britain did not take place in a relative vacuum, but was moderated by centuries of state-interventionism and other non-capitalist traditions. Countries that came of age after America have been influenced as much by the soul-destroying excesses and tremendous disparities of wealth that unbridled capitalism gave rise to in America during its first century as by capitalism's obvious virtues.

Most nation-builders are inspired by a sense of community, of bringing a people together so they can help one another out. Americans were very interested in staying out of each other's way. In the new republic, the lives of ordinary citizens—and the workings of business enterprises—were at all costs to be shielded from government, which was perceived as a meddlesome and even pernicious force. America's founding fathers were greatly inspired by English philosopher John Locke and other European thinkers then dissenting from absolutist rule. Like the classical economists, Locke thought that society was properly viewed as being subservient to man rather than the other way around. Thus he was in favour of unshackling the constraints imposed on the individual by, for instance, the communal voice of government and the arbitrary moral codes of organized religion. Locke and

---

2   A more commercially fortuitous coincidence is that both the Statue of Liberty and Coca-Cola celebrated their hundredth birthdays in 1986.

his contemporaries in the realm of political philosophy defined five "natural" laws for social organization, which complemented the natural laws framed by Smith, Malthus, and Ricardo, and which not only took root in the U.S. Constitution but have endured in the American corporate psyche: (1) the importance of individualism, (2) the right to private property, (3) the need for competition, (4) an insistence on limited government involvement in the lives of citizens, and (5) an emphasis on scientific and other empirical laws and values over religious ones.

The manifestation of this body of work in America's history is evident in the country's devotion to individual values and goals over communal ones. Indeed, a narrow focus on self-fulfillment has characterized America from the beginning. Even Ben Franklin, better known for his commentaries on thrift, was moved to pen a variant on the current "shop-'til-you-drop" ethic: "Is not the hope of being one day able to purchase and enjoy luxuries a great spur to labour and industry? May not luxury therefore produce more than it consumes, if, without such a spur, people would be, as they are naturally enough inclined to be, lazy and indolent?"

In the early nineteenth century, French historian Alexis de Tocqueville toured the United States and observed everywhere that people were riotously exercising their right to pursue happiness. "I know of no country, indeed, where the love of money has taken stronger hold on the affections of men," de Tocqueville wrote in 1835 in *Democracy in America*. "The lure of wealth is therefore to be traced, as either a principal or accessory motive, at the bottom of all that the Americans do; this gives to all their passions a sort of family likeness."

That collective harm could come of all this individual striving was not apparent until the economic empire-building of a later era, the late 1800s. At this point, the dubious ethics of commercial titans who had taken the pursuit of personal wealth as an overriding goal raised questions about America's underlying economic ethic. To be sure, just as settling the West had not been easily accomplished, harnessing America's potential economic might was bound to be a messy task. While settlers in the West were taming the hinterland with rifles and lariats, the financial frontiersmen in New York, Philadelphia, Chicago, and Cleveland adopted the brutish weapons of bribery, stock manipulation, and ruinous price wars. In the mighty struggle among a few dozen supercapitalists vying to build the infrastructure of the modern U.S. economy — its transcontinental railroads, its steel mills, its auto plants — great fortunes were made and lost overnight, and morality seldom made the acquaintance of self-fulfillment. For all that, though, grasping was deemed a meritorious activity. In the late 1800s, the Episcopal bishop William Lawrence told his wealthy New York parishoners, J.P. Morgan among them, that, "The rich man is the moral man. Godliness is in league with riches."

Among those less certain that these activities met with divine approval was novelist Theodore Dreiser. In a 1916 autobiography, Dreiser recalled the spirit of the last decades of the nineteenth century: "[America] was just entering on that vast, splendid, most lawless and most savage period in which the great financiers, now nearly all dead, were plotting and conniving the enslavement of the people and belabouring each other for power." The name most indelibly etched on this era is that of John Davison Rockefeller, an erstwhile bookkeeper who went into the oil-refining business at age twenty-three. By thirty-nine — in 1878 — Rockefeller had won control of 90 per cent of the oil refineries in the United States and a virtual monopoly over marketing facilities. He built his Standard Oil Co., a small Cleveland oil refinery, into a gigantic corporation through cutthroat competition. As he stepped into ever larger and more competitive markets outside his Cleveland home base, Rockefeller often sold his products at prices far below even his own low costs in order to drive his competitors over the brink; he then recouped his losses by raising prices once he had the market to himself. Eventually Rockefeller's huge share of the market enabled him secretly to extract generous rebates from the infant railroad industry, which was itself ruinously competitive and prepared to do anything to keep Standard Oil's business. Rockefeller's oil rivals became still more disadvantaged when Standard Oil gained a near monopoly in pipelines, which were supplanting railroad tank cars as carriers of petroleum products.

There was little sympathy for the railroad barons, however, for they too were a roguish lot. The Robber Baron era of the late 1800s takes its name from an influential 1934 book entitled *The Robber Barons*, which describes the knavery of Jay Gould. Gould was the most hated man in America, possibly because he candidly acknowledged his ruthless aims rather than hiding them, as his peers were wont to do, behind the false pieties of good-will and noble enterprise. Shortly after leaving his rural home in New York's Catskill Mountains in 1852 — at the age of fifteen with $5 in his pocket — Gould was engaged along with other Wall Street buccaneers in constant battles on the floor of the New York Stock Exchange for control of America's emerging industrial giants. As often as they sought to gain something for themselves from a market ploy they were bent on destroying one another's companies.

Early in his career, the audacious Gould took on "Commodore" Cornelius Vanderbilt, an industrial titan far more powerful than himself. Yet Gould succeeded in thwarting the Commodore's plan to seize control of the languishing Erie Railroad; and, at the age of thirty-two, Gould emerged as head of the Erie. But the carnage from the battle was appalling: each side attempted to corner the market in the other's stock, ruining innocent small investors, and they each liberally bribed judges, who issued injunctions against the side that hadn't paid them off. The episode earned Gould a reputation for black-heartedness which never left him; his peers in the railroad community labelled him "an infernal scoundrel and a moral monstrosity" and "the worst man on earth since the beginning of the Christian era".

This censure didn't stay Gould's course. He responded to the Commodore's attempt to underprice him on the Buffalo-to-New York line by waiting patiently until Vanderbilt had cut his rate for carrying steers from $125 a carload to $1 — then bought every steer he and his friends could find in Buffalo and shipped them on Vanderbilt's railroad. In his most astonishing ploy, Gould tried to corner the gold market. The scheme was as abjectly unsuccessful as the Hunt brothers' daring bid to corner silver in the 1980s. Gould's plan fell apart when a bribe he offered President Ulysses Grant's personal secretary was rejected. Soon thereafter, the U.S. government sold enough of its own gold holdings to break Gould's corner. This action precipitated 1869's "Black Friday" panic selling by gold investors, and produced monumental losses for innocent bystanders.

But the corruption of the era extended far beyond the stock and commodities markets. A lot of the players simply didn't like the "rules" of capitalism. They preferred their own rules. A prime tenet of capitalism is that markets must be competitive, so that any and all entrants may join the game. Yet Rockefeller, the railroad barons, steel magnate Andrew Carnegie, and financier J.P. Morgan strove mightily to concentrate America's emerging industrial power and drive out all rivals. Indeed, King Camp Gillette, who invented the safety razor, considered competition a social evil. In his 1884 bestseller, *Human Drift*, Gillette argued that all the world's industries should be rolled into one huge, efficient corporation.

To be sure, competition in the late nineteenth century had become overheated and, ultimately, self-destructive. In 1870 alone, the number of business firms leapt from 430,000 to 600,000. Soon the country was flooded with products turned out by the new companies, and prices fell disastrously. The thousands of firms that could not survive either closed voluntarily or were "rescued" — that is, forcibly bought up by huge trusts. The aim of the trusts (or "combines", as they were called in Canada) was to control output and prices in entire industries in order to ensure a satisfactory level of profit. Many of these trusts were creations of John Pierpont Morgan, scion of a wealthy Boston family and arguably the greatest financier of all time. His most famous creation, the United States Steel Corp., formed in 1901, controlled the entire U.S. steel industry. Morgan justified his trusts on the grounds that he was simply halting duplication and wasteful competition so that each industry could keep prices down and prevail against offshore rivals. This argument is a familiar one, of course: it is used today by U.S. and Canadian conglomateurs to justify their own occasionally harmful concentrations of power.

At the turn of the century, however, small businessmen and farmers considered the new trusts threatening, and their fears eventually mushroomed into widespread public agitation against artificially raised prices and closed opportunities for struggling new small companies. This antipathy found expression in a new political movement, Populism, whose leaders were vociferous in their condemnation of "Big Business". Among the most strident Populist journals was *The Commoner*, soapbox of legendary orator and failed presidential candidate William Jennings Bryan. When J.P. Morgan allowed that "America is good enough for me", *The Commoner* retorted, "Whenever he doesn't like it, he can give it back to us."

At the time he assumed the presidency following the assassination of his predecessor William McKinley, Theodore Roosevelt and his Republican colleagues were confronted with a strong tide of anti-business sentiment sweeping through the land. Roosevelt's natural inclination, notwithstanding the popular depiction of him today as a man of the people, was to openly admire the wizardry and brute power of the new class of tycoons, whose successful manipulations at first struck him as a glorious confirmation of America's economic ascendancy. Roosevelt himself had once described Cornelius Vanderbilt — with whom he shared a Dutch ancestry — as "one of the most potent architects of the marvellous American industrial fabric".

Such open admiration of the robber barons had its limits, though. Intent on curbing Populist inroads, which threatened his administration's longevity, Roosevelt co-opted the budding political movement by becoming a zealous advocate of its most magnetic policies. To help seal his 1904 presidential victory, for instance, Roosevelt declared war on the trusts. Labelling J.P. Morgan and his ilk "malefactors of great wealth", Roosevelt ordered that the great railroad, beef, oil, and tobacco trusts be broken up. His invocation was only partly successful, but represented an unprecedented governmental intrusion into the private sector.[3] Roosevelt enhanced his reputation as a crusader against commercial corruption by introducing measures to protect consumers

---

3   The Standard Oil Trust, the first "trust" and probably the greatest industrial combination ever formed, was created by John D. Rockefeller and his business associates in 1882. The trust was declared an illegal monopoly by the Ohio Supreme Court in 1899 when its capital exceeded $1 billion. Rather than dissolve it, Rockefeller merely folded the trust into a company device, the Standard Oil Co. of New Jersey, which he headed until 1911 when the US Supreme Court declared it also to be illegal. Since that time, the Rockefeller family has sold most of its interests in the oil industry.

The magnitude of the Standard Oil trust is evident from the continued dominance of the U.S. oil industry by the Standard Oil progeny created by the anti-trust action: Exxon Corp., New York (formerly Standard Oil Co. of New Jersey), is America's largest oil company; Mobil Corp., New York (formerly Standard Oil Co. of New York), ranks second; Chevron Corp., San Francisco (formerly Standard Oil Co. of California), ranks fourth; Amoco Corp., Chicago (formerly Standard Oil Co. of Indiana), ranks fifth; and Standard Oil Co., Cleveland (known as "Sohio"), ranks eleventh. The combined sales of these companies in 1985 was $225 billion.

Exxon is the largest oil firm in the world, and before the recent drop in oil prices was the world's largest company. In 1984, Gulf Oil Corp., one of the few major U.S. oil companies whose history does not trace back to John D. Rockefeller, was taken over by Chevron.

from undesirable additives used in the food-packing industry; the first federal meat-inspection law; and the Pure Food and Drugs Act, intended as a means of cracking down on misleading advertising by the patent-medicine industry.

By the 1920s, however, the public outcry that ignited the Roosevelt reforms had faded, and business was riding tall in the saddle again. Just as business was seen to have revived America's spirits after the Civil War, now it was making America forget the suffering of the First World War; it was time, once again, to look to one's own prosperity. President Calvin Coolidge said, "The man who builds a factory builds a temple, and the man who works there worships there"; *Ladies' Home Journal* carried an article by General Motors director John J. Raskob on how "Everybody Ought to Be Rich". And in his bestseller about the life of Jesus Christ, author Bruce Barton was certain that if the Saviour were alive in the Roaring Twenties he would be an account executive at an advertising agency.

The supercharged economy of the 1920s transformed industrialists into folk heros. *Nation's Business* reported that the American businessman was "the most influential person in the nation". And because, as economist John Kenneth Galbraith recently put it, "nothing so gives the illusion of intelligence as personal association with large sums of money", the public became particularly enamoured of financiers such as Samuel Insull and the Van Sweringen brothers, men of great wealth who created vast empires in utilities and railroads, respectively. By piling a superstructure of holding companies atop a utility or railroad, Insull and the other so-called "pyramiders" (the term was used admiringly then) were able repeatedly to sell shares and bonds in their new shell companies based on the strength of the underlying utility or railroad — thus, apparently, creating wealth out of thin air. Inevitably, the economic collapse of the early 1930s caught up with the fragile, over-leveraged structures that Insull and others had assembled and the creations came tumbling down, erasing the life savings of thousands of small investors. The end for Insull came in 1932, when two of his major holding companies went into receivership. Insull found himself $60 million in debt with no hope of paying it off. Assisted by his thirty-six bodyguards, Insull led authorities on a merry chase through Paris, Rome, Athens, and Turkey. After finally being apprehended, he was declared innocent of any wrongdoing, since holding companies at that time

were not subject to regulation. This prompted Will Rogers to conclude, "A holding company is a thing where you hand an accom-
plice the goods while the policeman searches you."

To this day, economists are divided on whether overzealous
production by factory owners or the piratic machinations of 1920s
stock-market speculators did more to cause the Depression. Certainly it appeared that the speculators had at the very least *precipitated* the massive economic reversal with their panic selling in
October 1929. Insull and some of the other high-profile manipu-
lators found legal absolution, but did not fare so well in the court
of public opinion.

By 1932, about sixteen million Americans were out of work and
thirty-four million men, women, and children (nearly 28 per cent
of the population) were without any income whatever. In these
desperate times, men set forest fires in order to be hired to put
them out, and newspapers reported an outbreak of "altruistic sui-
cides" — men killed themselves rather than be a burden on their
destitute families. In these overcast economic conditions, businessmen were no longer the high priests of prosperity; they were
pariahs whose evil speculations had transformed the American
Dream into a nightmare.

Franklin Delano Roosevelt and the new Democratic Congress
of 1934 appeased a vengeful public's hunger for blood by launching investigations to root out villainy on Wall Street. The probers
uncovered no lack of wrongdoers, and found them in the most
surprising places. J.P. Morgan, through the skillful use of legal
loopholes, was revealed to have paid no income tax in the years
1929, 1930, or 1931. Colonel Robert Rutherford McCormick, owner of the mighty *Chicago Tribune*, had been sending Washington a
token $1,500 each year while urging his readers in lengthy *Tribune*
editorials to meet their tax obligations in full.

A startling number of highly placed bankers — or "banksters",
as *Time* took to calling them — were found to have surrendered
probity to cupidity. Albert H. Wiggin, head of the Chase National
Bank (now Chase Manhattan), had short-sold the stock of his
own bank and then lied about it. Charles Mitchell, Wiggin's
counterpart at National City Bank (now Citicorp), was charged
with tax evasion; after a ten-year court battle, he was acquitted of
felonious intent, but paid a $1.1 million settlement of a civil suit.
Banker Joseph Wright Harriman attempted to elude police by taking refuge in a Manhattan nursing home, then escaped to a Long

Island inn, where he registered under an alias; upon being apprehended, he tried to drive a butcher's knife through his ribs. Harriman survived to serve two years in prison for doctoring his bank's books and misapplying its funds. Saul Singer, executive vice-president of the Bank of the United States — the largest American bank to fail up to that point — was imprisoned on similar charges. "The belief that those in control of the corporate life of America were motivated by honesty and ideals of honorable conduct," observed Joseph Kennedy,[4] "has been completely shattered."

Probably nothing so poisoned the image of business at this time as the remarkably simple-minded larceny of Richard Whitney. Whitney was rich and influential, and had many homes, cars, horses, and influential friends. He was also something of a national hero: At 1:30 P.M. on October 24, 1929 — the first big day of the stock-market crash — floor-trader Whitney had kept his head while his fellow traders were losing theirs, and temporarily quieted the selling panic with his order to *buy* ten thousand shares of U.S. Steel. A Harvard graduate and protégé of J.P. Morgan, Whitney was president of the New York Stock Exchange for five years. He held magnificent society balls and gave to all the right charities; in a widely quoted speech, he addressed the Philadelphia Chamber of Commerce on the topic "Business Honesty".

Whitney's downfall began with a bid to cash in on the repeal of Prohibition. Unfortunately, soon after Whitney bought the company that made Jersey Lightning applejack, people stopped buying it. A series of get-rich-quick schemes designed to bail out that first bad investment all failed and to cover his losses, Whitney borrowed from his wealthy friends. When that wasn't enough, he began to steal. First Whitney stole $150,000 worth of bonds belonging to the New York Yacht Club that had been entrusted to him for safekeeping. Then he stole bonds from Harvard and the St. Paul's school, and raided his wife's and his sister-in-law's trust funds. By a stroke of luck he was named a trustee of the Stock Exchange Gratuity Fund, set up to assist the widows and families of

---

4 Kennedy himself was not above suspicion. One of the few significant investors to survive the crash, he would be plagued for the rest of his life by rumours spread by envious enemies that he had been a rum-runner during Prohibition.

deceased brokers. Whitney looted it of $667,000. Confronted over this last indiscretion, Whitney argued that no charges should be laid against him. "After all, I'm Richard Whitney. I mean the stock exchange to millions of people." He was charged anyway, and sentenced to five to ten years at Sing Sing. Naturally the Whitney revelations fired the zeal of the dreaded New Dealers.

In his inaugural address, FDR had promised action against the "unscrupulous money changers" of the financial community and had demanded "an end to a conduct in banking and in business which too often has given to a sacred trust the likeness of callous and selfish wrongdoing". Like his cousin Teddy, FDR used the presidency to bring business to heel. Many of the banks that collapsed in the early years of the Depression had speculated with depositors' funds in the stock market through investment-banking arms. The Glass-Steagall Act of 1933 forbade national banks from maintaining such affiliates, provided other measures to divorce commercial from investment banking, and created an agency, the Federal Deposit Insurance Corp., authorized to guarantee bank deposits up to $5,000. The Securities Act of 1934 required greater public revelation of the details of stock promotions; the Securities Exchange Act of the same year created the Securities and Exchange Commission, empowered to require the registration of all securities traded on stock exchanges and authorized to regulate the trading of securities on margin. The Public Utility Holding Company Act of 1935 gave the SEC power to supervise the activities of holding companies. And Roosevelt's overly ambitious National Recovery Administration, although it failed in its designed purpose of stabilizing the economy through price and wage controls and production quotas, brought about enduring social reforms in business. The NRA established the principle of maximum hours and minimum wages in the workplace on a national basis, reduced the incidence of child labour, and made collective bargaining a national policy.

A little more than 150 years earlier, America had been founded on the principles of minimalist government and laissez-faire economics. The New Deal reforms and the abuses that precipitated them made a heavy dose of government interference an irreversible factor in business life.

Still, in the post-war years, business regained public confidence to such a degree the reforms hardly seemed necessary. Business had changed: by the 1950s, the idiosyncratic entrepreneurs who once had dominated the business scene had all but disappeared, replaced by corporations that sold their shares to the public and which were run by professional managers. To the extent they were larger and more financially stable than the flamboyant entrepreneurships they replaced, corporations seemed to provide their employees with a more secure living and had the resources to gamble on innovative projects without putting the whole company on the line with each new bet. They appeared to be a democratizing force, too, as autocratic management styles gave way to leadership by consensus. And they appeared to be more socially responsible than earlier forms of business organizations, since they institutionalized ethical and charitable practices that once existed solely at the whim of capricious entrepreneurs.

Yet the proliferation of corporations introduced new problems. Blame for wrongdoing was harder to assess, since, in contrast to their high-profile predecessors, the people who ran most big corporations abhored publicity and seemed to have gone into hiding. Not only was the public no longer aware of who the captains of industry were; the average industrial worker found himself in the employ of a vast, impersonal bureaucracy whose direction and values were set by people whose motives he could only guess at. Toiling in far flung subsidiaries, employees often didn't know who or where their ultimate boss was, and seldom had contact with the anonymous factotums inhabiting the highest corporate echelons. As well, corporations often fostered a cult of conformity, in which iconoclasts and whistleblowers ran a high risk of ostracism and abbreviated careers. The search for consensus was not, after all, such an admirable thing, but instead a ritual in which executives learned "if you want to get along, go along" — a code that often meant holding personal and community moral standards in abeyance. In the 1950s, economist Galbraith described as "groupthink" this blind adherence to a "value-neutral" corporate ethic. "Groupthink" is a means by which executives at all levels of a corporation dodge responsibility for their actions. As new and mildly alarming as this corporate conformity seemed when social scientists and a few management professors began to examine it in the 1950s and 1960s, the phenomenon of the unaccountable, value-blind corporation was foreseen back in 1927 by Alfred P. Sloan, the managerial genius who founded the modern General Motors: "There is a point beyond which diffusion of stock ownership must enfeeble the corporation by depriving it of virile interest in management upon the part of some one man or group of men to whom its success is a matter of personal and vital interest. And conversely at the same point the public interest becomes involved when the public can no longer locate some tangible personality within the ownership which it may hold responsible for the corporation's conduct."

Still, in the 1950s, a period of post-war recovery and unprecedented materialism, few voices were raised against business — the engine of prosperity — or in particular against the modern corporation, a remarkable institution with no equal in history in its ability to efficiently provide goods and services and generate wealth for shareholders and employees. Awakening to their own importance, corporations began to see themselves as being at the centre of the economic universe. It was in the 1950s, when he was a flack for General Electric, that Ronald Reagan told TV audiences, "GE's most important product is progress." As long as progress was synonymous with the general welfare, it was possible to get a warm feeling inside about all the good works being done at GE — and at RCA, AT&T, GM, duPont, and the rest.

Eventually, of course, the haze of post-war affluence began to clear, revealing a variety of dangerous byproducts of the corporatization of business. Operating according to agendas entirely of their own devising, with little or no regard to community standards of right and wrong, corporations befouled the environment, manufactured cars and drugs that claimed the lives of people who used them, fuelled the world arms race, and manipulated the political and legal systems of foreign countries and even their homeland. For the first time, it seemed that the awesome power of these economic institutions should perhaps be checked — and also that this would be no easy task. With the Watergate-era corporate-morality crisis of the early 1970s, it became obvious that Galbraith's earlier observation about "the bland leading the bland" within large corporations was a widespread truism. Where the robber barons three generations earlier had openly acknowledged their avarice, believing themselves to be guilty of nothing more than acting according to the impulses of natural laws, modern executives guilty of equally rank indiscretions skilfully shifted the blame to shareholders, to lesser employees who supposedly had acted without authority, and even to governments which had compelled them to manufacture Agent Orange in accordance with the national defence effort or turn the local river into a toxic sewer in order to provide gainful employment to a community's workforce.

The standard explications that saw corporations through the

early attacks on them during the 1960s did not stand up well after Watergate, however. In the early 1970s, prosecutors and scandal-hungry reporters were looking for political skulduggery. But often the most tantalizing revelations had to do with nefarious business schemes concocted by Richard Nixon's confreres. Companies with strong ties to the White House, such as International Telephone & Telegraph (ITT) and United Brands Co., were found to have meddled in the affairs of foreign lands. Lockheed, Gulf Oil, and two dozen other giant U.S. corporations had bribed foreign-government officials to secure contracts. Still other major corporations were discovered to have sought the aid of Nixon officials in avoiding prosecution on charges of anti-trust, income-tax evasion, and bid-rigging; and scores of firms — often the same blue-chip corporations seeking favours from the government — had made illegal campaign contributions to federal politicians and had bribed state and local officials.

In the immediate aftermath of Watergate, American business was put under a microscope, and it was presumed as the 1970s drew to a close that the U.S. corporate élite had been cleansed. Many major U.S. firms hired professional ethics-consultants and held their employees accountable to new, internal codes of ethical conduct. But at the end of the decade, *Fortune* matched up the long list of successful prosecutions against major companies during the 1970s with its list of the 1,043 largest corporations in America during that period. In order to simplify things, *Fortune* limited its survey to bribery, including domestic kickbacks and illegal rebates; criminal fraud; illegal political contributions; tax evasion; and criminal anti-trust violations. Foreign bribes and kickbacks were excluded as were such charges as the manufacture of faulty and dangerous products, false advertising, pollution, and monopolistic practices. *Fortune*'s limited survey revealed a dismaying record: 117 of America's biggest companies, or 11 per cent of the total, had been involved in blatant illegalities between 1970 and 1980. There were 98 anti-trust violations, 28 cases of kickbacks, and 21 instances of illegal political contributions. The majority of these cases were heard in the late 1970s, well after the scandals of the early part of the decade, leading the editors to glumly conclude that "big-business crime hasn't been swept away in a tide of post-Watergate morality".

There has never been a shortage of capitalists who argue that business is somehow separate and apart from society, that it cannot be held to the same standards of moral conduct that ordinary people apply to one another. These arguments appear during high tides of economic prosperity, which invariably are periods of moral complacency, and recede when the economy does, at which point they are scorned for the specious utterings they are. It is a shame that the self-redemptionist spirit that infuses business in hard times — when everybody and his government want a piece of its hide — does not visit the captains of industry more often when they can best afford to reform themselves.

The history of capitalism has been marked by great swings of brutishly insensitive profit-seeking and the sobering punishment of constraints applied by government. At the turn of the century, John D. Rockefeller justified his family's monopolistic practices in terms of Social Darwinism: "The growth of a large business is merely a survival of the fittest. . . . The American Beauty rose can be produced in the splendor and fragrance which bring cheer to its beholder only by sacrificing the early buds which grow up around it. This is not an evil tendency in business. It is merely the working out of a law of nature and a law of God."

Then came the sweeping anti-trust and consumer-protection reforms of Theodore Roosevelt, a Republican who bore down on business not out of philosophical convictions but because the public demanded it.

At the dawn of the Depression, Henry Ford insisted that unemployment insurance would merely ensure the perpetuation of unemployment; besides, joblessness wasn't such a bad thing. "Why, it's the best education in the world for those boys, that travelling around!" said Ford. "They get more experience in a few months than they would in years at school." John E. Edgerton, president of the National Association of Manufacturers, was convinced the unemployed were malingerers. "Many of those who are most boisterous now in clamor for work have either struck on the jobs they had or don't want to work at all, and are utilizing the occasion to swell the communistic chorus." *Fortune* was convinced that business should reject social responsibility, because the introduction of non-economic factors in business would upset the benign workings of a free market.

Then came the unsettling reforms of Franklin Delano Roosevelt, again by popular demand, which so legitimized government interference in business for all time that many business people still curse FDR's name.

In 1958, the complacency that had set in during the remarkably consumeristic 1950s prompted Eugene V. Rostow to observe, in *The Corporation in Modern Society*, that "one is struck by the atmosphere of relative peace. There seems to be no general conviction abroad that reform is needed. The vehement feelings of the early 1930s, expressing a sense of betrayal and frustration at a depression blamed on twelve years of business leadership, are almost entirely absent."

Then came more than a decade of race riots and bitter protest over industrial pollution, discrimination in the workplace, corporate political payoffs and meddling in the affairs of Third World countries, and cynicism over the growing disparity between rich and poor. Governments responded with strict policies on fair hiring, pollution abatement, and political spending that placed an onerous compliance burden on business and a tax burden on the public, which had to pay for enforcement. Business responded with internal codes of ethical conduct, boardrooms opened to representatives of labour, religion, women, and minorities (Gulf Oil killed two birds with one stone, appointing a nun to its board), and by funnelling corporate funds into urban renewal, small-business development, and other community programs.

In 1970, economist Milton Friedman expressed his disgust with the efforts of business to reform itself. Businessmen who "speak eloquently about the 'social responsibilities of business in a free-enterprise system'," Friedman concluded, were "unwitting puppets of the intellectual forces that have been undermining the basis of free society these past decades." It was not the job of business, Friedman said, to help counter poverty by troubling to employ the hard-core jobless, to help stanch ruinous inflation by striving to keep prices low, or to help rehabilitate the environment by reducing emissions more than was legally required. "In each of these cases," Friedman argued, "the corporate executive would be spending someone else's money [that of his shareholders] for a general social interest. Insofar as his actions in accord with his 'social responsibility' reduce returns to stockholders, he is spending their money." As far as Friedman was concerned, if shareholders want to save the world, they'll use their own money. In the meantime, they expect chief executives not to lift their eyes from the bottom line.

A decade and a half later, Friedman's view appears to have prevailed, not only in business but throughout society. Apart

Popular Attitudes Towards Business, 1880–1987

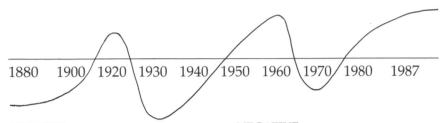

| 1880 | 1900 | 1920 | 1930 | 1940 | 1950 | 1960 | 1970 | 1980 | 1987 |

POSITIVE

Roaring Twenties:
A mere 1 per cent of the U.S. population owns 59 per cent of the wealth; Calvin Coolidge says the business of America is business, and millions of stock-market speculators giddily agree; Coolidge ignores a warning from Harvard's William Z. Ripley that "prestidigitation, double-shuffling, honeyfugling, horn-swoggling and skulduggery" imperil the economy.

Rampant Consumerism
Kids recognize the word "detergent" before they can read; a U.S. radio station plays a jingle that ends, "Buy, buy something that you need today" seventy times a day; Dwight Eisenhower appoints three Chevy dealers to his cabinet; *The Man in the Grey Flannel Suit* is a paradigm for corporate conformists.

Gilded Age Redux:
Right-wing governments in North America and Europe administer tax cuts to business as a balm for sixties-era business antipathy; Reaganomics — Ronald McDonald entertains at the White House; Jerry Rubin gets a job on Wall Street, then opens a chain of "business networking" nightclubs; Steve Jobs, Lee Iacocca, Conrad Black, and other tycoons are celebrities; Hollywood responds to the corporate crime wave with films such as *The Young and Indicted*, and *Toxic Avenger*, etc.

NEGATIVE

Robber Baron Era:
Jay Gould, Cornelius Vanderbilt, and other railroad magnates wage all-out war against one another, ruining small investors and corrupting judges in the process; J.P. Morgan and John D. Rockefeller build vast monopolies in steel and oil; Upton Sinclair, Ida Tarbell, and other muckrakers help pressure Theodore Roosevelt into imposing consumer and trust-busting reforms on business.

The Depression:
Millions of jobless ride the rails; destitute providers live in shantytowns named "Hoovervilles"; Wall Street's evil machinations are blamed for the Crash — and the apparent untimely end of the American Dream; FDR makes government intervention an irreversible fact of business life.

Psychedelic Sixties/Cynical Seventies:
Protests are raised against pollution, urban decay, workplace discrimination, the military-industrial complex, and political payoffs at home and abroad; flower power gives way to the rigours of runaway inflation and the oil crisis, both of which are suspected of unfairly benefiting business.

from a hard-bitten cadre of unfashionable relics of the 1960s, there is no one to man the barricades. Communal concerns have given way to urgent attention to self-fulfilment. So much to buy, so little time.

And yet in this new golden age of capitalism, more resplendent than any since the period between the two world wars, the rich are richer, the poor are poorer, and, surprisingly, the middle class has suffered a net *decline* in income, after inflation. Unemployment in most industrialized nations is still intolerably high. Generous tax breaks extended to business by right-wing governments in North America and Europe have gone not into job creation, new plants, new products, but have become a means of funding, at public expense, an epidemic of mergers and takeovers which, apart from lining the pockets of lawyers and investment bankers, contribute little if anything to the general economic health and may well detract from it. A relentless drive for profits, particularly after the early 1980s recession, has left a cruel legacy of layoffs and cut corners. The rallying cry of the 1970s, Paul Solman wrote recently in *Manhattan inc.*, was, "Free the Fortune 500. . . . The Fortune 500 are free all right: free to fail, to merge, to lay off, all in record numbers."

Unchecked, the zealous pursuit of material gain, in both business and personal lives, will lead inexorably to a great turnabout, as before. Already the strain is showing. Public distrust of business is on the rise, politicians are paying the price for alloying their interests too openly with business, and a generation of young business recruits grapples with the reality that not all of its members can quickly scale the heights of corporate success.

In 1851, the year in which, according to some scholars, Matthew Arnold wrote his poem "Dover Beach", England was at the summit of her imperial greatness. England was the wealthiest, most powerful, most industrially advanced nation on earth. Yet Arnold was saddened by what he saw as England's destructive self-confidence, and was filled with anguish that the advancement of intellect and industry should be accompanied by a loss of human feeling. As Arnold did more than 135 years ago, one beholds the vacant, soulless power of commerce and watches, with impatient hope, for signs of civility. And one thinks of "Dover Beach":

The Sea of Faith
Was once, too, at the full, and round earth's shore
Lay like the folds of a bright girdle furl'd.
But now I only hear
Its melancholy, long, withdrawing roar, . . .
. . . for the world, which seems
To lie before us like a land of dreams,
So various, so beautiful, so new,
Hath really neither joy, nor love, nor light,
Nor certitude, nor peace, nor help for pain;
And we are here as on a darkling plain
Swept with confused alarms of struggle and flight,
Where ignorant armies clash by night.

CHAPTER THREE
THE CANADIANS:
A GREED APART

Rarely have businesspeople in Canada come in for such high praise as was lavished on them by the authors of the *Canadian Biographical Dictionary and Portrait Gallery of Eminent and Self-Made Men*, published in Ontario in 1880–81. In the preface to their volume, the biographers insist that "To know how to achieve success is a laudable craving of the human heart; and to teach by example is the best method of satisfying that craving. . . . [Businesspeople are] examples [that] may spread the good seed, encourage the weary, give new life to the desponding and energy to the aspiring."

What the biographers intended, of course, was that Canadians would come to respect and even revere their budding entrepreneur class in somewhat the same way Americans thought of their daring industrialists as nation-builders. But this was not to be. Even today, Americans cling to their traditional view of business as a life-giving force in society; they indulge its excesses in the expectation that business will reward them by functioning as the well-spring of the general prosperity. Canadians, by contrast, have never had that kind of faith in business, the good intentions of the *Dictionary* authors notwithstanding. Indeed, for a variety of reasons business has traditionally been regarded in Canada with suspicion in good times and contempt in bad.

Canadians haven't embraced business quite so readily as people in some other lands in part because for the longest time business was something that other people did. Many of the "stars" of early Canadian commerce — from the pioneers of the Atlantic fishery and the founders of the fur trade, Canada's oldest businesses, to Cornelius Van Horne, enterprising builder of the CPR — were imports from Europe and the United States. A great

many of the native Canadians who eventually took up commercial pursuits were United Empire Loyalists who fled the American colonies at the time of the rebellion against Britain. "Historically," Northrop Frye has said, "a Canadian is an American who
rejects the Revolution." The loyalists also disdained the osten-
tatious lifestyles that encouraged popular idolatry of successful
tycoons in the United States. While in America money has always
attracted attention to itself, in Canada it traditionally has lain low,
and inspired a heightened sense of sobriety among those who
possessed it. During his brief stay in Canada in the early 1940s,
the English writer and painter Wyndham Lewis found that
money acted as a sort of depressant. "I have been living in this
sanctimonious icebox," Lewis wrote to a friend, "painting portraits of the opulent Methodists of Toronto. Methodism and
money in this city have produced a sort of hell of dullness."

French Canadians—more than half the population at the time
of Confederation—had a powerful bias against commerce; the
clergy preached that business was a debased calling. The defeat
of France by Britain on the Plains of Abraham in 1759 was followed by an exodus of merchants, lawyers, civil servants, and
other notables back to France; this "social decapitation" deprived
Quebec of a formidable business leadership and created a
vacuum which the clergy quickly occupied. Unfortunately, the
method for preserving the French fact in North America chosen
by Quebec's "priest-ridden" society consisted largely of clinging
to an outmoded agrarian lifestyle and forsaking the commercial
pursuits so closely identified with the English conquerers. By the
early twentieth century it was evident to some that Quebec had
been wrong in its attempt to reject the Industrial Revolution.
"Material power must support moral strength," Montreal financier Joseph Versailles exhorted his audience at a 1921 convention
of the Catholic Association of Canadian Youth. "To succeed, we
must do our utmost to launch our brightest young people in
economic and financial careers." Yet as late as 1937 the prevailing
view, as expressed by the influential University of Montreal historian and priest, Lionel-Adolphe Groulx, was, "In every respect
the agricultural policy remains for French Canada its vital policy."
Today, per-capita enrolment in business schools is higher in Quebec than anywhere in North America, but the emergence of a significant Francophone business leadership did not occur until

after the "Quiet Revolution" of the 1960s. In the many years prior to the sudden emergence of a native Quebec business class, the province languished in less-than-splendid isolation. In 1956, the then journalist Pierre Trudeau sketched the legacy of wasted years in dark strokes:

> A people vanquished, occupied, leaderless, kept aside from business life and away from the cities, gradually reduced to a minority role and deprived of influence in a country which, after all, it had discovered, explored and settled, could have but a limited choice of attitudes that might help it to preserve its own identity . . . .
>
> That is why, pitted against an English, Protestant, democratic, materialistic, business-minded, and later industrial environment, our nationalism's system of self-preservation glorified every contrary tendency; and made a cult of the French language, Catholicism, authoritarianism, idealism [and] the rural way of life, including later, the myth of a "return to the land."

As for the purported curative powers of business on the economy, Canadians of both official languages have in the main instead attributed these to what has usually been the real engine of economic growth in Canada — government. For while the American economic frontier was settled by rugged entrepreneurs, Canada has been built in large part by Crown corporations. Indeed, given the frequency with which governments have directed and financed business activities deemed vital to nation-building, one might even conclude that Canadians consider business too important to be left to businesspeople.[1]

It is difficult to think of a time in Canada when business was not largely an agent or ward of the state. Sir John A. Macdonald cossetted the fledgling industrial base of southern Ontario and Quebec with his National Policy, which erected tariff barriers to protect new Canadian factories from larger and lower-cost operations south of the border. Ottawa also underwrote the cost of

---

1 In 1983, government-owned and -controlled enterprises accounted for 26 per cent of the net fixed assets of all Canadian corporations; Crown corporations — of which there are 259, federal and provincial — accounted for 35 percent of government employment in 1982.

building a transcontinental railway, the completion of which was a condition of British Columbia's agreement to join Confederation in 1871. The Canadian Pacific Railway and, much later, the publicly assisted TransCanada natural-gas pipeline, have always been operated by private interests. But when a clutch of overzealous upstarts challenging the CPR's hegemony became fiscally derailed early in this century, Ottawa bailed out five of the largest and most beleaguered railways and amalgamated them under the banner "Canadian National". And this operation — the longest railway on the continent — remains state-owned, as does the airline it spawned, Air Canada.

Some notable government creations in business — such as Pacific Western Airlines (now part of Canadian Airlines, and originally set up by the Alberta government) and Ipsco Inc. (the only steelmaker on the Prairies, created by the Saskatchewan government) — have evolved into purely private-sector operations. As well, some businesses that have been bailed out by government — such as the aerospace companies de Havilland Aircraft of Canada and Canadair and the major fishery companies National Sea Products and Fishery Products International — have been returned to private-sector ownership after being nursed back to health by the state. But many companies taken over by government have remained state-owned, usually because popular sentiment demanded it.

Time and again, private interests have failed to legitimize their claim to vital core industries in the face of popular dissent. Telephone utilities on the Prairies were nationalized soon after the turn of the century. Very few major electric utilities have escaped nationalization: Ontario's private power companies were expropriated by Adam Beck — an erstwhile manufacturer, of all things — who galvanized public outrage over rapacious power pricing to garner support for his creation of Ontario Hydro in 1906. René Lévesque, when he was a Liberal provincial cabinet minister in the early 1960s, similarly capitalized on public disaffection with private enterprise when he swept most of Quebec's large privately held power companies into Hydro-Québec. In the late 1970s, when Lévesque's Parti Québécois came to power, Lévesque began a four-year-long campaign to nationalize much of Quebec's asbestos industry, the miserable labour-relations record of which had been a catalyst for the separatist movement in the 1950s.

Nothing has so damaged the image of business, and weakened its defences against the encroachment of government, as the inglorious conduct of many who have engaged in it. To be sure, though, the history of Canadian business is studded with inspirational figures whose conduct would seem to justify the adulation displayed by the authors of the *Canadian Biographical Dictionary*. Indeed, some of these men were noteworthy as exponents of high moral standards far beyond the borders of their Canadian homeland.

Samuel Cunard, son of a Halifax dockyard carpenter, succeeded in his audacious bid to dominate North Atlantic shipping by insisting his ships be well built, efficiently manned, and carefully sailed. While unprincipled competitors sacrificed safety for speed, and lost many ships and passengers as a result, Cunard's line stayed physically and fiscally afloat. It also inspired the Mark Twain line: "He felt himself rather safer on board a Cunard liner than he did upon land."

At the height of the robber-baron era of U.S. railroad building, Ontario-born railway tycoon James Jerome Hill distinguished himself by building his St. Paul and Pacific Railroad, which stretched several thousand miles across the U.S. Northwest, with the best materials, and by going around mountains rather than over them. This method produced low construction and operating costs, and thus was scorned by the construction-type railroad promoters of the day, whose very object was to inflate costs as much as possible. (Hill was vindicated when his railroad, renamed the Great Northern, was the only transcontinental line to survive the financial panic of 1893.)

In the 1940s, Quebec geologist John T. Williamson became something of a goodwill ambassador for Canada after discovering the fabulous Mwadui diamond mine in East Africa. Forsaking the practice of other mine operators, who billeted their African workers in monastic compounds far from their families, Williamson invited married men among his three thousand native workers to bring their wives and children into his compound. He provided them with comfortable homes, a good hospital, a modern school, and a clubhouse. His rapport with Africans was such that when Tanganyika and Zanzibar merged to become the independent nation of Tanzania in 1964, three years after Williamson's death from throat cancer, it was to Canada that the new Tanzanian president Julius Nyerere at once turned for technical aid.

Other pioneering Canadian industrialists became famous for their charity and benevolent paternalism at home. Farm equipment magnate Hart Almerrin Massey in many ways fit the stereotype of the parsimonious, tyrannical nineteenth-century industrialist. He was also possessed, however, of a deep-rooted philanthropic urge. Massey's public largesse—which, like that of so many industrialists, is likely to outlive the business he founded—includes the sprawling Hart House recreation complex at the University of Toronto and the Massey Music Hall (now known simply as Massey Hall) in Toronto, considered at the time of its 1894 opening to be one of the six finest concert halls in the world.[2]

In an era when merchants often unloaded shoddy goods at fancy prices, Irish immigrant Timothy Eaton launched his Toronto dry-goods business in 1869 with a stern warning to his employees that they were to "use no deception in the smallest degree—nothing you cannot defend before God and man". Eaton held himself to an unwritten social contract that made his company responsible for the well-being of its staff. Thus Eaton's was the first major Canadian retailer to cut its employees' work week; employed hundreds of "Welfare Secretaries" to administer financial, medical, and other aid to employees in need; and operated its own string of recreation clubs and summer camps. The Eaton beneficence extended far beyond the aisles of the family's stores, and included millions of dollars in donations to art galleries, churches (including the construction of Timothy Eaton Memorial Church in Toronto), and hospitals, most notably Toronto General, Canada's largest. "Eaton's have always recognized their public responsibilities," *Globe and Mail* financial editor Wellington Jeffers wrote in 1950. "There never was a time when the term 'social corporation' could not be applied to that firm except by men careless of the truth."

---

2   The Newcastle Foundry and Machine Manufactory, founded in 1847 by Daniel Massey, became the largest manufacturer of harvestors in the British Empire under the direction of Daniel's son, Hart, who merged his father's company with its chief competitor, A. Harris, Son and Co., in 1891. Under less gifted management, Massey-Ferguson Ltd. (a name adopted in 1958 after a merger with the Ferguson engine companies) recorded severe losses in the late 1970s and required government assistance and the infinite patience of its bankers to survive.

Often, of course, socially responsible behaviour is prompted by thinly disguised bids for self-redemption. H.R. MacMillan, founder of the forestry giant now known as MacMillan Bloedel Ltd., readily acknowledged his ruthless determination to prevail over his rivals. "Yes, that's what I am," he once confessed. "A buccaneer. I sink them all without a trace." Yet MacMillan, in an attempt both to ensure his firm's future prosperity and to overcome the taint of his early graspings, pioneered scientific forestry methods which he used to replace the trees he cut, in stark contrast to the practice — rampant then and, sadly, still common today — of exploiting forest resources with little thought to their replenishment.

The Seagrams distilling dynasty has also transcended the unrefined practices of its founders, the Bronfman brothers. During Prohibition, the Bronfmans flourished by manufacturing liquor for export — a practice that was legal in Canada during prohibition. The booze found its way to bootleggers who, by car, ferry, dog team, and almost every other known conveyance, smuggled it into the United States. By the standards of the times, the Bronfmans produced high-quality products; but like other primitive distillers of the day they often slapped phoncy labels on bottles attesting to false lands of origin; Scotland was a favourite. In the aftermath of Prohibition, however, Seagram worked assiduously to become a model of corporate social responsibility. Long before it was fashionable, Seagram urged moderation in the consumption of its products. "The House of Seagram does not want a dollar that should be spent on the necessities of life," read the text of a 1934 Seagrams ad. Two Montreal institutions — the Jewish General Hospital and the Samuel and Saidye Bronfman cultural centre — owe their existence to the generosity of the founding generation of Bronfmans; the succeeding generation that now runs the company has been tireless in its support of good causes — including, most notably Seagram chairman Edgar Bronfman's work as an emissary negotiating for the release of Jewish *émigrés* from the Soviet Union.

Still, it would take an oceanic dose of such goodwill to cleanse the image of business. The stigma is planted early in the minds of young Canadians, who are taught in grade school about the bad bargain Native peoples received at the hands of Hudson's Bay Co. and North West Co. fur traders. Alas, further readings of

Canadian business history easily encourage one to believe that this prototypical transaction—in which white men came away with valuable furs and the Native peoples were left with a debilitating addiction to "firewater"—is characteristic of how business is done.

For instance, early transportation magnates habitually getting in over their heads, prevailed on administrators of the public treasury to make good their ill-conceived investments. The Lachine Canal, one of the earliest examples of private-sector cupidity, was begun in 1821 by Montreal merchants. By its completion four years later, its feckless promoters had been bailed out by public funds; a few years later, governments assumed complete and permanent responsibility for the financing and operation of waterways. An identical pattern marked the subsequent development of railways. The hugely ambitious Grand Trunk Railway, completed from Montreal to Sarnia in 1860, amassed £800,000 in debt to British banks—one of which dispatched a representative to inspect the damage. He reported back to his superiors that the GTR was "a sink of iniquity".

The ferocious tussle between two private syndicates for the federal contract to build the Canadian Pacific Railway inspired an unhappy bit of zealotry when one of the bidders swelled Tory campaign coffers with $350,000. When the kickback was publicly exposed, it not only cost the bidder the contract he had sought thereby to obtain, but also precipitated the 1873 collapse of Sir John A. Macdonald's government. Finally completed in 1885, the CPR was a monstrous bleeding of the public purse, even though it was from the start (and remains) every inch a privately owned concern.[3]

Banking's formative years also were animated by cutthroat competition, rabid speculation, and unscrupulous self-dealing. The first Bank of Upper Canada, launched by Kingston, Ontario, merchants in 1818, collapsed four years later because, so far as a government inquiry could determine, "The conduct of its directors was . . . reprehensible inasmuch as no inquiry appears to have been made by them into the actual state of the bank." The

---

3 Ottawa generously endowed the CPR at the time of its construction with, among other things, $25 million in cash, twenty-five million acres in land grants, tax concessions, and a twenty-year monopoly on the Prairies.

Agricultural Bank, which obliged competitors to fall into step with its then-novel practice of paying interest on deposits (at the rate of 3 percent a year), had by 1837 been driven out of business by resentful rivals. And the Second (or Chartered) Bank of Upper Canada, despite a near-monopoly granted by the Family Compact, could not survive the consequences of its reckless land speculation; its collapse in 1866 so shook public confidence that another large lender, the Commercial Bank, tumbled into bankruptcy the following year.

In fact, banking in Canada was a very unstable business until well after the turn of the century, largely because of the roguish designs of bankers. Between 1867 and the outbreak of the First World War, there were twenty six bank failures, nineteen of them caused by illegal activities by bank employees against whom criminal charges were laid. During this period, the failure rate of Canadian banks was 36 per cent (compared with 22.5 per cent in the United States).

The banking watershed was the 1923 collapse of the Home Bank of Canada. The demise of this large and trusted institution, founded seventy years earlier by a Roman Catholic bishop to tend the financial affairs of his flock, was brought on by injudicious lending in speculative real-estate ventures and a profligacy of investments in deals in which the bank's own officers and directors had a stake. Bank president H.J. Daly had lent a furniture company he owned $120,000; director Henry Mill Pellatt ("the Plunger"), financier and sometime castle builder (Toronto's Casa Loma), had obtained $1.5 million for a real-estate deal he and the bank's general manager cooked up. The bank had even extended funds to a bootlegging company — owned by Daly and one of the bank's directors.[4] Nothing remains of Home Bank

---

4 Four months after the Home Bank collapsed, its president, vice-president, general manager, chief account, chief auditor, and five of its directors were arrested and charged with signing or approving false statements about the bank's financial standing. The executives were accused of manipulating the books in order to pay dividends out of depositors' funds rather than the bank's profits. President Daly died three months before the 1924 trial began; the others were found guilty on various counts, although convictions against the vice-president and the directors were overturned because the men had no direct knowledge the statements were fictitious but had relied on the management of the bank.

today (its last asset, a played out coal property, was sold in 1960) save lasting reforms, the most important being the creation of the office of the Inspector General of Banks, a federal department charged with monitoring the financial health of all Canadian chartered banks. Unfortunately, however, the lessons of the Home Bank collapse were lost on the executives who led the Canadian Commercial Bank, the Northland Bank, and a score of other banks and trust companies down the same path of indiscriminate lending and self-dealing in the 1980s. These few irresponsible operators have tainted the entire industry, which is now burdened with the formidable task of rebuilding public confidence in the financial industry.

Bankers, of course, were not the only sharp operators to pass through the pages of Canadian business history. Donald Smith, the grizzled gentleman in top hat and tails who drove home the last spike of the CPR on November 7, 1885, was a figure of towering business accomplishment. From a start as an apprentice clerk for the Hudson's Bay Co. counting muskrat skins in a Lachine warehouse, the Irish immigrant propelled himself to tremendous prominence. He was governor of the Bay for four decades, president of the Bank of Montreal for twenty-seven years, and was late in life appointed to the distinguished post of High Commissioner to Britain. Yet Smith also sealed his 1873 re-election to the House of Commons by temporarily transferring twenty-six Hudson's Bay families to his riding, and bribed them for their votes. (Smith was confirmed in his seat by a Manitoba judge, but it was revealed Smith held a mortgage on the judge's home. The Supreme Court reversed the decision.) Smith's financial backing was instrumental in the CPR's progress. But Smith and his colleagues in the CPR syndicate took exceptionally good care of themselves at public expense, selling five million acres of land granted free to the CPR to settlers at an average price of $6 an acre. They also sold CPR treasury stock to themselves at 25 cents on the dollar, thus guaranteeing themselves a personal profit before the first CPR train made its first trip. Upon his elevation to the peerage in 1897, Smith, now Lord Strathcona, appropriately chose for his official crest a beaver gnawing a maple tree.

Smith's accomplishments and infamy paled, however, beside the subsequent manipulations of Sir Herbert Holt. At his height, this one-man commercial colossus had a hand in the direction of some three hundred companies on four continents. His Montreal

Light, Heat & Power Consolidated was for a time the largest private utility in the world. Holt founded the predecessor companies to Consolidated-Bathurst, Dominion Textile, Canada Cement, and Dominon Coal and Steel; controlled Montreal Trust and Holt Renfrew & Co. (no relation); and was a leading figure in the syndicates that built the Famous Players theatre circuit and Montreal's posh Ritz-Carlton hotel. Holt also found time to serve as president of the Royal Bank of Canada; during his twenty-six-year tenure in that post, the Royal's assets multiplied fifteenfold.

Holt found time for his many ventures because he did not run any of them. A "paper entrepreneur" seven decades before that term was invented, Holt didn't build new companies. By means of complex stock manipulations he smashed existing companies together in great, often ungainly agglomerations. His methods were legal at the time, but unseemly. Holt's own interests frequently clashed with those of target companies, public officials, and even the shareholders of firms he already controlled. Holt built his Montreal power monopoly, for example, by methodically exchanging stock in his own company (thereby spending little of his own money) for shares in his rivals', and crushed those who refused to sell.

Convinced that business was inherently treacherous, Holt did not trouble himself to make friends in his business dealings, and was treated in kind. When it was reported that some of Holt's blood was used in a transfusion for one of his grandchildren, society gossips said the child must have frozen to death. During a strike against his utility companies Holt's life was threatened so many times Montreal newspapers set his obituary in type and kept it on hand in their composing rooms. When the richest man in Canada did die, the news was announced at a baseball game at Montreal's Delorimier Stadium. The crowd cheered.

Indeed, share-shuffling seems to inspire insensitivity among those who practise it. E.P. Taylor — dubbed "E(xcess) P(rofits)" Taylor by members of the Communist Party of Canada — hunted down the hundred or so companies that ultimately comprised his Argus Corp. empire with Holt-like ruthless efficiency. In the annexation of a brewery to his enormous beer conglomerate (which survives today as the much smaller Carling O'Keefe Ltd.), Taylor instructed his London colleagues to buy his own brewery's stock in order to inflate its value: Taylor was using his stock, not cash, to acquire the target company. After investigating the formation of Taylor's Canadian Breweries, the federal Restrictive Trade Practices Commission charged Taylor with attempting to form a brewing monopoly. In one of his letters to his London cohorts, Taylor had written, in reference to an enclosed list of ten breweries, "We know that with consolidation an accomplished fact and half a million cash in the bank, we would be in a position to make the operation of any one of the above listed companies so disastrous that they would be forced to consolidate with us or go out of business." In another letter Taylor explained he was prepared to wage "local price wars here and there to discipline small companies". Yet Taylor responded angrily to the RTPC report, insisting "every move made in the building up of Canadian Breweries was reported to the shareholders. At no time were we told by any government that what was being done was wrong." The RTPC backed off. Evidently, the spirit of Taylor's intentions, as revealed in his letters, was not sufficiently damning to take action against him.

The ease with which Taylor circumvented the spirit of anti-monopoly regulations was but an early example of the now widespread and chronic failure of government to rein in unseemly business practices. In 1986, the Law Reform Commission of Canada accused the federal Environmental Protection Service of having such a close relationship with the companies it regulates that it "has rarely chosen to prosecute — even when violations have been detected". The Canadian Radio-television and Telecommunications Commission devotes a great deal of energy tracking the number of hours of Canadian content provided by the radio and television stations it licenses. Yet the CRTC ritualistically renews the licences of broadcast outlets that load up their schedules almost entirely with American programming, and then sternly lectures the station owners to make a more earnest stab at complying with the law before coming back for another renewal.

Not surprisingly, lack of enforcement and inconsistencies among laws and regulations breeds patronage and confusion within the government branches charged with protecting the public interest, as federal environment minister Tom McMillan acknowledges: "The essential problem now is that in the area of toxic chemicals, twenty-six ministers of the Crown are involved and some fifty-seven pieces of legislation," he says. "The authority and the mandate are all over hell's half-acre."

Regulators in Ottawa and Ontario working at cross-purposes contributed mightily to the Astra Trust Co. fiasco, an episode that calls to mind Stephen Leacock's observation (in an essay commissioned by a trust company, ironically enough) about the sometimes dubious utility of professional fiduciaries. The question for those seeking to protect their savings, as Leacock put it, is "whether to let other people look after your money, or to lose it yourself in your own way".

From the time it was granted a licence to operate in 1977 until it went into liquidation in 1980, Niagara Falls, Ontario-based Astra diligently bilked hundreds of investors out of millions of dollars. Astra was in violation of its trust-company charter on its very first day of business, when its directors voted for a five-for-one share split without notifying regulatory authorities. Barely a trust company, it billed itself as "more than a bank", and peddled high-risk investments, usually in real-estate ventures Astra founder and president Carlo Montemurro and top Astra officers had personal stakes in. These investments were sold on the implicit understanding that all the goods Astra offered were guaranteed by the Canada Deposit Insurance Corp. (CDIC). Most were *not* covered.

Almost every regulatory agency and police force in the province — and a few outside Ontario, as well — knew about Astra's persistent breaches of the law: the federal superintendent of insurance (the department then in charge of supervising federally chartered insurance and trust companies); various arms of the Ontario consumer and commercial relations ministry, including the Ontario Securities Commission; the CDIC; the RCMP; the Ontario Provincial Police; and even the Niagara Falls police. Yet, each new discovery of legal infractions down at tiny Astra Trust sent the entire federal-provincial supervisory apparatus into a Keystone Kops routine. At various times, each arm of the regulatory system mistakenly assumed another arm was handling the Astra outrages. Anxious not to step on one another's toes or improperly claim jurisdiction, the regulators fiddled while Montemurro defrauded 320 investors of $12 million. Sadly, Astra was a mere foreshadowing of the state of financial-institution regulation in Canada that would figure in the collapse of the much larger Crown Trust Co. in 1983, and the demise of the Canadian Commercial and Northland Banks in 1985.

In the regulators' defence, it must be said that business indiscretions often are not so bald as to merit an official rebuke. Not so bald, in any case, as Harold Arviv's decision one Sunday morning in 1980 to dynamite his Toronto discotheque, Arviv's, in order to collect the insurance money—a crime for which Arviv was sentenced to four years' imprisonment. Or as primitive as the ploy by the owners of Koolatron Corp., a Brantford, Ontario, refrigeration-equipment maker, to hastily relocate their operations in Batavia, N.Y., in May 1987 after a whistleblower at the firm alerted provincial inspectors to the fact that workers were exposed to dangerous levels of isocyanates, a cancer-causing chemical used in the manufacturing of refrigerators. Within forty-eight hours of being charged with a violation of occupational safety laws, Koolatron laid off 150 workers and packed up its equipment for a quick trip south of the U.S. border. Koolatron president Kiran Kulkarni, whose plant is the recipient of a $1 million Ontario government loan, complained that the labour-ministry officials who had hounded him "do not seem to understand the urgency that private-enterprisers face".

More disheartening is the example set by the more substantial captains of commerce, whose indiscretions are not illegal but who also are not inclined to accept the *Canadian Biographical Dictionary* authors' challenge to "spread the good seed, encourage the weary, give new life to the desponding and energy to the aspiring".

One need only consider the record of businesspeople who have caught the public's imagination to wonder whatever became of the sense of public responsibility with which Timothy Eaton was infused. Conrad Black, probably the most well-known businessman in Canada, is certain of his own claim to privilege: "The only charge that anyone can level against us," Black once said of his and his brother's record at Argus Corp., "is one of insufficient generosity to ourselves." Unfortunately, though, Black is sometimes reluctant to grant lesser beings their due. When the time came in 1985 for Argus to shrug off its Dominion Store albatross and, in the process, put many Dominion employees out on the street, Black struggled to be sympathetic: "We had $30 million in produce stolen by employees [each year]. . . . It's sometimes difficult for me to work myself into an absolute lacrimose fit about a work force that steals on that scale. I'm sorry for honest people who are out of work, I honestly am. . . . But on the other hand, we are not running a welfare agency for corrupt union leaders and a slovenly work force."

Neither is there much to uplift the spirit in the example of Peter Pocklington, the Edmonton Oilers owner who at age six borrowed cherries from someone else's trees, poured tap water on them, and flogged them door to door as preserves. Many years later, in the early 1980s, Pocklington's empire of energy firms, car dealerships and a major trust company collapsed under the strain of overzealous expansion. As regulators representing taxpayers — who financed the bailout of depositors in Pocklington's failed Fidelity Trust Co. — sorted through the ruins, Pocklington's fortunes miraculously recovered. But his arrogant proprietorship of Edmonton meatpackers Gainers Inc., which was strike-bound for six months in 1986, is shaping up as an archetype of abysmal labour-relations, and is a strange tack for a man who sought the Progressive Conservative party leadership in 1983 in the hopes of becoming prime minister.

In their own ways, Black and Pocklington are reinforcing the venerable Canadian tradition in which business leaders feel themselves imbued with a sense of superiority that encourages them to decline taking responsibility for their actions, good or bad. Timothy Eaton's own progeny have seldom acknowledged their public-spirited agenda, as if to do so would encourage observers to hold them forever accountable to a course of goodwill. In the 1970s, when Toronto's Holy Trinity Church accused the family's Eaton Centre of encroaching unfairly on its own land, no one at the firm bothered to mention that the main reason Timothy Eaton had moved his original Toronto store in the early 1880s was to avoid having to demolish an adjoining Presbyterian church, which Eaton's rival Simpsons eventually did knock down when *it* expanded. The Eaton Centre débâcle ended with the massive development being replanned to accommodate Holy Trinity, but through the whole process Eaton's allowed itself to be portrayed as a villain — a posture that frustrated Eaton's own corporate historian, William Stevenson. "As far as I could make out," Stevenson wrote in a letter to *The Globe and Mail* in 1973, "Eaton's had done far more for Toronto than Toronto ever did, or has done, for Eaton's. But if it keeps its mouth shut when critics are all about it, Eaton's deserves everything it gets. I fully expect it to go down the drain one of these days, still muttering through clenched teeth, 'At least the beggars never ruffled my composure.'"

One of the few significant exceptions to this approach is Toronto's Olympia & York Developments Ltd., which is one of the largest real-estate companies in the world. O&Y's First Canadian Place office complex, the tallest building in Canada, dominates the Toronto skyline; and with about ten million square feet of office space in Manhattan, O&Y is the biggest office landlord in New York City. In an industry known for shady dealings and cost-cutting, O&Y has the principal distinguishing feature of enjoying a reputation for honesty and quality workmanship in the buildings it erects. For thirty years, the word of O&Y owners Albert, Paul, and Ralph Reichmann has been as good as a contract, and the brothers have insisted that every partner with which they deal must come away feeling it has gained as much as has O&Y — for the simple, sensible reason that O&Y might hope to do business with that partner again.

Indeed, the Reichmanns have always tended to place personal values ahead of business considerations — a practice that many observers have attributed to the brothers' strict Orthodox Jewish faith. Paul Reichmann, senior executive vice-president and chief strategist at the firm, insists his religion is not a factor. "I don't accept that we're any different," he says. "I'm sure there are many more businesspeople besides ourselves who live by their consciences. For us, it's a matter of simply deciding that if something is wrong, we don't do it. We are a large company, but we have no temptations to become bigger by any means. We'd simply be idiots to seek a gain that was wrongly gotten."

This attitude seems out of place coming from a family whose assets have been placed at about $25 billion, but Reichmann insists he and his brothers hold to it. "Business is not the purpose of my life," he says. "I never want to be subservient to my assets, but have it the other way around. What I enjoy about what we do is not the fruits of success, but rather that our success doesn't enslave or direct my life. When you are consumed by your business, you stop being successful."

So consistent was O&Y's business conduct that there was no reason to question Reichmann's sincerity, until O&Y engaged in two prolonged and messy takeover battles in 1985 and 1986. O&Y's takeover of Gulf Canada in 1985 was controversial for a $500 million tax break that was pivotal to the deal; and its 1986 acquisition of distiller Hiram Walker Resources Ltd. was one of the most hostile in Canadian history. The tax break was greeted by cries of outrage in Ottawa from MPs who wondered why the government was financing a takeover that led to layoffs when the Reichmanns found they had to cut costs to make the $2.8 billion takeover pay its way. The Walker takeover ultimately resulted in the dismemberment of the company — parts of which were quickly sold off to raise cash — and ignited fears about job security among unionized distillery workers.

The Reichmanns in fact have kept layoffs to a minimum, and their tax-break financing techniques are common practice in takeovers. The most significant cost-cutting effort had been the Reichmanns' decision in 1986 to bring Gulf's oil-drilling activity in the Beaufort Sea to a halt — a move that clearly contravened the family's avowed goal to mastermind deals they perceived to be in the best interests of Canada. Yet by January 1987, O&Y bravely reversed that decision and proceeded with plans for a $120 million drilling program, to employ as many as 120 workers in the Beaufort in the summer of 1987; Gulf thus became the first major oil company to return to the Beaufort following the disastrous plunge in world oil prices that began in 1986.

Still, it would be wrong to assume the Reichmanns' new plans have much to do with any desire to answer the critics. Paul Reichmann offers no apologies about deals that some government MPs and officials found questionable. "A certain type of [corporate] activity causes trouble," he says. "If someone's very active in business, it's very possible that certain things won't be perfect — or even if they are perfect, won't be seen to be perfect."

Indeed, a certain type of business activity *does* often seem imperfect. It's worth noting that no one seriously questioned the Reichmanns' ethics during their nearly three decades of doing business in Canada. Not, that is, until they strayed from the land development business whose customs they know so well and ventured into the unfamiliar, murky area of takeovers. Like so many other small and large investors alike in the 1980s, the Reichmanns' troubles began when they got involved in the stock market.

CHAPTER FOUR
INDECENT DISCLOSURES IN
THE STOCK MARKET

The world seemed a bright and generous place to Ivan Boesky in 1985, when he delivered the commencement address at the University of California School of Business Administration. Widely heralded as one of the most brilliant stock-market traders in history, he was eager to talk about the rewards of his calling. "Greed is all right," he boldly proclaimed on that occasion. "Greed is healthy. You can be greedy and still feel good about yourself."

Boesky's conviction about a year later on charges of illegal insider trading transformed him overnight into a pariah on Wall Street. But the consequences for the market as a whole were more dispiriting. The stock market is, after all, the nexus of capital formation in the funding of new and existing businesses. The promise of the system is supposed to burn brightest there: this is the place where sturdy investors risk their funds so that enterprises small and large might grow, and are justly rewarded when the companies they underwrite flourish.

Without question, the supposed sanctity of this hallowed capitalist institution had been conspicuously breached many times — most notably by the railroad speculators of the late nineteenth century and by boiler-room operators, who sold worthless or non-existent stock over the telephone, during the 1920s. But the 1980s, until Boesky, appeared to be the beneficiary of sweeping reforms dating from the turn of the century and substantially reinforced during the Depression. The major brokerage houses had become venerable institutions oozing respectability — if their ads were to be believed. And should their sworn commitment to probity waver, there was standing ready in the wings a corps of eagle-eyed regulators armed with a sophisticated battery of legal admonitions and computerized monitoring systems all designed to catch every swindler and curb each underhanded practice before it threatened to become a trend.

In the wake of Boesky, however, it has become apparent that the proud veil of honour and dedication to the concept of self-regulation that the securities industry has long draped itself in is a frail garment; and the network of federal and state securities watchdogs pose no serious threat to outlaws determined to twist the system to their own advantage. The great bull market that began in late 1982 — a period of greater share-price appreciation than any in history — proved too alluring to unscrupulous operators, who have not been content merely to ride the market's upward swing and take honest profits. Instead, as has always happened during bull markets, they have been determined to become multimillionaires overnight. And in so doing they have given new life to old assumptions that the market, almost by definition, is an arena of graspers where the ordinary, honest investor is bound to come up short.

In some cases, to be sure, the wrongdoing has been the work of mere mischief-makers. Since 1981, for instance, messengers of ill report have spread false rumours of Ronald Reagan's death, hoping thereby to profit, say, from short sales of defence stocks. (More than once, the White House has felt the need to issue a press release insisting the president is not dead.) Harder to combat are unlikely stories about radioactive sugar beets growing out of control in Eastern Europe after the nuclear accident at Chernobyl, and earnest reports that hog herds are being felled by acquired immune deficiency syndrome (AIDS). Sometimes the rumours are not whimsical. Cheap talk that the giant BankAmerica Corp. was on the brink of insolvency in September 1986 sparked panic selling of BankAmerica stock, which plummeted to $9.50 — its lowest point in decades. Alarmed at the potential for a run on the deposits of the bank — the second-largest banking organization in the U.S. — BankAmerica's then chairman Samuel Armacost called on the New York Stock Exchange and the SEC to probe the "maliciously planted false rumors".

Armacost was hardly alone in his plight. At least $6 billion worth of stock in companies such as Union Carbide Corp. that were coping with sharply lower profits were similarly vulnerable to "hit and run" attacks by rumour-mongers. Indeed, rumours work to the disadvantage of trusting investors who make their decisions on the basis of widely known information. But most market insiders remain sanguine. Says Frank Napolitano, chief financial officer of Collins Commodities in Chicago: "Rumors generate volume for people who earn commissions, and commissions benefit the whole industry."

The thought rarely occurs to brokers, it seems, that ill-gotten commissions are just the thing that periodically drives disillusioned investors out of the market. And yet between 1981 and 1986, during the greatest bull market in Wall Street history, the number of complaints about unscrupulous activities in the market lodged by investors with the U.S. Securities and Exchange Commission (SEC) shot up 55 per cent—to about twenty-five thousand, an all-time high. The likely reason is that at the tail end of that period the market began to soften, and securities firms began to exert tremendous pressure on stock salesmen to sell harder in order to stem the sudden slowdown in commission volume. Individual brokers who had become conditioned to the high life were faced with a sudden drop in their incomes. Engaging in dubious practices was too tempting for many salespeople.

Canadian stock-market officials often insist that the action is safer on this side of the border. "When you look at the number of transactions overall," says Investment Dealers Association of Canada president Andrew Kniewasser, "the remarkable thing is how few complaints there are."

Actually, the remarkable thing is what some brokers try to get away with. The case of Florence Ryder is instructive. Ryder is a widow in her late seventies who has no business experience and professes not to know the difference between a stock and a bond. She instructed her broker to administer a safe, conservative account on her behalf. Instead, according to an Ontario Supreme Court judgement in February 1985, the broker turned Ryder's account into a speculative one that traded for capital gains rather than dividend income, and generated $125,220 in commissions for herself during an eleven-month period. Ryder lost an estimated $272,295; the court awarded her that amount plus interest, a total of $400,000—probably the largest amount awarded in Canada to a brokerage company's aggrieved customer.

One of the most common broker abuses is "churning", which occurs when a broker executes an inordinately large number of trades in a client's account simply to generate commissions.

Stock-market officials deny that churning is a problem, but the practice is widely evident. "The amount of churning that goes on is incredible," says a Toronto broker who handles discretionary accounts, those like Ryder's in which the client has given trading authority to his or her broker. "If *I* was the client in these cases I'd damn well be suing the firms and the brokers involved."

Unfortunately, victims rarely report their brokers' malfeasance: The cheated clients often feel foolish for not monitoring their brokers' activities, or shrug off their losses as simply the result of being beaten by the market. As well, many clients, after taking a stock-market pounding, don't have the funds to pursue their brokers through the courts. Moreover, the punishment imposed on Ryder's broker and the securities firm that employed her is an extraordinary departure from the norm: Most fines are too puny to be an incentive for the industry to clean up its act. A doctor in his mid-seventies opened an account with a member broker of the Toronto Stock Exchange in 1981. The broker ploughed most of the $140,000 into options and, in less than a year, drove the value of the physician's intended retirement nest egg down to $23,000. The TSE frowned on such mismanagement: The broker was fined $2,000.

Disciplinary actions are getting a little tougher. In 1986, a sales rep employed by Richardson Greenshields of Canada Ltd., which has probably more experience serving small "retail" investors than any securities dealer in Canada, was found to have churned one of his client's accounts; the broker had also misappropriated more than $22,000 of the company funds. For this he was fined $21,500 by the TSE and barred permanently from selling securities. The TSE also took action against securities dealer Osler Inc., which between 1981 and 1984, according to the TSE, "through lack of vigilance" allowed trainees to deal with customers and prospective customers and permitted sales reps transferring from other firms to trade in securities before their registrations had been transferred. Since that time, Osler's ownership and management have changed; but the firm was assessed fines and costs anyway, totalling $50,000.

Yet securities firms have little need to fear severe discipline. The TSE investigates an average of two hundred complaints per year, and takes disciplinary action against individual brokers in about thirty to thirty-five of those cases. But the TSE disciplined only two *firms* in 1984, none in 1985, and two in 1986. And only

one Canadian firm has paid the ultimate price of losing its regis-
tration outright (meaning it is basically put out of business)—
Rademaker MacDougall & Co. of Vancouver, which was expelled
by both the TSE and the Vancouver Stock Exchange in 1983. Only
in 1985 did the TSE consent to begin disclosing the names of firms
employing salespeople who break exchange rules, and even at
that, action is almost always taken against individuals rather than
firms. Self-regulation is a cozy system; the TSE is, after all, owned
by its member firms.

Fraternalism is so strong among the forty-eight member firms
of the Vancouver Stock Exchange that it took a scandal that made
headlines across the continent to shake the VSE's complacency
about rules to protect investors. It is precisely the VSE's relative
laxity in regulating brokers and stock promoters that has made it
the most speculative trading arena in North America and a leading source of capital for fledgling resource firms. Never mind that
the vast majority of the penny-stock issues traded in Vancouver
have no real assets to speak of—a 1984 study of the more than
nine hundred gold stocks listed on the VSE turned up only half a
dozen companies with genuine production potential.

The VSE did nothing in response to several scandals in the early
1980s—including a stock promoter who was convicted of bribing
a VSE official, and another who was convicted of stock manipulation. But the collapse of Beauford Resources Ltd. in 1984 was different. During the summer of 1984, twenty or so investors (not
brokers working for securities dealers) created a buying frenzy in
the shares of Beauford and several related VSE-listed firms. Eventually, it became obvious to other veteran VSE investors that Beauford, a non-producing company, was vastly overvalued, and the
shares collapsed, from $10.88 to $2.00 in just twenty-one minutes
on Friday, October 19, 1984. The total paper loss came to $40
million; margin accounts containing shares of Beauford and companies linked with it were hit with $5 million in losses. "Black Fri-
day", as the catastrophe was quickly dubbed, prompted the VSE
to finally adopt reforms—including new regulations to raise the
standards for listing requirements in order to upgrade the quality
of shares traded on the exchange. At the same time, the VSE did
some serious housecleaning, instituting a policy of publishing the
names of brokers and brokerage houses that break VSE rules.
And, in 1987, the government of British Columbia finally created
a securities commission, becoming the last province with a stock

exchange to do so. As well, the B.C. Securities Act of 1987 — postponed for some eight years by bureaucratic inertia and investment-firm resistance — ushered in several reforms, including stiffer penalties for illegal insider trading and tougher measures to ensure that companies issuing shares provide truthful information to prospective investors.

Unfortunately, though, irregular trading practices often defy remedial or preventive action, as witness the case of Robert Brennan. Brennan's firm, First Jersey Securities, was until recently a major U.S. equivalent of the few "broker-dealers" operating in Ontario.[1] Most brokers provide a range of products and services, and buy and sell blue-chip as well as more obscure "junior" stocks for their clients. However, the specialty of Ontario broker-dealers, and of First Jersey, is the purchase and sale — mostly the *sale* — of obscure unlisted stocks for which a true auction market does not exist. The stocks are real enough, but the companies that issue the shares are usually struggling start-up entities. What's more, these issues do not actively trade on any stock market; their price, therefore, is generally what the broker from whom one buys them says it is, since the broker is usually the only party in a position to buy them back.

Brennan's story is an elaborate version of the American Dream. Born poor in New Jersey, Brennan started First Jersey with a tiny grubstake; by the early 1980s he presided over a brokerage with 1,000 salespeople, 35 offices across the United States, and 350,000 investors. He was an important political fund-raiser, and a major figure in the glamorous world of horseracing; Vice-President George Bush and New York mayor Ed Koch were among his many influential friends.

First Jersey, founded by Brennan in 1974, was inconsequential

---

1   Broker-dealers typically peddle stock over the phone to raise cash for very risky firms that cannot afford a conventional underwriting. Most conventional brokers keep only 5 per cent or so of the funds they raise as a commission; broker-dealers — as an incentive for flogging stock no one has heard of — keep back as much as 70 per cent of the funds they raise as a fee. The buyer of stock will never see this money again, of course, since it isn't used to explore for precious metals or build plants.

In 1984, the Ontario Securities Commission revoked the self-regulatory status of the six broker-dealer firms (the ranks had thinned from the 250 broker-dealers who thrived in Ontario in the 1960s) and brought the firms under its direct supervision. The osc was concerned that broker-dealers did not represent an "efficient means of raising capital".

by the standards of major Wall Street firms. But Brennan made it a household name by spending as much on advertising as did giants such as Merrill Lynch and Shearson Lehman Bros. In early 1980s TV ads, in which he invited investors to share his dream by purchasing stocks peddled by First Jersey, Brennan was displayed, with his limo, in front of the nation's Capitol, flying over the Erie Canal, or landing near the Grand Coulee dam: "The Grand Coulee dam," Brennan announced. "Built to harness the power of the Columbia River. That took bold imagination that made this country grow. Today I see the same kind of imagination in hundreds of small and medium-size companies whose new ideas, new technologies, and new jobs will continue to build America. At First Jersey, we specialize in discovering such emerging companies for today's investors with vision. First Jersey Securities: come grow with us."

There's something amiss in that pitch. The Grand Coulee was financed by government, not through any free-enterprise initiative (same goes for the Erie Canal). But most First Jersey clients didn't notice anything strange until they attempted to unload a stock purchased from one of the firm's eager sales people. The First Jersey system was designed to *sell* securities. Sales people were paid 10 per cent commissions, much higher than industry standards, on sales, and no commission when they consented to buy stock back. And the stocks were often crummy: stocks in companies that went bankrupt, that were delinquent in paying taxes and interest on loans, that overstated earnings or that in a few cases, were controlled or largely owned by Bob Brennan. There were some winners, to be sure, but not many. And when a stock did perform well, the firm encouraged the client not to sell, but to shift the winnings into yet another First Jersey offering.

The U.S. Securities and Exchange Commission went after Brennan in 1979, alleging such improprieties as price manipulation. Its case was stalled for five years, during which Brennan sued the SEC three times. "[Brennan has] brought every dilatory and frivolous motion possible," an SEC official said. Brennan based one appeal on the grounds that a SEC lawyer was prejudiced because a dog belonging to a First Jersey executive had bitten the SEC's man's son a few years earlier. During the course of the SEC proceedings, 200,000 pages of documents disappeared from the SEC's offices at New York. In 1979, the National Association of Securities Dealers, of which First Jersey was a member,

charged First Jersey with, among other things, artificially inflat-
ing stock values. *That* case dragged on: Brennan sued the NASD;
and, in 1985, 20,000 pages of documents relevant to the NASD's
case went missing.

In 1984, soon after *Forbes* magazine published a cover story
accusing First Jersey of operating "a clever and apparently legal
system for fobbing off shoddy and overpriced merchandise on a
not very well informed public", Brennan settled the five-year-old
SEC action by signing a consent decree: First Jersey admitted no
guilt but consented to abide by securities laws in the future. Two
years later, however, Brennan was in trouble again. The NASD
fined First Jersey $300,000 and Brennan $25,000 for excessive
mark-ups on securities transactions. In the summer of 1986, with
new SEC allegations of manipulating prices facing his firm, Brennan stepped down from the chairmanship of First Jersey; in
December 1986, Brennan sold First Jersey's retail brokerage
operation to another securities trader, and basically took himself
out of the securities business.

In Congress, John Dingell, chairman of the House Energy and
Commerce Committee, scheduled hearings on the SEC's handling
of the First Jersey case, which he labelled an example of the SEC's
"inability to enforce the law. For a decade, the SEC has been aware
of serious problems with the way First Jersey has operated. But
[it] has failed to carry out its responsibility to protect the
thousands of trusting victims of First Jersey." What the unchari-
table Dingell failed to appreciate is that regulators work in the
dark, with little political support (and occasionally a good deal of
non-constructive political interference) in attempting to prove
their suspicions about unscrupulous operators. Sadly, only after
those suspicions have blossomed into full-fledged scandals do
the politicians descend, eager to be seen closing the door of an
empty barn.[2]

---

2 At Dingell's request, the U.S. General Accounting Office in late 1986
   launched a wide-ranging inquiry into the supervisory and surveillance
   capabilities of the SEC, the New York Stock Exchange, the American Stock Exchange, the National Association of Securities Dealers (NASD), the Chicago
   Board Option Exchange, and other major markets. Dingell insists stock-
   market surveillance authorities are ill-equipped to build convincing cases
   against unscrupulous insider traders and other stock-market criminals. The
   SEC, for its part, frets that Dingell's and the GAO's probing may upset the SEC's
   pending cases against suspected offenders.

Despite his sudden eclipse, Brennan is sanguine. "I feel terrific," he said upon quitting his job. "I'm excited about the things I'm going to be doing," which include a possible run for political office in New Jersey.

Certainly Brennan has a high profile, and not just in New Jersey. By December 1986, about the time Brennan sold most of First Jersey's assets to another broker, "60 Minutes" decided to see what he was all about. In the modest living-room of an elderly First Jersey investor, Mike Wallace had a sheaf of pretty but valueless stock certificates waved in his face. Wallace couldn't quite make out what the bespectacled lady was saying—something about wallpaper?—so he asked her to repeat herself. "Toilet paper!" the First Jersey victim shouted. "That's all it is, Mike," she said, letting the multi-hued certificates spill into her lap and down to the floor, "just good-for-nothing *toilet* paper!"

Even the most reputable brokerages are seldom vigilant enough in protecting the interests of their clients. In particular, most securities firms have trouble keeping their research and underwriting functions separate.

The underwriting department's job is to raise funds for companies through bond and stock offerings; the research department's role is to provide the brokerage's clients with objective advice on the merits of relative investments. In order to keep one camp from putting pressure on the other, securities firms are required to maintain a "Chinese wall" whereby employees performing the two functions work in the same premises but keep knowledge of their activities for the firm to themselves. Too often, though, securities analysts working in a broker's research office are pressured to put out the good word about a stock or bond issue the firm is trying to peddle, and it is rare that analysts will speak frankly to their clients about a stock offering their firm is preparing. At best, analysts simply refrain from discussing a stock at all.

As well, most brokerages trade in the market for their own account and it is tempting to act on confidential information in order to protect the firm's own portfolio. First Boston Corp. of New York, one of the most prestigious securities houses in the United States, was fined $264,000 in 1986 for acting on inside information, information not available to the public that could have a big impact on the value of securities. In the First Boston case, a corporate client of the brokerage informed First Boston's underwriting department in confidence that it soon would suffer a severe financial setback. Unfortunately, that news leaked to a manager handling First Boston's own portfolio, which included some stock in the troubled client; the manager dumped the shares from the brokerage's portfolio. It was a good investment move but a breach of securities regulations, since information about the client's troubles was not available to the investing public.

By early 1987, as the SEC insider-trading probe netted its dozenth investment-banking suspect, it had become apparent the securities industry's Chinese Wall had massive cracks through which the likes of disgraced traders Ivan Boesky, Dennis Levine, and Martin Siegel had passed. Each had profited illegally by gaining access to supposedly confidential material on mergers being planned by prestigious investment-banking firms, and which was on no account supposed to find its way into the hands of stock-market traders who could use it for their own — or even the investment firm's — gain. "Chinese walls didn't keep the Mongols out of China," says Dingell, "and they haven't kept the miscreants on Wall Street out of the money pot either."

Through pension funds and other indirect means, most North Americans have a stake in what takes place on the stock market, but not surprisingly, only a small portion of the public — about 22 per cent of Americans and 18 per cent of Canadians — risks its funds in the market *directly*. The Canadian figure is a tremendous improvement over the 11 per cent of people willing to risk a stock-market investment just a decade ago.

But the upturn may prove short-lived. It was caused by the biggest bull market in history; the new provincial stock savings plans which offer tax incentives as a means of encouraging investors to underwrite local firms; and a buying spree of mutual-fund investments.

By 1987, however, the market was showing signs of peaking, after the Dow Jones Industrial index pierced the 2400 level in the spring. The Quebec Stock Savings Plan and the other provincial schemes had begun to run dry of credible blue-chip investment opportunities, and poorly capitalized ventures whose prospects

were not as bright—funeral homes and flower shops, for instance—had begun to offer shares in the hopes of attracting investors. When some of these latter firms performed poorly, the
sheen came off the provincial share-purchase program. And the
lustre of mutual funds—never much of an indicator of confidence in the market since they are professionally administered
and considered the safest of market investments—had dimmed
by 1987 as it became apparent that they had been bought by
everyone and his brother-in-law's uncle. Too many people had
bought funds, and they had become overpriced. Finally, small investors, particularly in the United States, had reason to believe
that they were victims of traders with inside information, and
that the market had been poisoned.

Investment banking is built upon many things. Capital, surely.
Distribution, definitely. Brains and stamina, certainly.

But standing above it all is a single idea: the integrity of the
people involved. The integrity of their standards, their thinking,
and their behaviour.

It is what we look for in whom we recruit. And acknowledge
by those we promote . . . To our clients, this fabric of integrity
translates into a fragile thing called "trust." To us, it is that nonne-
gotiable idea that echoes down the halls at night, and remains the
ultimate bottom line.

—advertisement in *Business Week*
placed by leading New York
securities dealer Shearson
Lehman Bros., December 1986.

In 1986, insider-trading abuses gave rise to one of the biggest
scandals in Wall Street history—a scandal that did for business
what Watergate did for politics.

Securities regulations in most jurisdictions define "insiders" as
officers and directors of a corporation, and shareholders who
own 10 per cent or more of a company's stock. It is not illegal for
these individuals to trade actively in their company's stock; indeed, it is considered a sign of confidence if they're buying or a
warning to other investors if they're selling. The key, of course, is
that insiders must promptly report their stock transactions,
which are published by the Securities and Exchange Commission

in the United States and in Canada by provincial securities commissions. As well, insiders are required not to act on vital information they are privy to until it has been released to the public.

Oddly, Congress never has passed legislation that specifically outlaws improper insider trading. Instead, the SEC merely drafts rules about the practice under the Securities Exchange Act of 1934. And it took a dazzling Canadian mineral discovery in the early 1960s to clarify just what constitutes "inside" information.

In the mid-1960s, senior executives of New York-based Texas Gulf Sulphur Co. loaded up on company stock while concealing from the public details of a 1963 find the firm had made near Timmins, Ontario. When news did get out in the spring of 1964 about the Kidd Creek mine, the world's largest single zinc-copper-silver ore body, Texas Gulf shares soared to $80 from little more than $20 in the previous fall. In pursuing insider-trading allegations against thirteen Texas Gulf officers and employees, the SEC forced a landmark 1968 decision by the U.S. Supreme Court, which held that a person violates the law if he buys or sells stock on the basis of material non-public information about his company. The information is deemed "material" if it is something the average investor would want to know before he buys or sells.

In the late 1970s, the SEC brought several dozen insider-trading cases — more in a three-year span than in the previous four decades. The campaign led to widespread reforms on Wall Street. Brokers worked harder to restrict sensitive information to those with a "need to know", used code names when writing or speaking about takeover deals, hired electronics experts to sweep their premises for eavesdropping devices, and became vigilant about locking up or shredding confidential documents. Most firms also undertook to warn employees repeatedly that spreading inside information or using it for personal profit was grounds for dismissal.

Thus the fall of former *Wall Street Journal* reporter R. Foster Winans in 1985 came as a surprise to those who thought the disease of insider trading had been cured. Winans, who as a city-hall reporter had once lost a night's sleep worrying whether he had compromised himself by letting a politician treat him to a spaghetti dinner, was convicted of fraud for leaking, prior to publication, the contents of his *Journal* tipster "Heard on the Street" column, of which he was co-writer, to two New York stockbrokers. That information produced about $700,000 in illicit gains for the brokers, who paid Winans for his help.[3]

But this was a mere hiccup in the insider-trading scandal that would blossom during the next few months.

The then SEC chairman John Shad had decided to test the integrity of Wall Street when he became the securities industry's top watchdog in 1981.[4] Dismayed that a campaign to curb insider trading in the late 1970s had failed and convinced that insider-trading abuses were widespread, if latent, Shad vowed to ferret out wrongdoers and come down on them "with hobnail boots". Few took Shad's intentions seriously: how could the SEC, which was to endure staffing cutbacks as the laissez-faire Reagan administration wore on, throw a scare into the industry when past efforts had failed? This time, however, the market undervalued the SEC's resolve.

Shad's attack was three-pronged. In careful co-ordination with major stock markets, the SEC fine-tuned a computerized stock-monitoring system of great sophistication, which probed unusual, and potentially illegal, trading in thousands of stock issues. As well, by 1984 Shad was equipped with a bigger club: People found guilty of insider trading could no longer merely pay a fine and give back their illicit profits. New legislation stiffened the fine, lengthened the potential jail sentence, and empowered courts to order offenders to return the profits with damages equal to three times the ill-gotten gains. Most important, though, Shad sensibly calculated that if his crackdown was to have a significant effect as a deterrent, the SEC would have to stop going after cabdrivers who overheard sensitive conversations about mergers and print shop employees who had access to confidential financial documents.

During the first four years, however, the SEC's strategy of going after high-profile targets had uncovered few noteworthy crooks except Foster Winans and then undersecretary of defense Paul Thayer. And Shad was disappointed in the press accounts about

---

3 Winans, thirty-eight, was convicted on fifty-nine counts of conspiracy and stock fraud in 1985. In the summer of 1987 he awaited the results of an appeal of his conviction to the U.S. Supreme Court.

4 In 1987, Shad, a former vice-chairman of E.F. Hutton & Co., Inc., stepped down from the SEC post after being appointed ambassador to the Netherlands by President Ronald Reagan.

Thayer and Winans. Thayer's stock-market transgressions were treated as merely symptomatic of the petty corruption eating away at the Reagan administration; and, the papers seemed less interested in Winans's finances than his homosexuality. But soon Shad's investigators hit paydirt.

In May 1986, the SEC charged Dennis Levine with violations of securities regulations—to which Levine would shortly plead guilty—involving an elaborate system for generating illicit profits from insider information obtained from a network of confederates. The case had all the ingredients to get the attention of Wall Street—and Main Street. Levine & Co. had engaged in cloak-and-dagger stratagems, employing fictitious names, dummy Panamanian companies, and a Bahamas based broker. Best of all, Shad's latest quarry was not familiar with the business end of a taxicab.

Dennis B. Levine, mastermind of the biggest insider-trading scam the SEC had uncovered, was a managing director of the New York securities firm Drexel Burnham Lambert Inc., and the first senior investment banker implicated in an insider-trading case. Levine was raised in a small, one-storey red-brick house in Bayside, Queens: there he was known as "Dennis the Menace" because of his fondness for innocent mischief, fast cars, and noisy motorcycles. For a couple of years after high-school graduation, he helped his father, Philip, run the small family business, which sold aluminum and vinyl siding to homeowners in Queens and Long Island.

At Baruch College, a branch of the City University of New York, Levine didn't grow his hair long, and kept his distance from the anti-war demonstrators. Instead, he concentrated on gaining an entrée to the snobbish confines of New York investment banking, a profession that even by the 1970s was still dominated by patricians who preferred to recruit from among the Ivy League-educated offspring of the Northeast's oldest families. But by the mid-1970s, when Levine graduated from Baruch, investment banking was the hottest career choice in America and he was determined to be part of it. In his master's thesis, Levine wrote, "The investment banker's reputation [is] an essential part of his business."

At first, things went badly for Levine, who was to be repeatedly frustrated in his attempts to cut an impressive figure on Wall

Street. Levine hustled, mailing out résumés, pumping his professors for contacts, and buying for new suits for his interviews. When Levine did not get a job in investment banking, he blamed his lack of Ivy League schooling.

Eventually, Levine accepted a low-level position in the currency-exchange department of Citibank. After his first promotion thirteen months later, Levine was ready to jump. The prestigious investment banking firm Smith Barney, Harris Upham & Co. was impressed with his résumé, but would not give him what he wanted — a posting in the field of mergers and acquisitions, the most lucrative and glamorous area of investment banking. Levine joined Smith Barney anyway, as a clerk in its Paris office. Still, after only two years, in 1978 Levine realized his dream: Smith Barney called him back to New York, put him to work in its mergers department, and paid him well. Levine was twenty-seven.

Two years later, Levine travelled to the Bahamas to open a secret bank account under the name "Mr. Diamond". With an initial deposit of $125,000 transferred from a Swiss bank, he launched a frenzied covert campaign to make himself very rich very fast by using his knowledge of pending mergers to buy and sell stocks. According to evidence entered against him by the U.S. Justice department, Levine and a cohort at another investment firm often met late at night at the latter's office and rummaged through the offices of people who worked in the mergers and acquisitions department in search of private data that could be used for profitable trading. Levine also, on at least two occasions, tipped off newspapers such as *The New York Times* and the *Chicago Tribune* to pending mergers in the hope of driving up stock prices.

As the Bahamas account became swollen with booty, Levine's power and influence on the home front grew. A superstar salesman who mesmerized his clients, Levine became a hot property. He was lured away by Shearson Lehman Bros., America's second-ranking brokerage, and after only a few years there traded up again to the lofty post of managing director at Drexel, the most aggressive broker in funding the wild takeover craze of the early and mid-1980s. Levine was one of a select few employees Drexel featured in its glossy annual report.

In order to guard against security breaches, Drexel had started administering lie-detector tests to prospective new employees.

But Levine, who had been operating his insider-trading scam on the side for several years, was not subjected to one. "Typically that's not the kind of situation where we would use it," Drexel CEO Fred Joseph would say later. "[Levine] was a well-regarded, well-known professional that we spent a lot of time with. We were sure he knew the rules."

Levine knew the rules. He put a lot of effort into circumventing them — including, according to SEC allegations, destroying documents and testifying falsely in a November 1984 SEC deposition. In the end, Levine couldn't stop. He hadn't spent any of the close to $10 million socked away in the Bahamas (the ill-gotten gains came to $12.6 million in total), yet even after he learned the SEC was investigating him, Levine attempted to devise a new arrangement that would allow him to continue the inside trading. At the time of his arrest in 1986, Levine's day job was paying him an estimated $3 million in salary and bonuses per year, enough to put him behind the wheel of an $80,000 red Ferrari Testarossa and cover the cost of an elegant Park Avenue apartment and a summer house on Long Island. The SEC charges against Levine in May 1986 outraged ordinary investors across the country — never had such a senior executive been accused of exploiting confidential information for so much personal gain for such a long period of time. And Wall Street, to Shad's delight, was finally thrown into a panic. Levine, glib socialite that he was, knew everybody and had done *business* with almost everybody. "A lot of people knew Dennis," one New York trader said after the charges were announced, "and I would suppose a number of them are sweating bullets right now."

Indeed, Levine, who drew a two-year prison sentence and was fined $362,000 (U.S.), sang to his captors, and by the summer's end the SEC had hauled in about a dozen more crooked traders. Yet, few dared imagine the trail would lead to the market's most sophisticated traders and certainly not to the kingpin of speculative takeover trading, Ivan Boesky.

"Ivan the Terrible" (a nickname Boesky relishes) had profited mightily from his declared specialty, risk arbitrage, which involves purchasing and selling stocks in companies that appear on the verge of being taken over. So long as "risk arbs" act on information not obtained from company executives or others legally defined as insiders, they are on the right side of the law. It is in the nature of their work, however, for arbs to tread dangerously close to the line, since their success hinges entirely on their ability to collect as much market data as possible — often from elaborate networks of lawyers, accountants, and securities dealers privy to valuable inside information. By the mid-1980s, when 2,500-plus mergers with a total value of more than $100 billion were taking place each year, a shadowy clutch of risk arbs had emerged to exploit sudden share-price swings. The dozen or so top risk arbs were a valuable catalyst in the market, driving prices up with the risky bets they placed on erratic stock issues. But they were mostly a subdued lot, partly because their potential for profit would be trimmed if outsiders guessed their strategies, and partly from fear that the more that was known about them, the more they would be perceived as greedy opportunists whose activities should be curbed.

Boesky, however, was proud of his work and loved attention. Like Levine, he had struggled at first. "Ivan the Bum", his wealthy in-laws called him; they felt he lacked direction and wouldn't amount to much. To this day, Boesky's estranged sister-in-law, with whom he tangled over control of a Beverly Hills hotel in which they both had shares, says, "He is the most avaricious, arrogant piece of sewage I've ever met."

Boesky, fifty, is the son of a Russian immigrant who, with his four brothers, ran several popular delis in Detroit. At age thirteen, Boesky drove an ice-cream truck around Detroit — without a driver's licence. He attended three colleges before graduating from Detroit College of Law. He drifted through a series of jobs, including stints as a law clerk and an accountant. But after his father-in-law set him and his wife, Seema, up in a Park Avenue apartment in the late 1960s, Boesky found his calling. At the age of twenty-nine, he took up the arcane trade of risk arbitrage with a passion, out-finessing his elder peers and shocking them with his ruthless obsession to become wealthy. His career was stayed only temporarily in the early 1970s, when, while running the arb department of a small New York brokerage, he was fined $10,000 by the SEC for breaching a securities regulation.

Bent on exceeding his father-in-law's net worth, Boesky slept but three or four hours a night, craming two normal person's workdays into each day he spent at his sprawling white marble suite of offices high above Fifth Avenue. There, stationed behind a three-hundred-line telephone console and a battery of video screens monitoring stock-trading activity, the tall, perfectly tailored Boesky fuelled himself with gallons of coffee and a constant stream of market data and gossip as he methodically built his fortune. Had he not been blessed with a death wish along with his uncanny talent for out-guessing the market, Boesky might still be toiling in his marble palace today.

John Kenneth Galbraith, assessing the fate of the Hunt brothers of Texas when they failed to corner the world silver market in the early 1980s, concluded that "in all but the rarest cases the great speculators are the victims of their own speculation and the great swindlers almost invariably end up swindling themselves. Both kinds of operator are victims of the publicity that they have generated, and which they have come to believe."

In 1985, Boesky's name appeared prominently on the cover of a ghost-written book called *Merger Mania*, which was subtitled, *Arbitrage: Wall Street's Best Kept Money-Making Secret*. This scholarly work was Boesky's attempt to dignify risk arbitrage by dressing it up as a respectable science. Boesky also spent a lot of time on the lecture circuit, where he depicted himself as the small investor's friend. The public service he provided, Boesky explained, was to snap up shares in the market from small investors, thus allowing them to make a killing on a takeover play while he, Boesky, absorbed all the risk.[5]

But the book, the tours, and a bevy of charities Boesky gave money and his time to were a sharp departure from character. In private, Boesky seemed to be trying to prove Galbraith's point, bent on self-destruction. As if he were tempting fate, Boesky built his last offices in a Fifth Avenue suite recently vacated by a company affiliated with Marc Rich, a notorious fugitive from justice who is wanted by the United States on tax-evasion charges. Associates recall that when all the deals were working,

---

5   Among Boesky's believers was Foster Winans, one of the many Boesky adulators in the media who were taken in by the man and his "crystal ball". "I interviewed him as a *Wall Street Journal* reporter," Winans recalled soon after Boesky, too, had been convicted. "There was a time when I wanted to work for Ivan Boesky . . . because if I was entertaining the idea of [switching from] watching Wall Street to participating, certainly Ivan Boesky was at the top of the heap. What he does takes good research and I thought I would make a good researcher for him."

  Boesky also beguiled his ghostwriter, Jeffrey Madrick. "I feel completely duped," Madrick said after Boesky's confession. "He completely denied to me that he ever had traded on inside information."

Boesky would try to get a piece of every deal on the Street. Time and again he bet the entire shop on one risky deal, and seemed surprised — almost disappointed, some said — to emerge unscathed. Asked in late 1985 how things were going, Boesky joked, "'So far, so good,' said the man falling out the thirty-fifth-floor window."

But in the spring of 1985 Boesky had almost guaranteed he would not escape injury. According to SEC evidence, he struck up a partnership with Dennis Levine, in which Levine received a share of the profits Boesky earned on Levine's tips. Boesky was begging for trouble. Levine had been under investigation by the SEC for several months. A year and a half later the SEC announced its biggest catch in insider-trading abuse: On November 14, 1986, Ivan Boesky agreed to a settlement of insider-trading charges brought against him. The fine: $100 million. And Boesky was barred from professional stock trading for the rest of his life. After amassing a $200 million-plus fortune, Boesky was suddenly the man falling out the window.

Now the enormity of the insider-trading scandal became clear. Levine, who had focused attention on insider abuses, proved a mere bit player. For the better part of a year, Boesky had been using his massive $1-billion arbitrage fund to play the merger game, and had dabbled in almost every major takeover of the period. Just about every securities dealer had executed trades with him. The SEC soon confirmed everyone's worst fear: Boesky, presumably in a bid for leniency, had allowed himself to be wired for sound, and had spent his last few days before being revealed as a disgrace talking shop with all his old friends and building the feds' case against still more culprits. Many of the biggest and most prestigious brokerages in New York had already had their reputations sullied during the SEC's dragnet, which scooped up employees of Drexel, Shearson Lehman Bros., Merrill Lynch, Kidder Peabody, Lazard Frères, Goldman Sachs and other prominent firms. After the Boesky revelation, brokers talked fretfully about a "Wall Street Watergate", and nervously speculated about whom the SEC investigators — or "Boesky-constrictors", as they became known — would crush next. Congressmen, reacting to the outcry on Main Street, began to press for legislation to stop the trusting public from being ripped off by high-rolling New York miscreants.

Two weeks into the panic, Shearson ran its "Fabric of Integrity" ad. It was an audacious PR patch-up job, considering that Levine and another of that summer's apprehended brokers had carried on insider-trading abuses while in Shearson's employ. But drastic measures were needed. "The popular perception is that this kind of Boesky crap goes on all the time," said Robert Hanisee, president of Seidler Amdec Securities, a Los Angeles brokerage. "The real tragedy is that we keep living up to people's worst expectations." Boesky, to no one's surprise, suddenly assumed a low profile. In one brief public statement, he was contrite. "My life will be forever changed," he said following the SEC announcement of his downfall. "But I hope that something positive will ultimately come out of this situation."

Securities regulators in the United States and other countries immediately set about making that happen. By Christmas 1986, the SEC was probing trades in dozens of stocks that had been involved in takeovers. In many cases leads were generated by Boesky, Levine, and the traders they had implicated. British authorities, who acknowledged that insider-trading was chronic on the London stock exchange, investigated eight hundred such suspected cases in 1985. In an effort to step up the number, they asked for and received copious documentation of the Boesky case and others from the SEC in order to probe Boesky's many deals in the United Kingdom. British legislators tightened laws against insider abuses, and Switzerland's Parliament approved a bill that made insider trading a criminal offence. "No one can be in any doubt that we regard insider trading as a thoroughly pernicious practice," declared U.K. corporate and consumer affairs minister Michael Howard, "that we are determined to do all in our power to root out."[6]

---

6   Working with leads from the U.S. investigation of Boesky, British regulators soon discovered treachery in a distinguished place—the boardroom of the venerable brewer Guinness PLC. In late 1986, Guinness was revealed to have sought Boesky's assistance in its titanic struggle earlier that year to take over Distillers Co. PLC, maker of Johnnie Walker whisky and Gordon's gin. Boesky obliged: His role in the hostile takeover was to purchase Guinness shares, thus propping up their value. Indeed, Guinness succeeded in enlisting the aid of several parties in this share-buying scheme, a ploy expressly prohibited under U.K. securities law. The efforts of Guinness's allies were vital since Guinness was offering a combination of cash and its own (artificially inflated) stock in exchange for Distillers shares. In early 1987, when the scheme was exposed, several Guinness directors and senior officers, including the firm's CEO—who had masterminded the ultimately successful Distillers takeover—were forced to resign from the company.

Even Wall Street brokers, who have long insisted on their ability to regulate their own affairs, have begun to call on an external source for help in cleaning up their image. "It is now obvious if it was not before that effective remedial measures are needed to deal with the problem if a loss of public confidence in the markets of potentially devastating proportions is to be avoided," Donald Marron, chairman and CEO of Paine Webber Inc., a leading New York investment dealer, told a Senate subcommittee in 1987. "Congress' assistance in this endeavour is essential. I reluctantly conclude that Wall Street cannot solve this problem alone. The stakes are too high." And there was, according to most observers, no doubting that the avarice giving rise to the insider-trading scandal was deeply entrenched, and was not just the overreaching of a few naive "yuppies". Of the greed inspired by the manic pace of merger and acquisition activity in the 1980s, and the huge fees the craze generated, the anonymously quoted head of one Wall Street investment firm told *The New York Times*: "It was like free sex. You saw the abuses growing, but you also saw an absence of people getting caught, so the atmosphere grew relaxed."

At first, the Canadian reaction to the greatest Wall Street scandal in decades was understandably sanguine. Canada's high level of corporate concentration leaves few widely held companies vulnerable to takeover. And Canada's community of risk arbitrageurs numbers only three or four. These players, most notably the Belzberg family of Vancouver and Toronto trader Andrew Sarlos, invest much, if not most, of their money in the same prominent U.S. (and occasionally U.K.) merger targets from which Boesky profited. Unlike Boesky and Levine, Sarlos — for years the only risk arb of consequence in Canada — long ago learned his limits. "You can get blinded by your success and lose touch with reality and danger," Sarlos said back in 1983, after suffering a disastrous reversal during the early 1980s recession. "You reach a stage where your success is so great anything you touch turns to gold. You don't recognize the danger signals."

Securities regulators in Ontario, Canada's biggest trading arena, have successfully prosecuted only one insider-trading case, and there hasn't been a single such case in twenty years under British Columbia's securities legislation. On closer inspection, though, there are troubling signs that a significant amount of illegal insider trading *does* take place in Canadian markets. Concerned about markedly increased trading prior to several takeovers of Canadian firms, regulators drastically stiffened penalties for insider-trading abuses and began probing cases of suspected improper insider trading. Mostly they concentrated on the $2.6 billion takeover of Vancouver's Genstar Corp. by the tobacco giant Imasco Ltd. of Montreal in April 1986. Genstar shares jumped $11 in value, or 27 per cent, in the two trading sessions before Imasco's bid was announced. Regulators are also concerned about suspicious price hikes immediately before takeovers of Standard Broadcasting Corp. Ltd., Daon Development Corp., Union Enterprises Ltd., Bank of British Columbia, and Canadian Tire Corporation Ltd. But by the summer of 1987 the investigations had yet to reveal evidence of wrongdoing. Given the chronic and hard-to-detect nature of insider abuses, Ontario Securities Commission chairman Stanley Beck is thankful that takeover activity is more subdued in his bailliwick than it is in the United States. "Insider trading is easy to hide and it's an enormous amount of work to track hundreds of trades," he says. "Many times we are suspicious, but we can't prove anything."

A case against Boesky was proved, but the SEC was ultimately forced to play according to Boesky's rules. In order to enable him to pay his enormous fine, the SEC had to consent to Boesky's last fling—selling $447 million worth of securities from his main portfolio a few days before his fine was announced. The SEC's logic was that share issues propped up by takeover speculation would be in trouble once the news got out that Ivan the Terrible had been banished. True enough: Many such stocks plunged after the Boesky announcement, costing other speculators about $1 billion in lost share value. "It's the irony of ironies," said one disgruntled observer. "The biggest insider-trading information is that Boesky is being put out of business, and he gets to trade on it first."

In April 1987, Boesky pleaded guilty to one count of conspiring to make false statements to the SEC, and at a sentencing scheduled for August he faced up to five years in prison and a fine of $250,000 (U.S.). In addition, six civil lawsuits had been filed against him by investors who claim they lost money as a result of his market manipulations. Boesky himself is not cash-strapped, although he put a huge apartment in Paris, a block from Christian

Dior's showroom, on the market in 1987 (asking price: $2.5 million) along with a New Castle, N.Y., house for which he outbid tennis star Arthur Ashe in the fall of 1986 (price: $3 million). And his wife helped him through a liquidity crunch at tax time, lending him a seven-figure sum but taking care to put liens on another Boesky house in New Castle, a sculpture collection, and some rare books in order to ensure she got the funds back (the Boeskys, who in the spring of 1987 were rumoured to have split up, keep their finances separate). But Boesky's three bottles of 1961 Château Mouton Rothschild in storage behind a false wall in the basement of the 21 Club just a few rows away from Richard Nixon's stash of Dom Pérignon are safe and will, insists the wine steward, be waiting for Boesky when he gets out of prison.

Boesky had hoped to be remembered for elevating risk arbitrage to the status of a respected science. "There are no easy ways to make money in the securities market," he earnestly declared in *Merger Mania*. Undue profits are not made: "There are no esoteric tricks that enable arbitrageurs to outwit the system." Unfortunately, in proving his point Boesky blackened the eye of all business, because the market is the most prominent symbol of capitalism. Still, for a while the "small investor's friend" had a lot of believers. Said one lawyer acquaintance of Boesky's: "He beguiled everybody about his exhaustive research and canny stock analysis when he really made money the old-fashioned way: He stole it."

The rank indiscretions of a relative handful of roguish traders at first seemed like some kind of serialized entertainment, but as the indictments and convictions rolled along throughout 1987 the larger costs began to be calculated. Growing distrust of stock-market investments was driving small players out of the market — thus undermining long-time efforts by the brokerage community and public finance officials to popularize stock-market investing — and the sophisticated investors who remained flocked to trustworthy blue-chip issues, not wanting to touch riskier small companies in need of capital but lacking a track record or name recognition. And as major companies who claimed that takeovers they had completed had been artificially inflated in price because of the machinations of Boesky and the other marauders, it became clear that those inflated costs would be passed on to the consumers of products and services offered by those companies.

Naturally, a cry has gone up that someone has to pay for this disaster, and that future outbreaks of underhanded trading must be prevented. But the sad truth is that, in most jurisdictions, internal reform is a hollow promise and the political will to impose reforms from without is not likely to materialize. For all its huffing and puffing, the SEC has concentrated on a few high-profile cases which it hopes will serve as an example, while all but ignoring the vast majority of miscreants. Between 1981 and 1986 stock-trading volume in the United States tripled—and the SEC's staff *declined* by 4 per cent. The SEC, like every agency of the Reagan administration, has done its best not to be a burden on the taxpayer. Indeed, the SEC—which pays its own way through fees it collects—has, since 1983, been running a budget surplus; in 1986, it collected twice as much as it spent, and rather than hire more investigators it has turned its earnings over to the U.S. Treasury's general fund.

It's possible, of course, and certainly to be hoped, that political and regulatory officials—along with market players themselves—will start taking this form of white-collar crime seriously. But those who looked to government administrators for moral direction were bound to be disappointed, for in the mid-1980s the public sector appeared for all the world to be deriving *its* ethical standards from none other than the stock market.

CHAPTER FIVE
INDECENT DISCLOSURES
IN GOVERNMENT

As scandals have erupted in the stock market and elsewhere in business in recent years, the focus of public attention has shifted to government. People naturally wonder how the government and its formidable regulatory apparatus let the stock market once again become a playground for scoundrels. And they demand to know what proposals their elected officials have in mind for curbing the widespread scourge of corporate corruption.

But these demands will not be satisfied quickly or easily. For it seems these days that to shift one's gaze from, say, the stock market to the local legislature is to look from one den of thieves to another. Indeed, the remarkably low moral tone of our governance lately makes absurd the suggestion that public officials should presume to monitor the ethical conduct of businesspeople — a proposition akin to pressing agnostics into service as tour guides at St. Peter's Basilica. Worse still, as far as the image of business is concerned, the current epidemic of public-sector cupidity and malfeasance throughout North America can be traced in large part to businesspeople-turned-public officials who have tainted public service with lax moral standards they picked up during their previous careers in business. Lesson One for executives who do hope to derive ethical guidance from the example set by public officials would appear to be: don't let businesspeople run the government.

To pick but one recent case, Peter E. Voss had a clear idea what was expected of him when he agreed to help Ronald Reagan win the presidency in 1980. But after turning in an admirable performance as co-chairman of Reagan's campaign in Ohio, Voss became confused about the precise nature of public service when the new Reagan regime invited him to continue serving his country. In May 1986, Voss stepped down as vice-chairman of the U.S.

Postal Service Board of Governors after pleading guilty to federal charges of embezzlement and receiving illegal payments. According to court documents, within three weeks of being appointed to the board in 1982 Voss had begun an elaborate scheme of billing the government for tens of thousands of dollars in first-class air travel while travelling in coach. He also admitted to participating in an arrangement in which he would have collected more than $800,000 if a favoured supplier had been awarded a $250 million mail-sorting contract—a deal which federal prosecutors said had set back automation by two years and cost the federal government hundreds of millions of dollars. At his October sentencing, at which he was handed a four-year jail term and ordered to pay an $11,000 fine, Voss attributed his errant behaviour to his "training as a businessman. . . . I'm used to being involved in intricate business deals.... I did not think of the total ethics of the situation."

Of course, for many observers who were already of the opinion that business ethics are invariably lax, the consequence of swelling the ranks of public service with businesspeople was predictable. "This is a businessman's administration," says Charles Dempsey, who was inspector general of the scandal-ridden Housing and Urban Development department and then the Environmental Protection Agency during Reagan's first term. "This administration is loaded with guys bringing the business morality to Washington, and some of them never learn. It's like they flunked a course in basic civics."

Still, the idea that business ethics do not travel well has come as a revelation to Reagan and to Canadian prime minister Brian Mulroney. After all, both men have staked their reputations on the notion that business values make good politics. They have each sought to cure the economic lassitude gripping their nations by setting business free of governmental restraints; and both leaders expected that with the assistance of practical administrators recruited from the private sector they would be able to honour their campaign promises to rid government of its bureaucratic waste and to eradicate the last traces of petty corruption left behind by previous regimes.

During the 1984 election campaign that swept his party into power, Mulroney was emphatic about his desire to transcend pork-barrel politics and purify the process of appointing senior officials. He promised "a brand new dimension [to government appointments] of objectivity and representation and fairness for all Canadians", and decried as "vulgar . . . shameful and scandalous" a series of eighteen patronage appointments hurriedly pushed through by John Turner during his own short-lived tenure as prime minister. (The appointments included retiring former Liberal cabinet ministers Bryce Mackasey and Eugene Whelan to comfortable ambassadorial posts.)

Just one week after that denunciation of rank patronage practices, however, Mulroney revealed his own confused thoughts on the matter in what was intended as a private discussion with the press aboard his campaign plane. "Let's face it," Mulroney told the reporters, "there's no whore like an old whore. If I'd been in Bryce's position, I'd have been right in there with my nose in the public trough like the rest of them." Towards the end of the conversation Mulroney looked around and said, "I hope this is all off the record. I'm taking the high road now."

Post-election, this route has turned out to be a high road through a low place. True to his oft-repeated dictum that "Ya dance with the lady what brung ya", Mulroney has taken care of his party faithful, making 1,280 patronage appointments within a year of making hay from Turner's 18. It would be an odd thing for a new government not to make a slew of personnel changes, but the indiscretions that forced a series of cabinet-level departures from Mulroney's government raised questions about the qualifications of the hundreds of other appointees Mulroney has entrusted with positions of power — many of whom appear to have been selected for service primarily because they were school chums of Mulroney or associates from his days in business and law practice. Most of the Liberal appointees who were pushed out to make way for the new brigade went quietly, but Timothy Porteous was an exception. Porteous, who was axed as head of the Canada Council in September 1985, held a press conference to voice his criticism of the caprice that occasioned his abrupt departure. Two years later he was still licking his wounds when he told *Globe and Mail* columnist Stevie Cameron, "The standards of morality and idealism have deteriorated badly in Ottawa and the concept of public service has deteriorated. The idea that you can run a government like a corporation is wrong."

As for the defrocked ministers, their ousters were usually prompted not by greed but by an astonishing inability to avoid activities that carried a sufficient whiff of taint to destroy their political careers. Their reasons for leaving included a visit to a West German nightclub that features strippers, conflict-of-interest allegations, and a decision to allow a fishery plant to release one million tins of sub-par-quality tuna to the public. By May 1986 a total of five ministers had quit Mulroney's government during its first year and a half; only one of the fallen, Marcel Masse, who was cleared of charges he had exceeded the legal limit on campaign spending in the 1984 election, was reinstated to his cabinet post. At this point, Mulroney, under tremendous pressure to clean house, insisted his Progressive Conservative government was "erecting a new standard of morality day by day in Canada". Yet within nine months two more ministers were gone: André Bissonnette was nudged out of his post as secretary of state for transport pending an investigation into soaring land prices for property bought by a defence contractor locating in his riding; and Minister of State Roch LaSalle quit in February 1987, saying he was "exhausted morally and physically" after coming under fire for hosting a party in July 1985 for which about thirty businessmen had paid an individual admission charge of $5,000 in the hope of being awarded government contracts. (LaSalle insisted he was unaware his guests had paid to attend.)

The repeated instances of questionable conduct have had the same effect on Mulroney as they would on the average company: Everyone involved in the enterprise — in this case the entire country — has been distracted by the run of shoddy episodes, and as a result the government has had a difficult time sticking to its public agenda of free trade, remedying the unemployment problem, restoring the environment, and so on. And Mulroney is paying a heavy political price. His party is the third-most popular of the three major parties, having slipped to its lowest point in the polls since 1942 — a fate that recalls the experience of the Tories under Sir John A. Macdonald. Macdonald's party dominated Canadian federal politics in the nineteenth century, but was ultimately undermined by a rash of scandals. These included revelations that Canada's first prime minister himself had accepted graft in exchange for supporting in Parliament the interests of railway promoters seeking a government contract (Macdonald's plea to railway lawyer J.C. Abbott in 1872 — "I MUST HAVE ANOTHER $10,000" — is the most famous telegram in Canadian history, and precipitated Macdonald's defeat at the polls one year later). Today, Mulroney contemplates his own political future from the prime minister's suite of offices in the Langevin Block, an imposing structure erected in the 1880s and named for Sir Hector-Louis Langevin. Sir Hector was not only implicated in the Pacific Scandal that brought down his boss, Macdonald, in 1873, but, following the political rehabilitation of both men, was caught up in yet another railway-contract scandal and in 1891 was forced to resign his cabinet post in disgrace. The Liberals capitalized on the lingering public disaffection with the Tories' string of moral lapses at the time of Sir Wilfrid Laurier's 1896 victory, and — with the short-lived exceptions of the Diefenbaker, Clark, and Mulroney governments — have dominated the federal scene ever since.

The moral lassitude in Ottawa draws most of the headlines, but unethical behaviour is hardly a special problem afflicting only federal politicians or Tories. The young government of Ontario premier David Peterson suffered three ministerial resignations in just six months beginning in June 1986. The first two ministers to quit were found to have contravened the premier's conflict-of-interest guidelines; the third briefly stepped down from his post as solicitor-general after it was revealed he faced a charge of consuming liquor on an Ontario Provincial Police boat only a few days before issuing a province-wide public campaign against the practice of drinking and boating. (After being convicted of the charge and paying a $53 fine, the embarrassed minister was quietly reappointed to the post.)

In the run-up to the 1986 contest to replace William Bennett as premier of British Columbia, three obvious contenders from Bennett's cabinet disqualified themselves. One minister quit the cabinet after pleading guilty to failing to disclose all of his investments; another admitted to being assaulted by the husband of a woman he was seeing on the side; a third testified in a prostitution trial that he had sought female companionship through an escort-services firm called Top Hat Productions. In October, the Nova Scotia legislature passed a special bill to eject one of its members, former culture minister William Joseph (Billy Joe) MacLean, who had pleaded guilty earlier in the year to four counts of issuing forged documents to justify almost $22,000 in official expense-account spending. Following his ejection and the payment of a $6,000 fine, the popular former Port Hawkesbury mayor was easily re-elected to his Inverness South riding in a by-election, and now sits in the legislature once again as an independent.

In November 1986, a telecommunications arm of the state-owned Manitoba Telephone System that had already come under fire for discriminatory hiring practices connected with contracts in Saudi Arabia was revealed to be rife with bribery, kickbacks, and maladministration. Alvin Mackling was forced to resign his post as minister responsible for MTS, several top executives of MTS and its telecommunications subsidiary resigned or were fired, and the Saudi Arabian operations were promptly wound up. At the same time heads were rolling in Manitoba, the former leader of the Liberal party in the Yukon was sentenced to three years imprisonment on drug-trafficking charges. The brazen culprit, Robert Coles, twenty-eight, had conducted one of his deals with RCMP undercover agents in the cafeteria of the Yukon Government administration building, and another in the Liberal caucus room at the Legislature. One month later, Peter Pope, a Tory member of the Prince Edward Island legislature who once had been transport minister, was convicted of assaulting a woman at her home in St. Eleanor's, and resigned from the provincial house of assembly early in 1987. Opposition-party critics had a field day with such revelations, of course, but even the accusers were not unbesmirched. In October 1986, federal Liberal MP Don Boudria, possibly the most tireless and vocal critic of Mulroney patronage, was himself discovered to have voted, while serving as an Ottawa-area councillor in 1979, to award a firm operated by his brother-in-law $82,000 in construction contracts. Confronted with the apparent past breach, Boudria explained that, while he had indeed failed to report the conflict, the guidelines for councillors did not specifically rule out voting on matters involving one's brother-in-law and, besides, it was no secret to Boudria's fellow councillors that the firm in question was run by someone to whom he was related. So undaunted by the revelation was Boudria, in fact, that he was soon back on the Mulroney government's case, accusing Maureen McTeer, wife of external affairs minister Joe Clark, of using her husband's government staff to assist her with the monthly column she produces for *Chatelaine* magazine.

Small wonder, then, that a public-opinion poll in late 1986 showed 54 per cent of Canadians believed federal and provincial politicians were less than honest. Yet the Canadian system, for all its apparent weaknesses, is inherently designed to encourage a higher standard of moral conduct in its public servants than is the U.S. system. An important facet of the Canadian political tradition has been the development of a professional civil service. Mulroney has made his hundreds of politically inspired appointments, to be sure, but these comprise a very small portion of all public-service posts, most of which are filled by well-paid employees who expect to make government a lifetime career.

The United States, by contrast, has a strong tradition of citizen politicians and bureaucrats. With each new presidency, thousands of people, most of them partisans of the presidential victor and with no training in government service, move into government for a few years and then return to private life. During their time in public office, which may last only as long as "their" president holds on to his job, these recruits make the most of the perks of office. At the higher rungs, the greatest perk usually is the chance to build a reputation and a network of high-powered contacts that should last a lifetime. Michael Deaver earned only $75,100 (U.S.) in salary as Ronald Reagan's deputy chief of staff, but soon after his departure from the White House in 1985 he peddled his continued access to top government officials — and especially to Reagan himself — with such avidity that within a year of quitting formal government service he was offered $18 million for the essentially one-man public-relations firm he had set up. (The value of the firm quickly plummeted, however, when Deaver came under fire for allegedly trading on his influence too quickly after retiring from the White House — particularly in a deal to help Canada lobby for acid-rain-prevention legislation on Capitol Hill.)

Similarly, former Reagan budget director David Stockman, also paid $75,100 while in office, was rewarded with a six-figure job at a Wall Street brokerage upon quitting government. He also nailed down a $2 million advance for a book he wrote describing how he helped Reagan plan the dismantling of the welfare state, and how the administration deceived the U.S. public by concocting a regime of tax cuts that required social programs to be cut back in order to fund tax reductions for America's wealthiest citizens.

The theory giving rise to the U.S. system is admirable enough. The founding fathers, repelled by the practice of European monarchs and their courtiers living high off the avails of public service, were determined that government employees in America not get rich at the taxpayers' expense. Unfortunately, in practice the relative low pay of even the best government jobs in the United States has required that talented administrators recruited from business and academe accept large pay cuts to take the positions. These people, along with less talented opportunists who hope to use public service as a stepping stone to lucrative jobs after retiring, are thus encouraged to perform their jobs in such a way as to secure a very comfortable living immediately upon departing the halls of political power. Thus the short tenure of government postings, whether elected or bureaucratic, has been a cause of public-service corruption since the earliest days of the Republic.

George Washington, who bought his way into the Virginia House of Burgesses in 1758 by supplying the voters with twenty-eight and one-half gallons of wine and copious other imbibements, was an unsuccessful — and, some historians claim, unscrupulous — land speculator who got in over his head. The general's solution was to marry rich, but after wedding the wealthy and recently widowed Martha Curtis, he became over-extended again with his liberal purchases of land and slaves. "I have swallowed, before I knew where I was, all the money I got by my marriage," he said. "Nay more, brought me into debt."

The richest man in America at the time of the Revolution was Robert Morris, a member of Congress and a partner in a Philadelphia brokerage and shipping house. After becoming a member of the congressional committee charged with procurement of military supplies, Morris absconded with $483,000 of the $2 million the committee spent to outfit the army. This was in addition to the profit Morris accumulated by importing goods for his own account on government ships carrying public goods, for which he paid neither charter fees nor insurance.

In the great Yazoo land scandal, the entire 1795 Georgia legislature (save one member) was bribed to grant millions of acres to land speculators at a price of one or two cents an acre. Later, Joseph Smith, founder of the Mormon Church, opened a bank in order to pay his debts; the vaults of this institution held reserves consisting of a thin layer of half-dollar coins covering a mound of sand, lead, and bits of old iron.

The third wife of President Ulysses S. Grant's war secretary was "Puss" Belknap. She used her husband's position to sell Indian post traderships on the quiet. Newly elected President Benjamin Harrison complained in 1889 that, "I could not name my own cabinet. [The party managers] had sold every place to pay the election expenses." At the height of the Robber Baron railway-building era, Credit Mobilier agents ladled out bargain-priced shares to more than a score of congressmen, including future president James Garfield and Secretary of State James Blaine.

Warren G. Harding's administration ushered in the hedonistic Roaring Twenties, and was every bit as consumed with unseemly grasping as the times. Harding's veterans' bureau director, Charlie Forbes, sold "surplus" hospital supplies and received huge kickbacks from building contractors. His attorney general, Harry Daugherty, sold liquor permits, pardons, and paroles at fancy prices. Daugherty's henchman Jess Smith sold "B permits" — which allowed liquor sales on medical grounds — to bootleggers. Harding's interior secretary, Albert Bacon Fall, secretly leased the U.S. Navy's oil reserves at Teapot Dome, Wyoming, and Elk Hills, California, to private interests in exchange for more than $250,000 in "loans". Harding's treasury secretary, Andrew Mellon, much loved by businessmen of the era for his tax-cutting regime, was exposed in the early 1930s as a tax cheat. Harding himself was a member of the Ku Klux Klan; he desecrated the White House by being inducted into the white-supremist society in a ceremony held in the Green Room of the presidential mansion.

No subsequent presidency would be so gripped by unbridled greed as Harding's had been. Indeed, most of the transgressions that surfaced during the next few decades were venial. The perception was growing, however, that public servants should be held accountable to a higher standard of moral conduct than they had been in the past. By the 1950s the mere hint of impropriety could scuttle a political career. In the process of absolving himself of accusations of wrongdoing during his 1952 bid for the vice-presidency on the Eisenhower ticket, Richard Nixon became one of the first major public figures to discover how damaging the adverse public perceptions could be. In one of television's most memorable addresses, Nixon faced the cameras to deny being the recipient of lavish campaign financing from a secret treasury funded by millionaires. Nixon was indeed not guilty — his campaign fund was neither secret nor improperly run — but he insisted on winding up his statement of innocence with a mawkish flourish: "One other thing I should probably tell you," Nixon said in conclusion, "because if I don't they'll be saying this about me, too. We did get something, a gift. . . . It was a little cocker spaniel dog in a crate . . . black and white, spotted, and our little girl Tricia, the six-year-old, named it Checkers. And you know, the kids, like all kids, love that dog, and I just want to say this, right now, that regardless of what they say about it, we're going to keep it."

Where Nixon was able to conquer the perception problem, Eisenhower's chief of staff, Sherman Adams, was not. No previous presidential aide had so thoroughly won the confidence of his boss; Adams had a hand in every decision. "Whatever I have to do he has in some measure to do," Eisenhower had said of Adams, and it was Adams's job to say "no" for the genial Eisenhower, who often could not bring himself to do so. Adams thus was known to political enemies as "the Abominable No-Man". His conspicuous integrity had gained national prominence during the Truman administration, which he had decried for its mink coats, freezers, and influence peddling and had called an "Augean stables". Once installed in the White House, Adams paid for the stamps he put on personal letters and insisted on being billed for personal phone calls.

In the summer of 1958, however, congressional hearings into the affairs of a corrupt New England textile manufacturer named Bernard Goldfine proved Adams's undoing. Goldfine, under investigation for allegedly looting his own firms of tens of thousands of dollars and appending misleading labels to his garments was revealed to have bought the affections of several public servants. Adams was not "bought"; no one even dared think he could be. But Adams and his family, ignorant of Goldfine's shady dealings, had become enamoured of the self-made Lithuanian immigrant, a public-spirited millionaire who had refused to join other textile makers in their pilgrimage to the cheap labour and low taxes of the South and had instead resolutely stayed put in Adams's native New England. Adams and Goldfine became friends, and Adams ascribed no ulterior designs to Goldfine's generosity — which extended to such gifts as a $2,400 Oriental rug from Macy's, picking up the tab for twenty-one stays by the Adamses at Boston's plush Sheraton Plaza Hotel, and a vicuña coat.

When the gifts became public, Adams admitted he had been

imprudent. But he claimed ignorance: He had been under the impression that the hotel suites at the Sheraton, for instance, were rented permanently by one of Goldfine's companies and would have been empty if his family hadn't used them. Adams insisted he had extended no assistance to Goldfine that he would not also have gladly offered any businessperson confused by Washington bureaucracy. Ike was determined to keep Adams on. "I need him," he told the press. But in 1958 the "vicuña scandal" was grist for every Democrat running against the Eisenhower administration. As the enormity of Goldfine's corruption became clear, Republican campaign funds dried up and the pressure on Ike to remove Adams became overpowering. Eisenhower described Adams's removal as "the most hurtful, the hardest, the most heartbreaking decision" of his presidency. In the end, true to form, he could not do the firing himself; he handed the task to an unfortunate subordinate.

Like Adams, Richard Nixon had once seemed a figure of immense moral rectitude. Indeed, he assumed the presidency in 1968 in the guise of "Mr. Law and Order", vowing to impose moral discipline on a society strife-torn by rioters and looters in the urban centres. At the beginning of his second term in office, however, Nixon would endure the political ruination he had so narrowly escaped in the early 1950s. He was preceded in this fate by his own vice-president, who was not able to defend himself as Nixon had in 1952: Spiro Agnew, who had placed third on the Gallup poll's 1969 list of "Men Most Admired by Americans" (after Nixon and the Reverend Billy Graham), resigned in 1973 after admitting he had falsified his federal income tax return.[1] Nixon's time would come ten months later.

---

1   Agnew was the first vice-president to resign in the face of criminal charges. He was fined $10,000 and put on probation for three years. In protracted plea-bargaining, Agnew extracted an assurance he would be treated leniently in court in exchange for tendering his resignation and allowing a forty-page statement of evidence to be entered into the court record. This statement, which Agnew denied, alleged he had received payoffs from contractors of more than $100,000 while serving as Baltimore County executive and Maryland governor and later as vice-president. The relaxed hand of justice in the Agnew case gave rise to an expression common in plea-bargaining sessions. Criminals seeking lenient sentences often spoke of their desire to receive "the Agnew treatment".

On August 8, 1974, after eighteen months of denials and coun-ter-charges, Nixon stepped down from office — the first president ever to do so. In another memorable TV address, Nixon obliquely confessed his participation in a conspiracy to obstruct justice by covering up his knowledge of the 1972 break-in and attempted bugging of the Democratic National Committee headquarters at the Watergate hotel in Washington, D.C., by White House opera-tives. When the nightmare was over, and the televised activities of the Senate and House investigative committees and the Water-gate special prosecutor had wound up, a record number of presi-dential officers had been hauled into court. Twenty-one people who worked for Nixon were charged with crimes arising from Watergate; seventeen were convicted.[2] The charges related to wiretapping, obstruction of justice, burglaries, and illegal cam-paign contributions, among other misdemeanours. After a fashion, Nixon ended up becoming a law-and-order man after all. The moral laxity of his administration bore the fruit of reform, principally the 1978 Ethics in Government Act, passed during President Jimmy Carter's administration but aimed at curbing Watergate-type offences. Hundreds of top presidential appointees now must report their income, assets, and liabilities to the Office of Government Ethics.

But the post-Watergate reforms held out a hollow promise. For one thing, they have seldom been matched by similar initiatives at other levels of government. In 1980, the Federal Bureau of In-vestigation reported that corruption by state and local officials outran bank fraud and embezzlement and was the most wide-spread form of white-collar crime. For another, the reforms

---

2   Nixon was granted a full pardon by his successor, Gerald Ford; it was the first pardon of a president for alleged criminal acts. At the time of his resig-nation, Nixon faced certain impeachment in the Senate. Three "Articles of Impeachment" were likely to be passed to it by the House of Representa-tives. The first Article, which accused Nixon of obstructing justice, was borne out by an Oval Office tape recording Nixon released a few days before his resignation, in which he said, "I don't give a shit what happens. I want you to stonewall it, let them plead the Fifth Amendment, cover up or anything else, if it'll save it, save the plan." In a tearful farewell talk with his White House staff on the morning of his last day in office, Nixon allowed that his financial position was shaky: "Now I've got to find a way to pay my taxes." He did. Nixon's political memoirs have earned the ex-chief executive more than $1 million.

appear to be an ineffective guard against federal impropriety, or so the epidemic of wrongdoing in the Reagan administration is proving.

In fairness, the handful of Reagan officials who have faced criminal charges is no match for the Nixon era. But the number who have gotten into trouble is. An unprecedented 110 senior Reagan appointees have been accused of unethical or illegal conduct. And unlike the Nixon lawbreakers, whose actions, however misconceived, were prompted by a patriotic belief that keeping Nixon in office was good for the country, the Reagan-era misconduct arises mostly out of naked greed, and has been characterized by personal enrichment, favouritism, and conflicts of interest.

To be sure, many of the transgressions have been of a venial nature: Daniel K. Benjamin resigned as chief of staff at the labour department in 1984 after disclosures that he had free use of a sailboat belonging to a lobbyist who deals with the department. Donald I. Hovde, undersecretary of Housing and Urban Development, reimbursed the government $3,100 for improper use of a government car and driver, which he used to pick up his laundry and to take his neighbours to the Kennedy Center and his parents on a sightseeing tour. Nancy Harvey Steorts, former chairperson of the Consumer Product Safety Commission, had her government driver take her to the hairdresser and pick up dresses at a boutique.

Some appointees have merely displayed questionable judgment. Ernest Lefever withdrew as a nominee for assistant secretary of state for human rights after a Senate committee rejected him, partly on the basis that his conservative think-tank had distributed material promoting infant formula to Third World mothers after receiving a $25,000 donation from Nestlé, a major infant-formula maker. Marianne Mele Hall quit the Copyright Tribunal in 1985 after editing a book that said blacks "insist on preserving their jungle freedoms" and stay on welfare to enjoy "leisure time and subsidized procreation". Eileen Marie Gardner quit as special assistant in the education department after eyebrows were raised over her published remarks that handicapped people had "selfishly drained resources from the normal school population" and that efforts to help the disabled were "misguided". James Watt stepped down as interior secretary after joking that a new advisory panel he had set up would reflect the government's official commitment to equal opportunity since it was to comprise "a black . . . , a woman, two Jews and a cripple". And R. Leonard Vance, director of health standards at the Occupational Safety and Health Administration, explained to congressional investigators in 1984 that he could not produce his appointment calendars showing his meetings with a chemical manufacturer because his dogs had been sick and vomited on them.

There has, however, been a great deal of more serious wrongdoing, and disturbingly, the malaise is deepest among government departments and agencies charged with supervising the activities of business. Both of Reagan's attorneys general—the highest law officers in the land—have been accused of ethical violations. William French Smith, Reagan's first attorney general and Reagan's own personal lawyer, agreed to forgo tax deductions from an oil-and-gas tax-shelter scheme the Internal Revenue Service had declared abusive; and he repaid $11,000 for improper use of a government limousine by his wife. Smith's successor, Edwin Meese III, was accused of helping arrange federal jobs for six people who had helped him financially during a previous posting as White House counsellor and failed to report on his financial disclosure form a $15,000 interest-free loan to his wife from a family friend who later worked for Meese at the White House. An independent counsel's inquiry in 1984 found no criminal violations by Meese on these and other allegations of impropriety. But Meese, whose department oversees anti-trust, insider-trading, and other business-related investigations, is at this writing one of the subjects of another probe, this one involving federal assistance to a government supplier named Wedtech Corp.

Ten top officials have quit or been fired from the Environmental Protection Agency following charges of wrongdoing; seven senior Housing and Urban Development department officials have departed under a cloud; and two successive heads of the now-defunct Synthetic Fuels Corp. have quit amid conflict-of-interest charges. In 1986, three senior officials who regulate the U.S. savings and loan industry billed the Federal Home Loan Bank Board several thousand dollars in personal expenses that included tickets to Wimbledon matches, greens fees at the tony Pebble Beach golf course in California, and chauffeur-driven limousines for sightseeing in London. A Securities and Exchange

Commission investigatory panel absolved a local SEC office from guilt in a sexual-harassment complaint brought against it by an employee with the sanguine explanation that, "All in all, an atmosphere exists [at the local SEC office] where drinking and sexual involvements among staff are not unusual, and where most of it is engaged in by members of upper management." The complainant's problem, apparently, was that she had failed to become a team player.

Despite the rampant immorality in high places, the Office of Government Ethics failed to discipline a single federal employee for ethical violations between 1983 and 1986. The mood in Washington reflects that of the president, who didn't see anything wrong in former White House chief of staff Deaver using his diplomatic passport to try to buy a BMW luxury car at a discount in West Germany. Reagan called the ploy a "standard practice that's been used for many, many years". Strange times, indeed. William H. Rehnquist told the Senators deciding whether to confirm him as the sixteenth chief justice of the Supreme Court, that he had not signed the deed to his summer house in Greensboro, Vermont, which he bought in 1974. Therefore he could not know that the deed contained a clause added to the standard printed document that bars sale of the house to "anyone of the Hebrew race". But then Rehnquist also had not seen or signed the deed on a previous home, in Phoenix; that deed included a covenant against transferring ownership of the property to anyone not of the "Caucasian race". Rehnquist, of course, was easily confirmed — no doubt, the first lawyer who doesn't read his personal legal documents to be elevated to the Supreme Court.

The problem seems to be that politicians are well-intentioned in matters of personal morality, but just can't seem to follow through on those intentions. "We cannot turn our democracy over to an aristocracy of money," Senate majority leader Robert Byrd said in a Senate address on the opening day of Congress in January 1987. "Without campaign finance reform, we will continue to subject our democratic process to control by the special interests and, more often, to the appearance of improper influence." This was no idle musing: Byrd himself only a month earlier had convened with two hundred lobbyists and directors of political-action committees and on this occasion, according to *The Washington Post*, had told his guests that if they were able to pledge $10,000 each towards his political efforts they would have the opportunity to sit down and chat with the leader on a regular informal basis during the 100th Congress.

And Reagan, who came to office in 1980 promising to restore "family values" and rid government of "waste, fraud and abuse", sets great store by high morals. "I am for morality," he said in the spring of 1987. "In fact, I wish there were more of it taught in our schools."

Of course, a great many people in society — everyone from school children to business leaders — take their cue as to what constitutes social mores from the person at the top. In this regard, *Fortune* in a September 1986 cover story, thought America was well served, and that businesspeople, in particular, could learn from the president's example. "A close look [at Reagan's administration] reveals lessons executives everywhere can put to work," the magazine said. Chief among these lessons, according to the the manager-in-chief himself: "Surround yourself with the best people you can find, delegate authority and don't interfere." Two months later Reagan was ensnarled in a crisis that seemed certain to greatly weaken the effectiveness of his administration during his remaining time in office — the sale of arms to Iran in exchange for the release of Americans held prisoner there, and the subsequent diversion of funds realized from those sales to armed rebels seeking to overthrow the government of Nicaragua. Only a month before officials in Reagan's National Security Council got the go-ahead to commence the arms shipments — approval for which was allegedly granted on August 8, 1985, eleven years to the day after Nixon's resignation speech Reagan had labelled Iran a prime example of "outlaw states run by the strangest collection of misfits, Looney Tunes and squalid criminals since the advent of the Third Reich". Now it appeared that the United States had sold arms to these Looney Tunes, despite an avowed White House policy never to trade arms or money for hostages; and the funds from this bizarre transaction were then dispatched to anti-government *contra* fighters in Nicaragua — a clear contravention of the will of Congress to curtail U.S. funding of efforts to overthrow the Central American government. As Reagan's officials either dissembled or took the Fifth Amendment, the chief executive himself said he simply could not remember if he approved the first shipment of arms to Iran on August 8, 1985.

"It's possible to forget," he said, asking a group of visitors to the White House if any could recall what they were doing on that date. None could. As for the constitutional abridgements and other alleged improprieties arising out of the so-called Irangate affair, all Reagan could offer by way of an apology was, "Mistakes were made."

Events in Washington and Ottawa have indeed set an important example for business. The consequences of failing to take responsibility for one's actions and those of subordinates are grievous, and they derive chiefly from an absence of clear guidelines as to what constitutes just and proper conduct by all of the individuals in an enterprise. In the wake of three resignations from his cabinet in the short space of a year, Ontario premier David Peterson realized, too late, that, "Our [conflict-of-interest guidelines] are so unclear. There is no ongoing monitoring and no enforcement." In the private sector, which has produced so many political recruits who have stumbled in public life, there is now a growing awareness of the need for preventive ethical maintenance. As the more ambitious examples in the following chapter indicate, business is slowly coming round to being worthy of the emulation that Reagan and Mulroney — perhaps a little too soon — thought it merited.

PART TWO

In Pursuit of the Honest Buck

CHAPTER SIX
MORAL ENTERPRISE:
PROFITING BY
THE LIGHT OF DAY

Ethical vacuity—the lack of a sense of right and wrong in a corporate culture   can have dire consequences. With increasing frequency, the victims of companies that befoul the environment, peddle unsafe products, deceive consumers, and cheat their shareholders feel empowered to hold corporate miscreants to account. At the very least, companies with no sense of social responsibility court negative publicity, fines, and lawsuits. In extreme cases, unscrupulous CEOs and other senior executives are being sacked and imprisoned; companies weakened by immoral conduct are exposed to the threat of takeovers or driven into bankruptcy; and entire industries are suffering the imposition of harsh new government regulations. Meanwhile, behind the sensationalist headlines describing pollution, product-liability, and insider-trading scandals, the toll exacted by white-collar malfeasance—crimes committed *against* companies, not by them—is rapidly mounting.

Moral decay is costing business its credibility and cold hard cash. That is why most businesses these days are re-examining the ways in which they operate. It is not an easy job to turn profit-driven companies into principle-driven ones. "Most managers think of profits and market share as moral," says Jim Waters, former dean of graduate studies at Boston College and former dean at Toronto's York University. "Their professional training has encouraged them to think that making as much money as they can for their companies is a primary moral obligation in itself." And the profit imperative usually subverts all other considerations. "Hard, measurable performance criteria—for example, profitability, sales volume, costs—tend to drive out softer, less measurable criteria such as social responsiveness and ethical practices," says Waters. "Because the former are easier to discuss, agree on, and control, they attract more executive time and energy than the latter."

Traditionally, corporations have relied on the audit process to guard against wrongdoing by their employees. Accounting, or "internal control", systems are intended to prevent the misuse of company funds by providing that transactions are properly authorized and all assets are accounted for. Yet breaches of health and safety regulations, violations of pollution laws, discrimination in hiring practices, price-fixing, and false advertising are just some of the many common illegal acts that may leave no traces in the books. And, as often as not, financial transactions that accompany unethical acts are duly authorized by corporate officers who believe, however wrongly, that they are acting in the best interests of the company. The only effective safeguard against ethical breaches, then, is to make ethical concerns an integral part of all corporate activities. And this, in turn, requires that the highest-ranked executives overtly and consistently commit themselves and their companies to doing well by doing good. As *The Wall Street Journal* recently put it, "Many corporate employees have behaved improperly in the misguided belief that the front office wanted them to. If standards are not formulated systematically at the top, they will be formulated haphazardly and impulsively in the field."

With this concern in mind, many major North American companies are implementing multi-faceted ethics programs. Large U.S. corporations such as General Dynamics Corp., McDonnell Douglas Corp., Chemical Bank, and Primerica Corp. (formerly American Can Co.) and leading Canadian businesses such as Imperial Oil Ltd. and the Royal Bank of Canada have in recent years developed elaborate ethics programs that include the drafting of codes of conduct, training workshops, ombudsmen, ethics directors, and special committees of management and directors which deal with moral issues. Less ambitious companies do not adopt all of these measures, but most major firms are taking at least some steps towards creating an ethical framework within which to conduct their business. Of the 279 leading U.S. firms that responded in 1985 to a 1,000-company survey on ethics conducted by the Center for Business Ethics at Bentley College in Waltham, Massachusetts, 208 reported having formal codes of

conduct, 99 had training programs, 40 had set up ethics committees whose members were drawn from senior management, and
17 had either ombudsmen or special hot lines to handle ethics-
related problems that employees might otherwise fail to report
because they feared the consequences of going through normal
channels.

To be sure, some of the most extensive drives to "get ethics"
have been face-saving exercises undertaken by companies exposed in defence-contract frauds, money-laundering activities,
and insider-trading scandals. More often, though, rescuing a
public image — or, ideally, heading off the need ever to do so — is
only one factor prompting the growing interest in ethics. Volatile
business conditions — deregulation, foreign competition, and
hectic merger and acquisition activity, for example — create new
problems that could lead to moral missteps by companies that fail
to take precautions. And companies that take ethics seriously
aren't just securing negative benefits — the vital but intangible
benefit, for instance, of not spilling contaminants into the environment at an untold cost to the community. The process of
raising a company's ethical consciousness requires that the firm
put itself through a comprehensive and critical re-evaluation of
how it goes about its business. And in that process of integrating
ethical considerations into every financial, manufacturing, marketing, and employee-relations decision, managers and workers
at all levels of the company rediscover the very nature of their
business and gain valuable new insights into the concerns of
every group with which the company deals: employees, customers, suppliers, shareholders, regulators, and competitors.
When properly introduced and constantly reinforced, a company's ethical values become just another important management tool, every bit as useful as cost-benefit analyses, new-
product research, and marketing surveys.

At most firms, the drive to raise the level of ethical consciousness begins with the creation of a corporate code of ethical conduct. Published codes are an overt and durable expression of a
firm's moral values, and as such are the most common foundation upon which a corporate ethical framework is built. Their
value was recognized long ago by a few enlightened companies
such as J.C. Penney Co. and Johnson & Johnson, which have
held themselves to corporate-values statements for several gene-

rations. The practice of drafting codes of ethical conduct did not become common, however, until the post-Watergate era of the mid-1970s, when many major U.S. corporations were implicated in scandals over illegal campaign contributions and overseas bribery. And only today is the practice of promulgating codes becoming truly widespread, prompted by the belated recognition that ethics-related crises do not always trace their origin to high-ranking executives nor are they confined to multinational concerns with extensive operations abroad.

Codes are often dismissed as mere window-dressing, a charge not easily refuted. At their worst, industry-wide codes of conduct are cynical bids to secure a self-policing status which in turn functions to keep pesky regulators at bay. The drug, tobacco, and construction trades are among the many industries with codes behind which firms have hidden while committing unsavoury acts with apparent impunity. When individual companies go to the trouble of adopting their own codes, some skeptics remain unimpressed. "Codes are meant only to be protective devices, not a means of establishing a higher moral standard," says H.T. (Tom) Wilson, an ethics professor at York University. "They're often meaningless, like putting up a warning sign outside the whorehouse."

But the alternative—having no code, and letting employees play it by ear—isn't very attractive, either. "A code is a good start, a reference point," says Allan Taylor, chairman of the Royal Bank of Canada. "Otherwise, you've got nothing. If you've at least highlighted obvious and common problems in a code, corporate officers can refer to it and say, 'My God, we can't do *that*.'" Employees need the guidance of a code, says Shell Canada Ltd. CEO Jack MacLeod, because "the social and legal definitions of right and wrong are becoming increasingly complex with the result that an employee may act in an unethical manner 'in all innocence'." And codes, unlike moral instruction received in the home, church, or school, are able to blend real-life issues facing a particular company and its industry with universal ethical values. "A code of corporate conduct is the primary documentation for moving business ethics from the area of ideas to that of action at the various levels of a corporation," says Arden Haynes, CEO of Imperial Oil. "Much of the content has its origins not in theory but in experience—and the need to co-ordinate diverse interests and activities, to accommodate the individual and the firm to environmental expectations and to avoid conflicts. It improves the quality and efficiency of relationships by providing common understandings."

Yet, while a consensus has emerged on the need for codes, attitudes vary widely on how best to put them to work. The most common approach is to make the ethics code part of the company's thick corporate policy manual. It's an effective method of implementation, since managers who use the manual are constantly reminded that their company cares as much about adherence to high ethical standards as it does about observing preferred procedures in areas such as finance, marketing, and manufacturing. Unfortunately, though, not many companies go beyond this step. For instance, at steelmaker Dofasco Inc. and forest products giant MacMillan Bloedel Ltd., codes are distributed only to managers; employees with ethics-related concerns are encouraged to take them up with their supervisors, who consult the codes for guidance. This approach has the effect of sidelining ethics, of making morality something that only managers have a special knowledge of and responsibility for. It also encourages the idea that managers, as keepers of the ethical codes, may have the power to interpret them to their own advantage.

While it is impractical to distribute a company's bible of operating procedures to every employee, the ethical directives contained in that daunting volume can easily be condensed and disseminated to all. Imperial Oil, for instance, tries to make ethics an everyday issue throughout the ranks by putting a copy of *Our Corporate Ethics* in the hands of all of its 12,500 employees. Everyone who works at Imperial is required to read the twenty-page publication and sign a statement "to demonstrate your understanding of and compliance with policies contained in the booklet". At the Royal Bank, all 38,200 employees receive copies of the bank's *Code of Conduct: Principles of Ethical Behaviour*, the contents of which are reviewed and discussed at the time of each employee's annual or semi-annual performance-appraisal interview.

When companies take the extra step of incorporating ethical values into their overall "mission statements" — snappy credos that describe a company's primary goals as a competitive enterprise — the commitment to ethics can be conveyed in an even more widespread manner, both inside and outside the company.

For instance, Johnson & Johnson's *Our Credo*, a motto first drafted in the 1940s describing J&J's responsibilities to a multitude of "stakeholders", hangs on the walls of hundreds of company offices throughout the world, where it is a constant reminder of J&J's operating principles—not only to employees but to customers and suppliers. And at J.C. Penney Co., employees receive wallet-sized cards bearing *The Penney Idea*. The *Idea* consists of seven objectives, the last of which is, "To test our every policy, method and act in this wise: 'Does it square with what is right and just?' "

Some companies find that sort of general statement so appealing they construct their ethical frameworks entirely out of general principles and disdain the creation of rules outlawing specific practices. "We're against rules," says Willard L'Heureux, managing partner of financial services at Hees International Corp., a publicly traded management company through which Edward and Peter Bronfman of Toronto control such major companies as the conglomerate Brascan Ltd. and land developer Trizec Corp. Ltd. "Ethics is pervasive, you can't put it in a box. So instead of rules we talk about the values and principles we believe in, which can be applied to every situation." L'Heureux's fear, of course, is that a manager, confronted with a list of specific prohibitions in a formal code of conduct, might take this as an invitation to search for loopholes and to contravene the spirit if not the letter of the code. It's hard to contravene the spirit of a code if the spirit is the only thing it conveys.

The drawback to that approach, however, is that individual managers are left to interpret the company's values and principles as best they can, and have no formal guidelines to help them cope with specific problems that come up. Many companies are more comfortable with a combination of the general and rule-based approaches.

Thus Imperial Oil's corporate-ethics booklet begins with the straightforward declaration that "This company cares about how it gets results." In the pages that follow, however, employees are instructed not to give or accept gifts or entertainment worth more than $25 and are provided with elaborate descriptions of what constitutes insider-trading, conflict-of-interest, and restrictive-trade practices. Putting specific prohibitions in writing also guards against the temptation among employees to wilfully fail to recognize the ethical dimension of a problem—or, having recognized an ethical conflict, deciding out of expedience or fear of reprisal not to report it. The Royal Bank comes down on this aspect of ethical accountability with an iron hand. In the introduction to its guidebook on ethical behaviour, the bank declares that, "The provisions of this Code are mandatory, and full compliance is expected of all employees, as a condition of employment. Further, any employee who becomes aware of a contravention of the Code, or of a grave infraction of the Employee Rules referred to in it, must report the facts promptly to his or her superior or to higher authority, or see that they are so reported."

Regardless of its contents, a code is sure to fail if it is perceived as a creation of "staff" versus "line" personnel within the company. The function of employees with staff jobs (accountants, lawyers, and human-resources and public-relations specialists) is only to advise the line-of-command side of the business—the plant managers, marketing experts, and sales reps who actually conduct the company's business and bring in the revenues. The latter have no patience with anything that appears to be a make-work project cooked up by an isolated staff department operating far from the field.

To carry conviction, a code of conduct must bear the imprimatur of the CEO and have the active support of senior finance, marketing, and manufacturing executives. Ethics at many firms is still a hobbyhorse of the human resources and PR departments—a sure way to sabotage a corporate social-reform movement at the outset. By contrast, the frequently revised ethical guidebook at Imperial Oil is distributed to employees with a covering letter from Arden Haynes, the top person at the company, who says Imperial's "high standard of ethics is among our most valued assets. . . . No one in the company, from myself to the newest member of our staff, is ever expected, for any reason, to commit an illegal or unethical act or to instruct other employees to do so." At the Royal Bank, "the board of directors expects me to live by these rules, and I myself have a hand in drafting them," says CEO Allan Taylor. "The code is dealt with by my office and reviewed by the executive committee of the board; it's not the kind of thing that's written up by the personnel department and then filed away."

The single most important function of codes is that they hold people and companies accountable. Computer maker Digital Equipment asks its clients to provide an annual appraisal of the ethical conduct of its own sales force; and Leaseway, a Cleveland-based trucking and truck-leasing firm, makes its internal standards of conduct known to customers and suppliers, who are encouraged to report stealing and other transgressions. Pitney Bowes holds itself accountable to its *rivals*: In a section entitled "Responsibilities to Competitors", the firm's *Business Practice Guidelines* booklet prohibits such tactics as criticizing the products of rival companies or strong-arming potential clients into cancelling orders placed with competitors.

Critics of codes of conduct are fond of comparing them with the legendary showmanship of Grigori Potemkin, the eighteenth-century Russian statesman who, according to some accounts (almost certainly apocryphal), gained Catherine II's confidence in his daring colonization campaigns by conducting her on tours of whole new towns that appeared to have sprung out of the wilds of the Russian steppes but which were later discovered to consist entirely of elaborate fake storefronts and other facades. Just as Potemkin's real-life accomplishments as a superb government administrator have tended not to get their due, corporate ethical codes have a substance that skeptics deny too readily. Having formally committed itself to a course of action — whether related to ethical conduct or a drive to obtain a given level of market share — a corporation has handed its potential critics the best weapon they could ask for: Its own sworn promise to act. Far more than is the case with ordinary individuals who don't live up to their stated intentions, companies that stand revealed as ineffective or hypocritical on account of their failed undertakings soon find themselves under tremendous pressure to make good on their promises.

In that context, the degree to which Hees International, for instance, chooses to have itself called to account is remarkable. In its annual report — about as public a forum as a company can select short of taking out newspaper ads — Hees demands that shareholders turf senior management if they feel their interests are being abused or neglected. "The corporate system breaks down when shareholders and managers who fail to perform their responsibilities are able to avoid sanction," Hees's own managers say in a two-page treatise entitled "Business Principles". "Shareholders, more often than not, tend to vote with their feet or have a policy of not wanting to take sides. In these circumstances, management, particularly through their control of the proxy process, can entrench and reward themselves free of any accountability to the owners." The Hees managers make an explicit promise not to feather their own nests. "Hees believes large salaries and generous benefits are an invitation to managements to become more interested in salary increases than in promoting the creation of wealth for shareholders. They also send confusing signals to other employees, thereby creating resentment and destroying any incentive to control costs or exercise restraint in their demands. . . . [At Hees] there are no management contracts and tenure is based solely on performance. With few exceptions, limousines, corporate aircraft and other such perquisites are considered inappropriate and an improper use of shareholders' funds."

Ultimately, codes are merely an acknowledgement of reality, the reality being that corporations sooner or later *are* held accountable for their actions. It is realistic to expect codes can help ward off the more unpleasant consequences of that reality. The Royal Bank ethical code's section on deceptive marketing practices is blunt and strict: "The Bank's word is its bond. . . . The Bank expects all employees to use only fair and honest sales and negotiating methods, and scrupulously avoid 'sharp' practices." Harsh though it may be, this directive is no match for the outcry consumer activists would direct at the Royal were they to uncover unsavoury selling practices. "We have to make people who come into our bank understand we're a no-nonsense organization, that we don't put up with anything that will catch us offside," says Allan Taylor. "Employees have to realize ethics is something you live with and learn about day by day. I shouldn't say every day there's an opportunity to do something that's immoral, but proposals of that nature are put to our people on the line with some frequency. Around the world there are more than thirty-eight thousand employees with the Royal's reputation in their hands. We have to count on them to know everything they do must stand the light of day. And that every decision, every judgment they make can be proudly defended."

In order to make the code of conduct a "living document" that does not grow stale with the passage of time, it must be updated frequently to account for changing conditions, and its directives must be articulated through a variety of means. Firms such as

American Express Co., Hewlett-Packard, Dayton-Hudson Corp., J.C. Penney, and Johnson & Johnson weave principles of honour and fair practice into most of their communications with employees and other "stakeholders". At some firms, an ethical flourish embellishes everything from the CEO's message to shareholders in the annual report to entry-level brochures for new employees and training manuals for sales and service personnel.

In order that these moral directives not be regarded as mere platitudes, firms with a serious commitment to moral enterprise train managers and supervisors to recognize that making an *honest* buck is a continuing part of their job. Companies such as Mac-Millan Bloedel, Imperial Oil, and Shell Canada operate training programs that instruct managers on ethics, with special reference to issues relevant to each firm's industry.

Ethics seminars are often greeted with suspicion and even hostility by managers who fear either that their own morality is being called into question or that the new ethical awareness will paralyse decision-making. Both fears are quickly laid to rest, however, by professional instructors who are careful to point out that the seminars are not part of a corporate witch-hunt nor are they designed to encumber anyone with impractical, time-consuming responsibilities. "What happens in the course of talking about ethical issues," says Jim Waters of Boston College, "is that managers see they aren't alone in facing ethical quandaries. Ethics is a seldom-discussed topic in business. These sessions open things up, giving executives the skills to talk about critical questions and thereby find solutions."

Ethics training is of limited use, however, unless it's backed up by compliance programs. Employees quickly learn that the ethics policy has teeth at Hewlett-Packard and J.C. Penney, where a record of ethical reliability is taken into consideration when managers are evaluated for promotion and eligibility for participating in profit-sharing plans. And some companies are generous with the stick as well as the carrot: Many firms that once hushed up the discovery of corrupt practices now engage in high-profile firings and demotions of wayward employees and even of workers who fail to report the wrongdoing of others. The failure to turn in a fellow employee is transformed from a relatively innocent sin of omission into a more serious sin of *commission* by companies such as American Airlines and CBS, which require managers to respond to an annual questionnaire asking them to identify any unlawful activities within the company that they have become aware of.

Snitches are not popular, of course, in business or any other kind of organization. And management guru Peter Drucker wonders if it isn't ultimately counterproductive to encourage a column of tattletales to take form within the ranks. "To be sure, there are misdeeds of the superior or of the employing organization which so grossly violate propriety and laws that the subordinate . . . cannot remain silent," Drucker says. But, citing Western societies such as Rome under Nero and the U.S.S.R. under Stalin in which informants were encouraged, Drucker insists a reign of whistleblowers promotes the decay of the relationship of trust between employer and employee. "Under whistleblowing, under the regime of the informer, no mutual trust, no interdependencies, and no ethics are possible." However, Drucker's argument fails on two counts. He presupposes a relationship of trust where often no such thing exists; indeed, the climate of trust may be *restored* by informants, and the need for snitching might therefore be eliminated.[1] And Drucker also wrongly assumes whistleblowing is always an effort to expose crimes by the company when, often enough, the whistleblower seeks to report crimes *against* the company — everything from simple embezzlement to elaborate schemes to fake or supress product-safety tests (a ploy that may secure sales in the short run, but which may ultimately land the company in court).

For example, the asbestos industry in North America is coping with $50 billion in lawsuits stemming from allegations it suppressed medical evidence pointing to the lethal impact of the mineral on people who worked with it. The Challenger space-shuttle disaster is an even more prominent case. In testimony before a presidential commission, engineers employed by Utah-based Morton Thiokol, Inc. — which built the solid fuel booster rockets for the Challenger — explained how they had protested

---

1 Most companies with formal whistleblowing programs take steps to ensure that complainants aren't exercising irrational grievances or plotting the unfair ousting of a superior. Usually this is accomplished by requiring the whistleblower to step from behind the veil of anonymity if his or her complaint hasn't been satisfied in the first few rounds of the complaint process.

on the eve of the space shuttle's ill-fated January 28, 1986, launch that the mission should not go ahead. But top managers at both Morton Thiokol and the National Aeronautics and Space Administration (NASA) ignored the engineers' warnings that the synthetic-rubber seals, or O-rings, between the booster's joints could fail in cold weather; the flight itself lasted only seventy-three seconds before the shuttle exploded, killing the seven Challenger astronauts. Only a month earlier, a DC-8 owned by Miami-based Arrow Air Inc. crashed at Gander, Newfoundland, resulting in the deaths of 248 U.S. soldiers and 8 civilian crew members. During a subsequent U.S. Senate investigation, a former Arrow Air pilot testified he had been relieved of flight status and then quit his job a year prior to the fatal crash after he had taken his complaints about the airline's maintenance standards to the Federal Aviation Administration. Whistleblowers usually pay a severe penalty for speaking out: a recent U.S. survey of whistleblowers found that 90 per cent of people who had gone public with their concerns had been fired or demoted or had quit.

Yet a system whereby employees feel free to express their concerns can be an invaluable distant early warning system — a way to "effectively and efficiently eliminate surprises", as Waters puts it. Waters says companies should endorse whistleblowing by creating "internal control systems that ensure that every employee is responsible for the auditing of corporate behaviour. The control climate must be managed in such a way that all individuals within an organization can initiate inquiries into known or suspected questionable corporate practices."

Indeed, some major companies have embraced this concept, which becomes more palatable when people with complaints are regarded not as "whistleblowers" but "social auditors". For the past twenty-eight years, IBM has operated a program it calls "Speak Up". Employees record their concerns on forms which are passed to Speak Up co-ordinators, who in turn detach the complainant's name and lock it in a safe, and pass the query to the appropriate manager. If the employee doesn't receive a written response within ten working days, he or she can ask for an interview with the manager. Many employees use the system because anonymity is guaranteed for those who wish it. At IDS Financial Services, the mutual-funds subsidiary of American Express, employees who feel their ethical concerns aren't being properly addressed have an opportunity to bring the problem to senior managers' attention through an "upward feedback" system in which supervisors are evaluated by their subordinates on their performance in terms of corporate values. And the Royal Bank, in the preface to its code of conduct, lends its unequivocable support to those who wish to raise concerns with superiors. "I wish to assure employees," reads the introductory letter signed by the bank's CEO, "that if they are faced with situations in which they believe their personal standards differ from those of the corporation, they have the right, without fear of reprisal, to discuss and resolve their concerns with their supervisor or with other appropriate officers, either directly or through the medium of R.S.V.P. [an employee feedback program]." At the Royal and other corporations with effective feedback systems, emphasis is placed on the propriety of employees going over the heads of superiors if necessary to have their grievances aired.

Several companies have taken the further step of institutionalizing ethical remedies by creating ombudsmen's offices or special committees to deal with ethical issues. Often these committees are struck in an ad hoc manner to cope with specific problems. The consumer-card division of American Express has a special committee that meets every two weeks to review the outpouring of AmEx ads and ensure that they are truthful and in good taste; by drawing representatives from the market research, legal, and consumer-affairs departments into discussions with the ad copywriters, the committee continually reinforces the notion that ethical standards apply to every corporate function. As a pre-emptive measure, the Royal Bank created a committee of senior managers in advance of the stock-market deregulation that took place in Ontario in 1987. This committee, which reports to two of the bank's most senior officers (a vice-chairman and a senior executive vice-president), is examining the potential for conflict-of-interest, insider trading, and other common stock-market abuses in anticipation of the bank's own plans to enter the investment-banking business. "When it seemed likely we would go into investment banking," says Royal CEO Allan Taylor, "right away we got to thinking of the problems that could come up. Investment bankers operate in an environment of fast and maybe easy money these days; anybody in that area has a difficult time keeping their head. We're going to have to be extremely careful about letting people reach too far in meeting profit targets, because that's an invitation to disaster in fast-moving markets."[2]

The Royal also has a permanent committee of the board of directors to deal with ethics and public-responsibility issues — a distinction it shares with very few Canadian or U.S. companies, Provigo Inc., John Labatt Ltd., and Royal Trustco Ltd. among them. Many companies disdain the idea because they feel it ghettoizes ethics, an argument that has some merit. "We have no ethics committee," explains Dofasco CEO Frank Sherman, "because the entire board considers the moral impact of any and all of its decisions as a matter of normal policy." This is an admirable sentiment. But in practice most boards are too caught up in the formidable financial and logistical details of a decision to consider its ethical dimensions. Ethics committees can provide that insight; and they can also bring to the full board's attention simmering issues that may be latent, and hence have escaped the board's notice, but threaten to cause trouble down the road.

Unfortunately, though, an ethics committee of the board would in many cases be something of a travesty since the full board itself may be badly in need of reform. Elaborate ethics programs — ethics committee of the board included — are only as good as the people administering them, and if the board members, the top officials in the company, are taking a moral holiday the reform movement at the grassroots level will soon come to a dead halt.

The tidal wave of liability suits that threatens to submerge many companies — and has already forced Manville Corp. and A.H. Robins Co. into bankruptcy — has focused attention on the role of directors in preventing corporate fiascos. The chief question is, if directors are powerless to stop their companies from getting into the kind of trouble that leads to lawsuits, what good are directors, anyway?

The theory is that directors, acting on behalf of shareholders, oversee the activities of the chief executive officer and his or her senior management team, who in turn run the company. However, in practice, the hired hands — and especially the CEO — are

---

2   Companies can never give too much thought to means of preventing such "disasters". Merrill Lynch, the world's largest securities dealer, is more than fifty years old but still has much to learn about the need for controlling overly ambitious traders. In 1987 the firm suffered $275 million in losses from unauthorized trading conducted by relatively inexperienced traders.

remarkably unhindered by the board as they go about their business. There is a good reason for this: It is a rare company where the CEO does not influence the selection of directors and decide who among these will sit on the powerful executive committee. Appointments to the board's nominating, audit and compensation committees must sit well with the CEO, who has only to say, "I can't work with that man" for a proposed nominee to be dropped by fellow board members. Outside experts — management consultants who promote the CEO's pet projects, accountants who put a pretty face on the cost of financing them, and compensation consultants who recommend healthy increases in the CEO's salary and bonuses — are themselves usually selected by the CEO and owe their own livelihoods to his or her decision to reward them over rival consultants also eager to secure the business of the CEO's firm. And while the CEO and the top management team make the firm the better part of their lives, directors have their own firms to run or are plucked from the busy halls of hospitals, academe, or public service. With as few as six meetings to attend each year, they often don't have the time, expertise, or access to information to grasp more than the most superficial details about how the companies they direct are faring.

The current boardroom crisis offers few unique insights into the perils of lackadasical stewardship, the precedents were all established long ago. For instance, the world probably has Sir Walter Scott's casual attitude towards the responsibilities of directorship to thank for *Ivanhoe*. "Went to the yearly court of the Edinburgh Assurance Co.," Scott wrote in his diary in 1825, "to which I am one of those graceful and useless appendages called 'Directors Extraordinary.'" Being too sanguine to notice that his inattentiveness was contributing to the decline of another firm — the publishing house Hurst & Robinson — Scott was horrified to discover himself being held personally liable for a portion of the debts when H&R went bankrupt. Scott attempted to write his way out of debt, but suceeded in producing only fifteen huge volumes (and retiring about a quarter of the £130,000 worth of debt assessed to him) before he died of exhaustion. Some 140 years later, the directors of Penn Central Transportation Co. seemed as surprised as anyone when America's largest transportation company became the biggest company ever to declare bankruptcy; dozens of shareholder suits alleging dereliction of duty by directors followed the 1970 débâcle, and were ultimately merged into a single action and settled out of court for $10 million. "You can't say we were any great success as a board," former Penn Central director Louis Cabot admitted a couple years after the court settlement. "In fact, it's a horrible example."

In 1934, just before he joined the staff of the Securities and Exchange Commission, future U.S. Supreme Court associate justice William O. Douglas wrote a prescient article for the *Harvard Law Review* entitled "Directors Who Do Not Direct". Managers of big business, Douglas thought, were inclined towards "skullduggery — secret loans and bonuses, undisclosed profit-sharing plans, insider trading" and other sins; and small stockholders, ill-equipped to put a stop to this, were themselves a "scattered, disorganized, lethargic and impotent" lot. His remedy? Limit the number of directorships a person could accept, and get rid of the "financial gigolo" director, a man recruited to the board to lend his prestige while posing no threat to management's control.

Some fifty years later, the presence of former U.S. president Gerald Ford on the board of Fidelity Trust Co. proved of limited value as the venerable Edmonton-based firm, controlled by Peter Pocklington, slid into insolvency in 1983. (Ford attended three board meetings in his one and a half years as a Fidelity director and consultant.) Former U.S. secretary of state Alexander M. Haig was similarly unable to arrest the decline into near-bankruptcy of Allegheny International, which makes Sunbeam appliances and counted Haig among its directors. A class-action suit filed against the company by a shareholder in 1987, soon after the firm's chairman resigned, alleged that top management wasted corporate funds and cited, among other things, the five-jet fleet of corporate aircraft, $32 million in low-interest loans provided to top executives, and a $16 million investment in a condominium project in which the CEO and other senior Allegheny officers owned apartments.

In case after case, from the near-collapse of America's seventh-largest bank (the Continental Illinois, whose board was graced by no fewer than nine CEOs of other *Fortune 500* companies) to the failure of Edmonton's Canadian Commercial Bank and the Northland Bank of Calgary, angry shareholders have demanded to know, "Where were the directors?" The answer is that they are present but not entirely accounted for, each having other, more pressing, responsibilities elsewhere and no particular reason to attend to those of a company they visit only six times a year. "Directors run virtually no personal risk for any amount of complacency, cronyism, or outright neglect of their duties," says Harold Geneen in *Managing*, a text he wrote soon after retiring from the chairmanship of ITT Corp. Geneen ran ITT for seventeen years and, thanks in large part to the timidity of his own board, did so without fear of rebuke despite a mediocre return on equity of 11 per cent during his tenure. "While the law holds [directors] responsible as fiduciaries to the stockholders, the courts have interpreted that responsibility very leniently. A director would rarely be found liable unless cupidity, a clear conflict of interest, or gross negligence (a vague concept) could be proved. Even then he is usually further protected by his company's indemnification and insurance policies, which in effect guarantee that any damages assessed against him will be paid by the company."

This picture of complacency is slowly changing. These days, directors run a one-in-five chance of being sued, and insurance to protect them is often not available. Even as the insurance crisis began to subside in 1987, it was apparent the shareholder revolt would not. From without, corporations have found themselves under attack by powerful institutional shareholders who now, for the first time, appear eager to step into the responsibility vacuum in many boardrooms by threatening to use their proxies to block management initiatives and even by proposing their own candidates for board membership. From within, meanwhile, companies with boards known to be ineffective and docile are undermined as morale declines throughout the ranks, sucking the level of efficiency, profitability, and moral conduct down with it.

Unfortunately, this is the area of ethical management that is most resistant to reform. In contrast to the widespread enlightenment that has manifested itself in codes of conduct, training, ombudsmen, and other corporate ethics initiatives, the hand of progress has barely touched the cozy, fraternal preserve of the boardroom. These days, however, cries for enhanced boardroom responsibility are at least becoming loud enough for entrenched directors and managers to hear: in some cases, the source of agitation is none other than retired executives and directors, who know too well how easily boardroom politics can be played almost entirely to management's advantage. Among the most important proposed reforms: separating the functions of chairman and CEO (how can the CEO's performance be honestly assessed when the CEO is also chairman of the body of his adjudicators?); instituting smaller boards, perhaps eight instead of the standard twelve members (larger groups are inefficient and thus easier to manipulate); paying directors more (the average CEO of a major U.S. company is paid $350,000 a year, and directors' fees for memberships on other companies' boards on average amount to a mere 6 per cent of that per board — not much of an incentive for diligence); having external accountants report directly to the board, not through management; and insisting that companies change auditors every few years to reinvigorate internal control procedures that may have atrophied; and encouraging directors to stand their ground when CEOs balk at their choice of board nominees or at lower-than-expected pay packages.

There are two broad approaches to ethical renewal within modern companies. There is the route forced on General Dynamics, the United States' largest defence contractor. GD, which for the better part of a decade has been battling allegations it defrauded the Pentagon, was told by the U.S. Navy in 1984 it would not be held accountable for any past misdeeds that surface in the future provided the company complies with a long list of Pentagon-conceived standards of ethical conduct which, in their entirety, impose a new way of life on GD. Company employees now cannot go on or off shift, or from one plant to another or even from one working area to another inside the same plant, without meticulously recording their movements on electronic scanners and timecards that bear warning labels reading, "MIS-CHARGING IS ILLEGAL". (Central to the allegations against GD are charges that the firm, or its employees acting independently in what they thought was the firm's best interests, shifted expenses from money-losing civilian contracts onto government jobs.) All 103,000 GD employees have been furnished with new twenty-page ethics booklets ("Be honest and trustworthy, responsible and reliable"); and many workers are inundated with dozens of legalistic documents describing how they are to handle a wide range of ethical problems. There is an ethics hotline for the use of whistleblowers wishing to remain anonymous; and an ethics director imported from the University of Chicago's business school tours GD facilities, where he provides both senior- and lower-level employees with formal instruction in corporate scruples. GD employees cannot so much as offer a visiting military or other government employee a free cup of coffee, and for their part cannot accept even a pen, calendar, or glass of fruit juice from a supplier. If there is the slightest doubt about the propriety of the most nominal sum charged to the government, employees are told to ask themselves, "How would this look on the front page of *The New York Times*?"

"Our employees are so hurt by the image that General Dynamics has that they will do anything to get that monkey off their back," says Stanley Pace, GD's new CEO, who was recruited in 1985 to help put the firm on the straight and narrow. This may be true, but the firm's employees are enduring the full force of reform when it was not the rank and file who created the apparent soak-the Pentagon climate said to have prevailed at GD during the past ten years. Many workers are chafing at the inconvenience and wasted time involved in living with the new order of things, to say nothing of a mood of paranoia that many feel has descended on the company. More to the point, GD is so deeply mired in alleged improprieties there is some question whether any amount of internal reform will buoy morale given the prospect of yet more revelations to come. Despite a daunting accumulation of tape recordings and other well-documented evidence, GD is stoutly maintaining its claims to innocence, thus ensuring that regulatory and congressional inquiries will drag on indefinitely — adding still more highly publicized material to the already rich vein of disclosures about $18,000 country-club initiation fees charged to the government and the $9,609 GD attempted to bill the Pentagon for a wrench. GD is a public whipping boy: when the Justice department announced in the spring of 1987 it would not seek an indictment against GD for allegedly filing false cost estimates with the Navy — apparently on the grounds that some Navy officials knew they were false, thus how could the Navy have been defrauded? — *Business Week* greeted the GD victory with the sour observation that the estimated $15 million cost of fighting two grand jury investigations, two Securities and Exchange Commission probes, and several congressional hearings will be built into GD contracts for which, yes, the Pentagon will foot the bill. And GD's ambitious clean-up effort struck *Fortune* as being too much, too late. "GD, [which] to many American newspaper readers [is] the symbol of waste and corruption in government spending, is behaving like a newly reformed sinner at a tent meeting," the magazine said recently. "It will take years for born again GD to turn many Americans into true believers."

By contrast, there is the route freely chosen by Domtar Inc., the large Montreal-based paper products company. In 1977, then CEO Alex Hamilton conducted an employee attitude survey. Thanks mostly to Domtar's sorry record of fractious labour relations, worker morale was low. "It seemed to Hamilton that the Domtar stance was the buck came first, people second," recalls Wilfrid Fournier, formerly vice-president of human relations at Domtar and now general manager of the firm's Eastern Canadian corrugated-container division. "Hamilton's response was to tell the senior management group that all the fingers pointed at him, and now *he* was saying if you want to work with me the policy is people come first."

The initial step in inculcating the new ethic was to find a more humane way of obtaining workforce reductions. During the next economic slowdown, which came in 1979, Domtar relied mostly on a voluntary-retirement program to trim the employee rolls, and when layoffs came they were made on the basis of employee performance rather than tenure. And rather than be the first in its industry to cut wages during a slowdown and the last to bump them up after a recession — a policy Domtar had had a reputation for following — the company decided it would try to keep compensation rates level. Domtar succeeded with the program — not only in 1979, but in the much more severe 1982–83 recession as well. Hamilton also developed Domtar's first code of business conduct, an elaborate document covering sixteen areas such as finance, engineering, R&D, and human resources.

Hamilton's successor, James H. Smith, has kept up the "people-first" policy's momentum by, for a start, being accessible: Smith has met with about eight thousand Domtar workers, more than half the total employee complement. In 1984, when Smith, Fournier, and other senior executives revised the code of conduct, Smith and Domtar's four group vice-presidents took it on the road to explain its provisions to managers at Domtar facilities in Montreal, Toronto, Calgary, and Chicago. "As a case in point, Smith talked about safety versus the dollar," says Fournier. "This is a simple one: safety is always the priority, because we are committed to a policy that people are what matter most."

By now, concern about employee welfare and a determination to work for labour peace are givens at Domtar. "Keeping wage levels steady during the 1982 recession was tough. But it was more important to do that in 1982 than it had been in 1979 because everyone was watching to see if we'd live by that commitment," says Fournier. "Once you start these things, there's no turning back or you lose credibility." Indeed, where employee-welfare initiatives were once greeted with surprise and a bit of suspicion, new campaigns such as 1986's hazardous-waste-handling training program are now accepted as the norm. (The latter initiative dovetailed with a Health and Safety Management Program that has achieved major reductions in the frequency of accidents every year for the past five years.) While Domtar had once been plagued by strike activity, the firm had no work disruptions in 1986—no mean feat given that it signed twenty-seven collective agreements that year. The state of labour-relations tranquillity has translated into flexibility, allowing Domtar to introduce tens of millions of dollars' worth of new cost-saving equipment within an atmosphere of co-operation rather than resistance and confrontation. Productivity, as measured by revenue per employee, has shot up 153 per cent in the past decade, which helps account for the fact that Domtar—whose earnings lagged in the mid 1970s—is now one of Canada's most profitable forest-products companies.

"I think we've benefited enormously from our consistent attention to ethical values, from realizing our company doesn't have an inalienable right to exist, and must abide by the values of society," says Fournier. "Businesspeople are fond of saying they need profits in order to survive in the same way people must breathe in order to live. The Domtar saying is that people do breathe to live, but they don't live to breathe. By the same token, there has to be more to business—in terms of job satisfaction, workplace harmony, and a sense of individual creativity—than merely making a profit."

There are many ways of becoming a moral enterprise, and more companies—each according to its fashion—are experimenting with them than ever before. Some methods of awakening and strengthening ethical values are more successful than others, though. This is true not only in corporations themselves but in the management schools where the next generation of business leaders is being trained—one hopes—not to make the mistakes that marked the passage of its predecessors.

CHAPTER SEVEN
ETHICS ON CAMPUS:
MORALITY AND THE MBA

Harvard University was founded by Puritan pastors. In the seventeenth century more than half its graduates became men of the cloth, and long after the one-time wilderness seminary had embraced new disciplines—medicine, law and, in 1908, business—Harvard kept faith with its founders, whose aim was to imbue every student with "knowledge and godlynes". But, in 1979, Harvard president Derek Bok detected that something was going wrong. In a barely disguised attack on his own distinguished business school, Bok complained, "Most classroom discussions still proceed on the unexamined assumption that growth and profits are the only concerns of the corporate manager. By remaining silent [about ethics], business schools not only fail to awaken their students to a larger sense of their calling, they neglect their responsibilities to their profession."

These days, Harvard and the other Ivy League colleges, most of which also started out as divinity schools, are paying dearly for failing to heed Bok's early warning. Their claims to high standards of instruction seem hollow in the wake of revelations about MBA grads who have been implicated in sensational scandals on Wall Street and elsewhere in business. As the epidemic of immoral business conduct has spread, chagrined administrators of MBA mills at Harvard, Yale and other prestigious schools are having the blame laid at their doorstep. Critics charge that business schools impart a facility with numbers and a craving for instant wealth but fail to inculcate a sense of honour.

It is businesspeople themselves, the people who actually work with MBA grads, who worry most about what the business schools are teaching. In *The Big Time*, a recent book about the latest crop of Harvard MBAS, Ned Dewey, class of '49, offers this unflattering appraisal of his newest fellow alumni: "These kids are smart, but I'd sooner take a python to bed as hire one. He'd suck my brains, memorize my Rolodex, and use my telephone to find some other guy who'd pay him twice the money." According to a recent survey of chief executives by Cornell University, nearly 80 per cent of CEOs are demanding that business schools place a greater emphasis on teaching human values. And John Shad, former chairman of the U.S. Securities and Exchange Commission, took time out in the spring of 1987 from his successful campaign of running crooked Wall Street traders to ground—many among them recent graduates of Harvard, Stanford, and Wharton—to tell a forum of financiers that business and law schools have a responsibility to teach that "ethics pay, that there are enormous benefits that come from quality and integrity".

In Canada, too, members of the business community are among the first to urge the inclusion of ethics in the curriculum. "In the aftermath of the Boesky, Guinness, and other scandals, it's obviously essential that ethics be taught at business schools," says Paul Martin, chief executive of the CSL Group Inc. of Montreal, one of Canada's largest privately owned transportation companies. "It has to be an urgent concern, because even if only 1 per cent of businesspeople are crooks, the negative impact on the image of business is devastating. We risk losing our sanction to operate."

Business schools admit they're feeling the heat, and most of them insist they're eager to help solve the ethics crisis. "We're coming to the painful realization that because we aren't putting the social concerns in their proper context, students are getting the message that any behaviour is okay," says Tim Reid, dean of the business school at Ryerson Polytechnic Institute in Toronto— which, with eleven thousand full- and part-time students, is one of Canada's biggest management schools. "We somehow have to bridge the two solitudes between instruction in high-level management techniques and awareness of the underside of business, which we haven't been confronting."

In response to the calls for reform, business schools across the continent are attempting to alloy management skills with a sense of ethical awareness and a dose of mind-broadening liberal-arts instruction. In early 1987, the business school at Toronto's York University—where enrolments in the MBA program are higher than at any other school in Canada — began offering a course in occupational and social ethics; and the faculty of management at the University of Manitoba announced it will insist that business students complete a course on ethics in their final year. Ryerson and the School of Business at the University of Western Ontario (arguably the most prestigious Canadian business school) both plan to add ethics instruction to their management-training curricula in the next year or two.

Training in business ethics is, however, more advanced in the United States than in Canada, where only the University of Toronto has a management-ethics course that dates from the 1970s. Most of the biggest U.S. business schools — Harvard, Yale, and Wharton, among others — have offered ethics classes for the past few years and have devised many other ways to "humanize" management programs. At Chicago's distinguished Northwestern University, business instructor Robert Bies immerses his MBA students in real-life experiences by sending them off to visit the homeless in Chicago shelters for the poor. Management instructors at several schools use literary classics in their classrooms, not only for the insights they provide into human behaviour but as a means of introducing their students to a larger world outside of business. "On Being Human", a course offered to business students at the University of Kansas, is based on readings from books such as Joseph Conrad's *Heart of Darkness* which offers insights into the complexities of social responsibility and moral reasoning; and at Hartwick College in Oneonta, N.Y., students of management professor John Clemens draw ethical guidance from Plutarch's *Parallel Lives*, Homer's *Iliad*, and the tragedies of Shakespeare. Among Clemens's unorthodox literary interpretations: King Lear lost his grip because he was not much of a delegator.

The new interest in ethics on campus has spawned a growth industry. Publishers of ethics texts are cashing in on the corporate-morality trend, a rarity on business campuses until recently, and suppliers of films, videotapes, and other instructional materials are coming in for their share. Specialized periodicals such as the *Journal of Business Ethics* and the *Business and Professional Ethics Journal* have sprung up to provide a continuing discussion of business-morality issues. And the ethics professors themselves, many of whom until recently toiled anonymously in philosophy departments and other dusty corners of academe, now achieve celebrity status on the lecture circuit and find themselves in great demand as consultants to corporations.

Unfortunately, though, these signs of progress are not merely the tip of the iceberg. They *are* the iceberg. An unprecedented number of unscrupulous business titans are squirming in the media spotlight these days, but this hasn't propelled many MBA students onto a higher plane of ethical consciousness. In a recent survey of students at the respected Fuqua School of Business at North Carolina's Duke University, most of those questioned thought disgraced insider trader Ivan Boesky was a crook who got off too easily with the $100 million in fines assessed against him. Yet 44 per cent of these same students said they would purchase stock on an inside tip that a company was going to be acquired — precisely Boesky's sin, of course — and half of them did not see any problem with price-fixing among competitors.

Indeed, the flurry of ethics-course start-ups and the attendant hoopla belie the fact that there is something less than a rush by students to sign up for these programs. In fact, enrolment for many ethics courses is down — most notably, for two of the oldest and best-known programs, those offered by Harvard and the University of Toronto. What's more, suspicions are being cast on the motives of students who do sign up. "Most kids regard these things as bird courses," admits William Dimma, deputy chairman of Toronto-based Royal LeP'age Ltd., Canada's biggest real-estate broker. Dimma, a former dean of York University's administrative studies, is an ardent advocate of ethics courses at business schools. "But for many students," he says, "ethics studies are a 'soft' alternative to the demanding, quantitative nature of most other management courses, and people opt for them because they're looking for something that will lighten their load."

Robert Figlio, an associate professor at Wharton who teaches a course on white-collar crime, shares Dimma's unease. He isn't eager to exaggerate the influence he has with his students. "They don't seem ideologically aware, and it's hard to provoke them," Figlio says. "They don't argue when I present them with unusual ideas. They're determined to keep their heads down and concentrate on getting a job. They do talk a lot about the Wharton graduates who became famous by going to Wall Street and then to jail, but always with a smirk. I can never tell whether they're talking about how wrong-headed those graduates were, or just about how stupid they must have been to get caught."

Yet it is business schools themselves that must be faulted for failing to engage the interest of more students. Universities, notoriously political places that they are, have a habit of squandering the opportunity to innovate by fumbling purposelessly at the moment of decision.

So it is with business-ethics courses. Almost without exception, they are offered in the final year of MBA studies and only as an elective. This despite a chorus of protest from educators and non-academics alike that if ethics training is to be taken seriously — on a par with such vital basic courses as accounting, finance, and marketing — it must be offered in first year, when students' minds are most open and receptive to new ideas, and must be mandatory, since making it an elective renders it a "holy course" taken by students already interested in the subject and ignored by many of those who may need it most.

The alternatives to that established format, however, require drastic change. And as the late Canadian educator Sidney Smith once observed, "Change within a university encounters all the difficulty of moving a cemetery." Better, one ruefully concludes, to attempt to set up a new college than fight for a new mandatory course. (When Harvard introduced "Human Resource Management" in 1981, it was the first new required course in twenty years.) "Creating a mandatory course requires a tremendous commitment," says Jim Waters, former associate dean of academic affairs at York University's business school, which did not exist when Harvard launched its *second*-youngest course in 1961. "Adding anything to the core curriculum is always a frigging big political joust. It affects enrolment and hiring of faculty and reduces the number of electives, and therefore the idea of having a choice in your studies." As well, ethics is competing with a crop of other hot new study areas for required-course status, including entrepreneurship, leadership, and computer technology. Meanwhile, severe government spending constraints mean many schools are stretching their faculty thin as it is, without taking on new courses. "Our finance department is undermanned," says Figlio, who is struggling to get tenure at Wharton. "So where do you think they'll create their next tenured position — in finance or ethics?"

Jeffrey Gandz, associate professor at the University of Western Ontario, is confronted with an even more severe predicament. He has the task of developing an ethics program at Western's business school. More ambitious than most educators working in this area, Gandz rejects both the elective and the mandatory approaches. Instead, he's trying to build an ethical component into every course at Western's business curriculum. "Ethics shouldn't be a special deal," says Gandz. "I want to make it a mainline business discipline, not something unusual or atypical. The way to do that is to make it inconspicuous, an integral part of every course from first year on. Believe me, it would be easier to teach ethics as a second-year elective: I'd be surrounded by socially conscious students and we'd all have fun. But that would be terribly inadequate."

But Gandz is climbing an awfully steep mountain. In order for him to get his way, every member of the business faculty will have to learn how to teach the subject — a demand many instructors are sure to balk at. "If you're a PhD. in marketing," says Max Clarkson, who has taught business ethics at the University of Toronto for several years, "the last thing you've been trained to teach is ethics."

If that view seems overly cynical, consider that even scaled-down versions of what Gandz proposes are proving tough to implement. MBA mills are scrambling to announce they have some sort of ethics program in the works, but many of them drag their feet over committing funds and faculty to actually get them underway. "The only reason business schools are so interested in ethics these days is hype," says Professor H.T. (Tom) Wilson, who launched York University's ethics course in the spring of 1987. "I can't take colleges seriously when they holler, 'We've got to get some ethics!' It's a hot topic, but maybe something else will be hot next year. In the meantime, talking about ethics is just a way for schools to appear to care." Harvard ethics professor Kenneth Goodpaster has similar misgivings. "In the same way that many companies these days are speaking ethically but still carrying a big stick to hurt people with, an ethics course can be a fig leaf in your university curriculum," Goodpaster says. "Far from truly integrating ethics into business programs, we haven't done much more than merely put them on the table. It will take some gutsy leaders — in business and academe — to advance ethics to the next, more meaningful level." Harvard, for one, could use some gutsy leaders. Ethics instructors throughout North America were stunned when John Shad, who made a fortune on Wall Street before becoming head of the SEC and decided to use a chunk of it to advance the cause of ethics training, made his $20 million bequest to Harvard. Harvard admits it doesn't know what to do with the money and has no plans to significantly upgrade its ethics program.

At the root of this confusion is the question of whether ethical behaviour is teachable at all. "In coping with corporate immorality, I just don't see how ethics classes are going to help," says Bernard Ghert, chief executive of Cadillac Fairview Corp. Ltd. of Toronto, one of Canada's largest land developers. To be sure, Ghert has problems with some high-priced business-school recruits. "Graduates from Harvard, in particular, have a win-at-any-cost mentality, and it's very hard to knock it out of them," he says. But Ghert, who took his MBA at the University of British Columbia and also taught several courses there, thinks ethics instruction may create more problems than it solves. "Students with sound values won't learn much that is new to them, and those who don't have integrity to begin with may just use the insights they gain to find new ways of getting away with immoral acts they are going to commit anyway."

For Wharton's Robert Figlio, however, the notion that students can't be taught ethical values they should have absorbed at home is a cop-out. "The dean of our business school says we have no responsibility for what Wharton students do after they leave," Figlio says. "But the truth is that problems often start here because we fail to tell students they don't have to surrender their morality for the sake of the corporation. Because business, law, and accounting are all taught as a sort of game, we're probably teaching a certain cynicism. The way these courses are currently structured, it's impossible to produce an altruistic businessperson or lawyer."

Many business leaders, too, are eager to see MBA schools take some responsibility for the moral bearing of the men and women who pass through their doors. Frank Sherman, chief executive of Hamilton, Ontario-based steelmaker Dofasco Inc., not only thinks ethics should be a "mandatory and formalized part of professional training in business schools", but would extend it to "high school, where more are likely to benefit from it". "Ethics instruction should be an implicit part of all educational programs," insists Jack MacLeod, chief executive officer of Shell Canada Ltd., who obtained some ethics training while earning his degree in engineering. It is important that ethics instruction no longer be "a discrete subject area without direct context" for business, because new and different moral quandaries are cropping up at the heart of business activity. "The social and legal definitions of right and wrong are becoming increasingly complex," says MacLeod, "with the result that an employee may act in an unethical manner 'in all innocence.'" And William Dimma, deputy chairman of real-estate broker Royal LePage Ltd., argues that while ethics should be inculcated at home, the fact that this often doesn't happen is all the more reason for schools to compensate for that failing. "It's precisely because so many kids these days are amoral when they enroll in business schools that we have to teach ethics," Dimma says. "We can't just send students who didn't hear about moral values at home into the business world without giving them some ethical background. Otherwise, MBA grads won't raise the level of ethical awareness once they get out into the business community. They'll succumb to the existing level."

It's no small irony that business schools are fumbling the ethics issue instead of finding in it some solutions to the larger identity crisis in business education. In plumbing the depths of their despair over having lost so much ground to the Japanese in the past several years, North American managers have come to realize that they have put too much store in numbers and maximizing profits in the short term. The most successful enterprises, whether they are located in North America, Europe, or the Pacific Rim, derive their success from creativity, intuition, and judgment, not merely from acumen in mathematical analysis. Yet MBA mills have always placed a greater emphasis on number-crunching than other values and skills, and this emphasis, combined with the rampant materialism in society during the past few years, tends to produce graduates who care more about making money than about the means by which they do so.

Of course, most of the students already have a keen desire to do well for themselves from the moment they arrive. The stated goals of Harvard freshmen, Bok glumly reported in 1986, are "money first, followed by power and then making a reputation." One in four U.S. students opts for business programs; fewer than 1 per cent expect to be English majors (English enrolments are down 80 per cent over the past twenty years), according to a survey of 280,000 college freshmen by the American Council on Education (ACE) and the Higher Education Research Institute at the University of California at Los Angeles (UCLA). In 1967, a year after the ACE-UCLA survey started, "developing a meaningful philosophy of life" was cited by 83 per cent of students as their primary goal. In 1986, close to 71 per cent identified their major objective as "being very well off financially". This new generation of students isn't inspired by coffee-house singers or an updated version of the Chicago Seven, but by icons such as William Gates III. Gates, founder of Seattle computer-software-maker Microsoft, became worth $350 million overnight when his young company went public in 1986. Gates is thirty-one. It is this kind of payoff that has attracted so many undergraduates to business programs: a record seventy thousand U.S. students will receive their MBA degrees in 1987, and a few thousand Canadians will also attain this academic laurel. Not all of the MBAs who are called by recruiters are chosen for the top jobs, those with $100,000-plus starting salaries, but a good 85 per cent or so accept positions within six months of graduation that pay a comfortable median starting pay of $25,000 to $35,000 and extend to the MBA holder a privileged entré to the corporate fast track wherever he or she is hired on.

Of course, MBAs were not always in such heavy demand. The first cadre of professional business managers, which emerged soon after the turn of the century, sprang mostly from engineering schools like the Massachusetts Institute of Technology because the essential requirement of managers at that time was an intimate knowledge of how the new mass-production factories worked. By the middle of this century, with the rise of the modern diversified corporations and the merger activity that brought them into being, the fledgling business departments at the University of Pennsylvania (the Wharton school), Dartmouth College, and Harvard — the three oldest U.S. business schools, in that order — began to emphasize financial-analysis skills. Still, demand for professionally trained managers grew very slowly: at the dawn of the Second World War, only half of all employers required management recruits even to possess a high-school diploma.

All that changed, however, just two decades later. By the late 1950s, the sole-proprietorships of the sort Henry Ford and Andrew Carnegie created had faded from the scene and the private sector had come to be dominated by elephantine and complex business organizations. These increasingly bureaucratic enterprises demanded that prospective managers have college degrees, and they soaked up the output of the now thriving business schools. In return, the business community and universities themselves — which noticed with some alarm that their business departments now often were the most vibrant force on campus — took a close look at what management schools were teaching their charges. A consensus emerged that in the main the schools were mere trade or vocational institutes, bereft of the rigorous academic training of Harvard and the other distinguished universities that had brought them into being. Business schools dutifully underwent a somewhat traumatic transformation, beginning in 1959. It being the age of Sputnik, which inspired a universal faith in technology and the scientific approach to all things in life, the road to respectability chosen by most management schools was to develop unimpeachable standards in the hallowed mathematical disciplines. The legacy of that upheaval is that even today, long after other academic disciplines had given in to the 1960s and 1970s demands for more flexible curricula, business schools drive their students relentlessly through a gruelling series of quantitative courses. The rewards, however, have been very generous: a bounty of job offers, high starting salaries, and a privileged place on the corporate fast track.

There are some obvious problems with this regimen, however. It tends to produce narrow-focused specialists rather than the well-rounded generalists that the business community desperately needs, particularly at its highest levels. In a recent analysis of Canadian MBA programs, Lynne Hall, a former executive-in-residence at the Queen's University School of Business in Kingston, Ontario, noted that business-school critics object to "what they perceive as an overemphasis on quantitative formulae, tools, and models, to the virtual exclusion of qualitative processes of thinking through and dealing with complex issues, options, and tradeoffs." Hall's survey of nearly ten thousand Canadian employers, MBA graduates, and academics, which turned up a frighteningly exhaustive list of failings among MBA grads, confirmed this perception. Among the conclusions in Hall's report, released in 1986, were that MBA students can analyse and compute but can't manage or communicate; they can solve problems, but have difficulty in recognizing and structuring them; and they understand accounting, finance, and marketing, but are lost when it comes to culture, accountability, and values.

By exerting tremendous pressure on students to perform and not exposing them to liberal-arts disciplines, MBA mills cannot help but produce students with a singular interest in getting rich in a hurry. "There is a danger that business education has become a marathon," say U.S. management professors Roger Dickinson, Anthony Herbst, and John O'Shaughnessy in a 1983 essay entitled "What Are Business Schools Doing for Business?" "With too much to absorb there is no time for depth of thought or questioning of assumptions, but there is enough time to generate unpleasant associations that inhibit the desire for further growth."

Ethics training, many educators believe, is an ideal means of broadening the interests of students. Beyond its usefulness as a means of instilling or strengthening moral values, ethics courses force students to confront issues — often ambiguous political, cultural, and social issues — that have more to do with the way business must operate than MBA students could guess from what they learn in their other classes.

To be sure, some educators promote ethics programs chiefly as a safety device. "The consequence of being caught in behaviours which peers, superiors, or the court of public opinion judge to be unethical may be personal and serious," Jeffrey Gandz writes in a rough outline of his plan for an ethical program at the University of Western Ontario's business school. "A manager's integrity may, over the long haul, prove more valuable than his or her MBA."

At Harvard, however, Kenneth Goodpaster strives to go beyond the view of ethics as something that produces negative rewards, and seeks instead to alter the fundamental character of his students. It isn't good enough to merely produce moral corporate-ladder-climbers. MBA students have to know there's more to life than getting ahead. Certainly on some campuses there is evidence that this ethic is not completely foreign to students. Yale business students raise money each year for a fund to subsidize classmates who forsake lucrative postings in the private sector between semesters in order to work in government or non-profit organizations. And in 1986, five Wharton MBA students spent their first summer after graduation cycling across Tibet to raise money for the Chinese handicapped.

But these are merely isolated signs of progress. "The degree of careerism among my most talented students is already amazing, and it can only become more pronounced when they leave Harvard," Goodpaster says. "If we reinforce our students' idea that the meaning of life is tied up entirely with the progress of their careers, and fail to mute that obsessive careerism — which I consider a form of mental illness — we're irresponsible as teachers." Still, Goodpaster has no illusions about how difficult it will be to imbue other business instructors with this sentiment. "How many business schools want to discourage ambition?"

The inherent problems in teaching ethics are on display in Professor Max Clarkson's classroom at the University of Toronto. Clarkson has equipped his students with "four basic commandments, with which you can't get confused or go very far wrong": Do not kill, do not steal, do not lie, do not oppress. The corollaries are: respect life, respect property, be honest, share power. It isn't Kant's categorical imperative, but it's admirably memorable, and an effective counterpoint to the overwhelming business imperative.

On the last day of the course, Clarkson notices upon entering the amphitheatre where he teaches that the previous class has left behind a commandment of its own in block letters on the blackboard:

QUESTION 2, GOAL #1:
MAXIMIZE TOTAL PROFIT

"Well, we'll just cover up 'Maximize total profit'," Clarkson says, pulling a projection screen down across the offending message.

On this final day of "MBA Course 2009 — Corporate Social Responsibilities" students present the last of their "social audits". Armed with a checklist of common ethical concerns, Clarkson's students have exhaustively probed the inner moral workings of several real corporations. It has been an untidy exercise, compared with their other straightforward, neatly organized MBA courses. The students have discovered that a great deal of what goes on at the average corporation is prompted not by internal directives or even by the competition but by the government, special-interest groups, the media, and other forces over which the executives they interviewed feel they have little if any control. In analysing financial performance, they have been surprised to find that luck and instinct have more often than not been the deciding factors in determining success or failure. And they have been appalled at the lack of genuine commitment behind many corporations' public platitudes about honesty, charity, and respect for others.[1]

Some of the social audits are uplifting. A large trust company earns high marks for preferring to be overstaffed for a few years rather than allow automated-teller technology to cause layoffs and for enshrining ethical concerns at the very top of the company in the form of a Business Conduct Review Committee composed of independent members of the trust's board of directors.

A mining firm that has suffered severe losses in recent years is credited with cutting its complement of top executives by more than half at the same time it cut back its hourly workforce by one third, and for making the latter reduction entirely through attrition and early-retirement programs instead of forced layoffs. A large electrical-equipment maker is praised for calculating the exact cost of worker injuries in order to impress on managers the need for enhanced safety conditions; and a utility company is lauded for managing to increase the number of women in its ranks by 18 per cent during a period when the total management ranks were being trimmed by 5 per cent.

In most of the cases, however, students have come away disheartened by what they have found. They are surprised, for a start, by the desultory manner in which many companies dealt with their inquiries. After one student's queries had been chan-

---

1 Professor Clarkson permitted the author to participate in his class on condition that the names of companies subjected to a "social audit" not be revealed. Clarkson keeps his students' reports confidential in order to ensure that corporations will make themselves available for inspections by successive classes of students. With the consent of his students, however, Clarkson often sends completed social audits to the chief executives of firms that have been examined.

nelled through the offices of nine executives at a major bank without advancing the cause one jot, he was offered a glib apology by a minor bank official. The banker's face fell when the student allowed that the way his questions were being handled was as important as the answers.

The answers, when they were forthcoming, revealed serious problems. Senior executives at a communications company boasted to a team of Clarkson's students about impressive productivity gains realized through staff cutbacks; but it became clear after a discussion with people farther down in the ranks that the firm's policy of making fewer people do more work was bringing many employees to the breaking point—some were even smashing equipment to vent their frustration. Other students documented incidents of chronic pollution, deceptive marketing practices, and unsafe working conditions. Many firms appeared only to pay lip service to such concerns as promoting women in management, pay equity, day care, setting up corporate codes of ethical conduct, and establishing a meaningful rapport between management and labour. Commenting on one bank's elaborate statement of principles, a student who had studied the bank tells the class, "Officially, the bank says it places customers first, then employees, then stockholders. But from what I could determine this is mostly just an internal ad. There's tremendous pressure on every employee to perform in order to get profits up, and I have the feeling that ethical issues are kept isolated from the basic business." For many students, listening to executives attest to their enlightened social attitudes was like watching a man furiously pedal a bicycle with the chain removed. They meant well, but for some reason never looked down to see why they weren't moving.

Clarkson himself seems unsure how to react as the presentations unfold. In an earlier career, he was a successful businessman in Buffalo, and his family made several million dollars when its graphic-controls company there was sold to Times Mirror Co., publisher of the *Los Angeles Times* in 1978. Now, back in Toronto, where he grew up, Clarkson lives in a splendid Forest Hill house, whose walls are lined with art; there is a Calder sculpture in the backyard. A former dean of U. of T.'s business school, Clarkson has many close friends in the higher reaches of Canadian business and serves on a few of their boards, including that of the oil giant Suncor Inc. In more than one case, the firms his students find morally wanting are run by people Clarkson sups with, and this annoys him. He doesn't say anything, but in the expression on his face one reads a question: If a bunch of students — *business* students, mind you, whose sympathy towards business is beyond question — can in a few weeks' time uncover all this malfeasance, how do these companies survive the glare of regulatory and media attention? But Clarkson only hints at his dismay. And while he's pleased by his students' ability to find what he told them to look for, he offers surprisingly little advice as to how they should cope if they find themselves working for companies where moral scruples are not part of the corporate culture.

A few weeks after the course winds up, two of Clarkson's students talk about the ethics sessions. Dan and David are both part-time MBA students; each has a full-time management job during the day and has several people reporting to him. At the rate of four courses per year, it takes part-time students about five years to obtain an MBA as compared to the two years most full-time programs require. Dan, twenty-nine, is a biochemist at a large pharmaceutical company in Toronto. Dave, thirty-one, is an engineering manager at a major utility firm. "I was looking for some answers, a sort of religion, I guess," says Dave, about the ethics course. "But there was no big solution."

"I thought there was too much emphasis on companies giving back to the community, as if attending church every Sunday made you a holy man," says Dan. "I'd be a lot more impressed if the companies studied in class just cleaned up their act rather than put so much energy into looking good. The company where we did our social audit had all the ethical goodies — a corporate-values statement, money for every charitable activity going, a woman newly appointed to the board. But it was all staged. There were hardly any women in middle management or running the plants, and the entire company was demoralized because of a series of layoffs and the fear of more to come. Not that the top executives would have much of a feel for the impact of that, since they can't bring themselves to fire people, to hurt them. I had to fire someone once. I know why they use consultants."

In the survey on students' attitudes towards ethics by Duke University's Fuqua School of Business, 61 per cent of the students said they doubted business schools could teach an effective course in ethics. Dan and Dave have, however, taken something from the Clarkson course. "I have to admit," says Dan, "that the class gave me a heightened awareness of what's going on. I wasn't expecting to be shocked by so many horror stories." "You came away thinking that the ethical approach is the only sensible one in the long run," Dave adds, "but more because you'll pay for it someday, not [because] you should just want to do what's morally right. It wasn't the warmest feeling. . . . "

As the two men part, Dan says to his friend, "You realize, don't you, that to get where we want to go, we're probably going to have to become unethical. I just don't see a way around it."

"Or turn a blind eye," Dan replies, "to the immorality all around us. . . . " Dan shrugs his shoulders. "I guess it amounts to the same thing, doesn't it?"

CHAPTER EIGHT
DISTURBERS OF THE PEACE:
Three Reformers who Broke the Circle of Corporate Moral Complacency

Muckraking has always been a dirty and almost thankless task. In 1918, the American essayist H.L. Mencken wrote: "For the habitual truth-teller and truth-seeker, indeed, the world has very little liking. He is always unpopular, and not infrequently his unpopularity is so excessive that it endangers his life. Run your eye back over the list of martyrs, lay and clerical: nine-tenths of them, you will find, stood accused of nothing worse than honest efforts to find out and announce the truth."

The historical precedents did not deter Upton Sinclair, Ida Tarbell, and the other pioneering, turn-of-the-century writers who first exposed the underside of Big Business. *Someone*, they felt, had to watch out for those who lacked the resources and cunning necessary to cope in the newly industrializing world—a world too much guided by philosopher Herbert Spencer's casual observation, "We have unmistakable proof that throughout all past time there has been a ceaseless devouring of the weak by the strong."

But the times were not kind to these first disturbers of the corporate peace. Their president, Theodore Roosevelt, was not eager to abandon Spencer's sanguine assessment of the natural order of man, even if in contemporary novelist Theodore Dreiser's words, it was becoming apparent that in business "men lived on other men". To be sure, Roosevelt was the first president to act on the crusaders' indictments and impose sweeping disciplinary measures on rogue industrialists. Yet Roosevelt was irked by the lack of faith in the new capitalist order expressed in the starchy put-downs of free-market wheeling and dealing that the reformers published, and he was not especially alarmed at the

evils that darted out from the rocks they lifted. Indeed, he publicly mocked the crusaders: borrowing a phrase from John Bun-
yan's *Pilgrim's Progress*, Roosevelt denounced "the Man with the
Muckrake . . . who could look no way but downward".

Later in life, Roosevelt would come round, concluding that, "If
a ring is to be put in the snout of the greedy, only organized
society can do it." Still, the words of the era that strike the most
respondent chord in society today are, sadly, from the pen of Ida
Tarbell, whose meticulous and devastating *History of the Standard
Oil Company* (1904) revealed the mean-spirited machinations of
John D. Rockefeller. "We are a commercial people," Tarbell pessi-
mistically asserted. "As a consequence, business success is sanc-
tified, and, practically, any methods which achieve it are
justified."

Latter-day peace-disturbers fare no better. Almost two generations after the original muckrakers had been interred, the
Princeton-trained son of a Lebanese immigrant restaurateur was
certain his story about a car that was a deathtrap on wheels could
never be told on American television because network executives
would not dare offend advertisers. So when *Unsafe at Any Speed*
was published in 1965, Ralph Nader promoted it first on the
Canadian Broadcasting Corporation public-affairs program "This
Hour Has Seven Days".[1] Auto safety legislation inspired by
Nader's book has prevented an estimated ten thousand highway
deaths every year since the book was published. The thirty-odd
pollution, nuclear-energy, drugs, food-safety, and other Nader-
linked organizations spawned by the book have saved countless
thousands more lives and prompted the passage of such vital
pieces of legislation as the 1966 Freedom of Information Act and
the 1970 Clean Air Act.

Yet, one would not wish for the media caricaturization of
Nader, who is now in his early fifties. He is, by most accounts, an
ascetic, humourless zealot born in the shapeless black suit he

---

1   The popular but controversial "Seven Days", which introduced the techniques of investigative and advocacy journalism to Canadian television and
drew an audience of more than three million each week, was soon to become
a victim of the very timidity Nader had come to Canada to escape. CBC
executives killed the program in 1966, less than two years after it was
launched.

favours. In 1966, *The Washington Post* celebrated the passage of the National Traffic and Motor Vehicle Safety Act—from which followed such commonsense innovations as seat belts, padded dashboards, collapsible steering wheels, and shatter-resistant glass—by saying, "Most of the credit for making possible this important legislation belongs to one man—Ralph Nader. . . . A one-man lobby for the public prevailed over the nation's most powerful industry." But these days, the man whose following of "Nader's Raiders" has included protégés as dissimilar as Robert F. Kennedy and former Montreal Canadiens goalie Ken Dryden is disparaged for the $400 cost per car of all those new safety features.

Yet, in a way it is their very unpopularity, their stubborn determination to be appreciated but not embraced by the public, government, and especially, business that makes Nader and the corporate reformers profiled on the following pages so effective. Only as outsiders, lone wolves who often alienate even their natural allies, can they agitate for lasting improvements in our way of life.

There is a grim tenacity in the toilings of Gar Mahood, Phil Edmonston, and Stephen Jarislowsky that even their sharpest adversaries would be hard pressed to emulate. It may seem to the average observer that the crusades against the tobacco companies, the automakers, and the executives who trample on their own shareholders' rights have been largely won. But these men beg to differ. Perhaps a perverse fear of being right after all—of succeeding and having nothing more to rail against—moves these reformers to deny victory. More likely, an indelible cynicism tells them the bastards on the other side always have energy enough for one more round in which to conjure up new, as yet unimagined, infamies. "We always fail," Nader once said. "The whole thing is limiting the degree of failure."

Fire and Pain

Gar Mahood, non-smokers-rights crusader

In tennis, the rite of victory is a solemn affair. Thus when the teenage German tennis sensation Boris Becker finished battling Sweden's Stefan Edberg into submission to secure the 1986 Player's International men's championship, a respectful silence

fell over Toronto's National Tennis Centre. Despite the oppressive heat — about 100°F — the crowd waited patiently as a red
carpet was rolled across centre court and a procession of tournament officials made its way into view.

At the centre of the procession was Paul Paré, a distinguished
figure with darkly tanned features. Paré was at the height of his
career. He could look back with justifiable pride on his twenty
years as the head of tobacco giant Imasco Ltd.of Montreal, a Brit-
ish-controlled company that Paré, a Quebec native, had transformed from a languishing victim of absentee ownership into a
diversified and highly profitable multinational enterprise. For
many people in the well-heeled audience, Paré was a stirring
symbol of Canadian business leadership; for those who knew
him only as a fellow tennis fan, Paré was greatly appreciated as
the principal sponsor of this tournament, the only Canadian
event big enough to attract the world's top tennis stars, and
which bears the name of Imasco's leading brand of cigarettes.
When Paré stepped forward to present Becker with a cheque for
$71,400, the applause that followed the announcement of his
name over the public-address system was almost as thunderous
as that which had greeted Becker in his moment of triumph over
Edberg. The two foreign tennis stars were, after all, only attrac-
tions of the moment. The crowd recognized Paré as a heroic
native son.

"Beu-tee-ful!"

In cramped offices above a mid-town Toronto pizzeria, a
middle-aged man with a monkish haircut cackled with delight.
Garfield Mahood, executive director of the Non-Smokers' Rights
Association (NSRA), summoned his top lieutenant, David
Sweanor, for an impromptu strategy session. "Look at this stuff,"
Mahood exclaimed. "Now we've really got the buggers!"

In the centre of Mahood's desk, between two precariously balanced stacks of research reports, was a collection of documents
describing the associations that Paul Paré, sworn enemy of the
NSRA, had struck with the Kidney Foundation and several Montreal hospitals. In Mahood's judgment, Paré's work as a fund-
raiser for hospitals and health-care organizations was a calculated
outrage.

In January 1987, scarcely five months after Paré's adulatory reception at the National Tennis Centre, Mahood held a press conference in Montreal at which he blasted both Paré and his beneficiaries: Mahood considered it intolerable that Paré, the "godfather" of an industry whose products cause bodily harm, should offer his services as a fund-raiser to health organizations, and condemned the "hypocrisy" of the hospitals and health-care associations that solicited his assistance. But in Montreal, Paré's home town, the criticism seemed to fly back in the face of Paré's detractor. Who was this little man to be questioning the character of a brilliant empire builder whose $4.3 billion conglomerate controlled half the Canadian cigarette market and owned Canada's largest trust company (Canada Trust) and one of the continent's biggest drug-store chains (Shoppers Drug Mart)? How could anyone fault Paré, an Anglophone business leader who had stood by Montreal when the Parti Québécois' restrictive language laws drove many English-speaking executives out of Quebec, and whose financial acumen had brought great economic wealth *into* the province; a man who had been recognized for his tireless fund-raising activities with induction into the Order of Canada, the highest civilian honour in the land; a man whose public-spirited firm had, only a month before, announced its intention to attack the problem of youth unemployment by helping set up a $7 million job-creation program designed to put a thousand young entrepreneurs to work?

Ultimately, it was Mahood's conduct that was judged outrageous. Montreal's renowned Royal Victoria Hospital and several other health-care institutions Mahood had condemned insisted the NSRA director had it all wrong. They couldn't very well comply with Mahood's demand that Paré be thrown off their boards, since Paré had not served on them for some time. The Kidney Foundation, just one of the groups Mahood accused of being an "offensive example of greed in the charitable community", attested to Paré's noble character; and Norm McDonald, president of the Canadian Tobacco Manufacturers' Council, castigated Mahood for "a despicable act in attempting to tear down a leading citizen of Montreal, and indeed, all of Canada".

But Mahood is unrepentant as he reflects on his sour reception in Montreal. He defends the apparent sloppiness of his research on that occasion by saying the health-care groups put out misleading data about their fund-raising activities, and once more goes onto the offensive: "Paré stands at the head of an industry that kills more people with its products than any other," Mahood says. "To fill the nation's hospital wards with people dying of tobacco-related disease and then raise funds for those hospitals as if you were some kind of good guy is almost an obscenity."

As it happens, any credibility problems Mahood himself might have suffered during the Montreal débâcle have since been eclipsed. In April 1987 a pair of federal cabinet ministers announced that a huge chunk of Mahood's agenda was about to become the law of the land. Treasury Board president Robert de Cotret, who quit smoking himself a day before joining health minister Jake Epp for the announcement, unveiled a program to eliminate smoking in all federal offices by 1989, a move that will affect hundreds of thousands of civil servants. But it was Epp who bore the more remarkable news that day. Citing tobacco use as Canada's most serious preventable health problem — a line he could have lifted verbatim from any of hundreds of NSRA ads, pamphlets, and press releases — Epp said Ottawa was phasing in a ban on all forms of tobacco advertising over a two-year period in order "to take away the means of educating people to smoke". There was more: tobacco firms will soon be forbidden to tie their brand names, trademarks, or related images to sports and cultural events they sponsor.

Indeed, Epp's new Tobacco Products Control Act even forbids tobacco firms from using cigarette packages themselves as ads. Calling the existing message on packs asking smokers to avoid inhaling "absolutely ridiculous", Epp said that in future, almost one-fifth of each pack's surface must be taken up with one of a series of rotating, blunt, health warnings. Moreover, the brand name and trademark and a new legally required list of major toxic substances in tobacco and cigarette smoke is all that may appear on each pack.

The tobacco firms, which had lobbied Epp during the winter in the hopes of preventing such drastic measures from being imposed, were enraged at the government's apparent resolve to bring the curtain down on the industry, which historically has been one of the most profitable in the history of both business and government tax-collectors. Jean-Louis Mercier, chairman of Imasco subsidiary Imperial Tobacco Ltd. and chairman of the Canadian Tobacco Manufacturers' Council, said he was "flabbergasted

that this government, which claims to be against useless regulations, uses laws and regulations to decide how Canadians should
behave in the workplace. The government has obviously decided
that you can't trust Canadians when it comes to their lifestyles."

Epp's proposed ban on advertising of a legal product alarmed
free-speech advocates and some civil libertarians. John C. Luik,
who teaches on the ethics of advertising at the University of
Manitoba, sympathizes with Mercier. "What is so deeply offensive about a ban on tobacco advertising is that, in restricting free
speech, it inevitably demeans us all by proclaiming that we are
insufficiently rational to understand the consequences of our
actions. If we cannot trust the rationality of the smoker who feels
his enjoyment is worth risking a shorter lifetime, can we really
trust the rationality of the fatty who refuses to start an exercise
program? Can we trust the good sense of the red-meat-eater who
stupidly prefers his steak to the latest in lean cuisine? And what
of the credit-card addict who, having been told never to leave
home without it, spends his way into insolvency?"

As domino theories go, however, Luik's is not compelling. Red
meat is not addictive; tobacco takes such a strong hold on
smokers that many cannot shake their habit even after being informed they have contracted a tobacco-related disease. And the
obesity or spendthrift nature of one person generally does not
present a risk to others; "second-hand" tobacco smoke, however,
has been implicated in dozens of studies as a cause of health disorders in non-smokers who live or work with smokers. Which is
why, in the wake of this extraordinary government initiative,
Mahood isn't pulling handsprings. "I'm pleased Ottawa is talking
tough," says Mahood, "but I'm not starry eyed. The tobacco companies will try to derail this legislation or thwart its intent. And
even if they don't, there's more to this issue than banning ads.
The ultimate goal is the elimination of tobacco products. We're
going to pour it on now. I want to see this thing sealed up."

It has been twenty-three years since the U.S. Surgeon General
first weighed in with a thick report about the health risks associated with tobacco, and issued a strong warning against continued
use of the product. It has been eighteen years since an all-party
committee of the House of Commons concluded that "there is no
longer any scientific controversy regarding the risk created by

cigarette smoking. The original statistical observations have been validated by clinical observation and the evidence is now accepted as fact by Canadian medicine. . . . " That evidence, updated and reinforced by some thirty thousand research reports by medical experts in Canada and abroad, represents a staggering indictment of tobacco products and, by inference, the people who make and distribute them:

* Tobacco-related diseases claim the lives of Canadians at the rate of one death every seventeen minutes, or a total of about thirty-two thousand deaths per year — roughly one-fifth of all deaths in Canada.
* Tobacco products cause 30 per cent of all fatal cancer cases, more than 80 per cent of lung cancers; tobacco use is responsible for one-quarter of all heart attacks and is a leading cause of death from emphysema, bronchitis, and pneumonia.
* In every eighteen-month period, more Canadians die from tobacco use than perished in the Second World War; the U.S. toll is 350,000 deaths per year, more U.S. lives than were lost in the Second World War and Vietnam combined.
* If the tobacco epidemic isn't brought under control, about four million Canadian smokers will die an average of eight years prematurely.

Yet despite this apalling toll, Canadians spent a record $6.1 billion on tobacco products in 1985, equal to about 1.3 per cent of the gross national product. Tobacco use is declining, but industry revenues continue to climb because smokers have endured a sharp run-up in prices. More ominously, the tobacco industry has succeeded in recruiting enough new smokers from the ranks of the very young to make up for many of the older smokers who have sensibly quit the habit.

For this reason the ad ban, despite seeming arbitrary to some observers, is indeed necessary. Cigarette ads, which depict smokers as athletic, fun-loving hedonists, are effective at baiting young people who identify with the adult smokers in the ads and aspire to the lifestyle of daring alpine-skiing tourneys and elegant romantic soirées shown in the ads.

Although the tobacco industry vehemently denies it, there can be no doubting the importance of convincing people to try cigarettes when they're young, since a large body of research shows that most people who have not smoked before the age of twenty never will take up cigarettes. Once hooked, smokers have a hard time breaking the habit: for some people tobacco is more addictive than heroin. Every year, more than 80 per cent of North American smokers attempt to quit smoking; obviously a great portion of them fail.[2] Such is the hold of cigarettes that 48 per cent of lung cancer victims who survive surgery start smoking again, usually within a year. There simply isn't much need to advertise to older smokers. In the foreword to the 1979 U.S. Surgeon General's report, former U.S. secretary of health Joseph Califano wrote, "It is nothing short of a national tragedy that so much death and disease are wrought by a powerful habit often taken up by unsuspecting children lured by seductive multi-million dollar cigarette advertising campaigns."

Unfortunately, Califano, who served in the administration of former president Jimmy Carter, got nowhere with his massive anti-smoking campaign, even though it was the most determined effort of its kind in North America until that time. The tobacco-industry lobby succeeded in gutting its most promising proposed remedies, and in truth the campaign itself was somewhat mis-directed. Like most anti-smoking initiatives undertaken by government agencies and non-profit health organizations such as the Canadian Cancer Society and the Heart Fund, Califano's campaign failed because it was directed at smokers. Mahood and the NSRA long ago gave up trying to convert the addicted. Instead, they have focused their firepower on the industry. "Sure, I'd like to reform smokers, particularly the thousands of kids in Canada who are hooked each year, 70 per cent of whom will be addicted for life," says Mahood. "But mostly it's the industry I'm after. I want to see it put out of business."

Government agencies and non-profit health-care groups — which Mahood disparagingly labels "the health establishment" — are non-combative by nature. In its own work to curb smoking, the establishment has consistently favoured such gentle tactics as poster campaigns, earnest research reports, and public-awareness events such as "Weedless Wednesday". Mahood regards

---

2 On the same day Ottawa announced its tobacco-ad ban, Ontario premier David Peterson was asked about the poor example he was giving young people by smoking in public. Peterson replied that he should quit. "But it's too hard," he said. "I've quit several times. I'm going to quit again."

these activities as so much teacup rattling. Among social-issue activists, he is a guerilla fighter who prides himself on being unpredictable. "We try to keep the smoking forces off balance," Mahood says. "I try never to let them know where we're coming from next."

Mahood and his staff of six constantly study the tobacco industry for signs of weakness, then strike at the most propitious moment. When asked to testify in court cases involving companies failing to comply with municipal anti-smoking bylaws or accused of subjecting their employees to smoky workplaces, Mahood seizes the opportunity to maintain that the underlying villainy rests with the tobacco makers. Outside the courtroom, his attacks can be petty, but they are always novel enough to garner press attention. Among his more offbeat ploys: Mahood exposed an Imasco ad in a program guide at Canada's Wonderland, a theme park north of Toronto, as an overt attempt to hook kids on tobacco (the guide was withdrawn), and raised a protest upon discovering that the real-life model who plays the "Macdonald Lassie" (the mascot who appears on the Export 'A' package) was only twenty years old—a clear violation of the industry's own code, which prohibits the use of models under age twenty-five to promote tobacco products.

Other NSRA campaigns are more elaborate, and audacious. In 1983, Mahood assailed the Canadian Ski Association for negotiating a $1.7 million sponsorship with tobacco-maker RJR-MacDonald Inc. A series of provocative NSRA newspaper ads headlined "Should the Canadian Ski Association get in bed with the tobacco industry?" sparked a controversy that culminated with Steve Podborski, a star of Canada's downhill ski team, vowing he would not take part in tobacco-sponsored events, and with a threat by Ottawa to cut off $2.5 million in federal financing to the CSA if the tobacco sponsorship went ahead.

In 1986, Mahood pulled out all the stops. A weighty NSRA research brief submitted to federal health minister Jake Epp in January labelled the tobacco industry's voluntary ad code "a public relations fraud". In the report, entitled "A Catalogue of Deception", Mahood identified more than 250 violations of the rule that tobacco billboards not be placed within 200 metres of primary or secondary schools, and concluded that health warnings on tobacco packages and in advertisements were often either missing or in type too small to read. In order to bolster its impact, Mahood reinforced the brief by placing an ad in *Maclean's* that bore the headline "30,000 Die While Feds Sit On Hands". Another brief in the fall to members of Parliament demanded the tobacco industry be severely constrained in its activities and deprived of all government subsidies. In this report, Mahood argued that "if death rates due to tobacco use are assumed to be proportional to the market share of each brand, then the Player's brands of cigarettes alone are killing Canadians at a faster rate than all traffic accidents from coast to coast. . . ." After sending off his brief to Parliament, Mahood took his argument to the public in a $125,000 ad campaign in twenty-three newspapers. One of the ads showed a man on crutches with a missing leg. The copy explained that smoking sometimes causes circulatory disorders: "Gangrene is only one of the consequences of the absence of government regulation of the tobacco industry."

Mahood's occasional extremism is his only way of coping with the painfully prolonged process of getting severe restrictions imposed on the sale of tobacco, while products such as saccharin, Red Dye #2, and ethyl carbamate in wine have long ago been banned or restricted, often on less evidence than has been amassed against tobacco. But there's more to it than that. Mahood, forty-five, is the angry young man who never grew up.

Born in Windsor, Ontario, the son of an insurance broker and grandson of a Presbyterian minister, Mahood smoked a little when he was fifteen but, unlike most children who take up the habit, kicked it while still in his teens. Although he is under 5'9", Mahood struggled successfully to get on the first string of varsity basketball and track-and-field teams; and while studying business administration at Waterloo University College in the mid-1960s went into business himself promoting basketball tournaments and ice carnivals. When a nascent waterski show he started went into fiscal arrest on its third day (the engine in Mahood's boat was improperly bolted down by the man who sold it to Mahood, and the boat flipped over), Mahood dropped out of school to earn enough money to pay his debts — and developed a lingering distrust of the very vocation he had hoped to make a fortune from. A successful businessman himself as an Encyclopedia Britannica salesman, Mahood began to doubt his calling soon after being named the company's top salesman in Canada. "We weren't supposed to tell prospective buyers the price until we'd given them the whole pitch," Mahood recalls. "It wasn't long before I was walking out of houses because I could see they couldn't afford the books."

Mahood peddled encyclopedias while his first wife obtained her degree in nursing, then returned to university himself. Soon he was swept up in issues that were hot on the campus of Toronto's York University in the early 1970s, including Canadian complicity in the Vietnam war and the spectre of foreign economic domination of Canada. By the time he decided to help Toronto nursing instructor Rosalie Berlin set up the NSRA in 1974, Mahood had already put in a two-year stint as executive director of the Canadian Environmental Law Association, where he had campaigned successfully for the passage of Ontario's Environmental Assessment Act.

By this point, Mahood had also become like the burr you can't shake from your trouser leg after walking through a field of wildflowers. Leonard Lumbers was one of the first people to discover how prickly the activist can be when crossed. Lumbers made the mistake of blocking Mahood's Volvo with his Lincoln in a parking lot at York. Mahood, guessing that the Lincoln could only belong to one of York's big-wig benefactors, hauled Lumbers out of a board of governors meeting and hollered at him in the cold winter night the whole way to the parking lot. When Lumbers, whom Mahood only later discovered was the head of Canada Wire & Cable, refused to apologise for the inconvenience he'd caused, Mahood sued. Mahood let the court date pass, but the story of the student who sued the member of York's board of governors was big news in the campus press and rated a small mention in *The Globe and Mail*.

His appetite for confrontation thus whetted, Mahood continued to make small waves. When his first wife took a tumble on a subway staircase after the heel of her left shoe snapped off, Mahood took the offending footwear back to Eaton's and demanded not only a replacement but a modest compensatory payment. When the department store refused to oblige, Mahood sought opinions from shoe experts in Canada and Britain — including a supporting report unwittingly provided by Eaton's own product-testing lab — and told his story to the papers and CBC radio. Eaton's eventually came up with a new pair of shoes and $200 in damages. In 1981, Mahood's mother, Evelyn, was bumped from a transatlantic British Airways flight. Mahood, who was seeing his mother off in London, commandeered a phone at the airline's own office and noisily plotted with his Toronto lawyer the lawsuit he planned to bring against Britain's largest air carrier. The airline paid Mahood off with an $850 out-of-court settlement after he threatened to subpoena enough evidence to fill a small plane.

Mahood revels in his self-appointed role as a David pitted against the tobacco industry and other Goliaths, often prefacing accounts of past triumphs with the words, "And then little old Gar had a great idea . . . ". Unfortunately, though, his habitual contempt for politicians and the health-care establishment has turned off many of his natural allies. Former alderman Pat Sheppard, a non-smoker who was a left-wing member of Toronto City Council in the 1970s, complained bitterly about the NSRA's high-pressure tactics. After being hounded over his alleged lack of concern about the tobacco issue once too often, Sheppard vowed never to speak with Mahood again and accused the NSRA of being "incredibly pious, self-righteous, and uncompromising in its positions". Toronto alderman Richard Gilbert, another sometime NSRA ally, says Mahood has "a zeal that sometimes borders on fanaticism, and this sometimes prompts him to bite the hand that feeds him". And there is something nervy about the accusation he levels against orthodox health groups of getting a "free ride" when he appends their names to his highly charged briefs and advertisements. Mahood doesn't stop to consider the credibility those names lend to the NSRA's media blitzes. Most importantly, though, Mahood's vituperation, particularly when it is directed against other members of what should be a united front, sometimes plays into the hands of the tobacco industry. The industry's most effective defence tactic has been to maintain a studied silence on the health issue, which by now it cannot fight without straining credulity. It maintains this silence in the hope that the anti-smoking faction will seem shrill by comparison, and perhaps even present itself as a threat to civil liberties.

For all that, though, Mahood's effectiveness cannot be denied. The NSRA can justly claim much of the credit for Toronto's landmark 1977 by-law against smoking in public places, and the Toronto Transit Commission's decision several years ago to sacrifice $200,000 in annual revenues by banning tobacco ads on transit vehicles. Mahood's highly publicized campaigns have been successful in stalling the creation of a national tobacco-marketing agency. And they have met with the approval of a good many highly placed politicians, including federal secretary of state David Crombie, who when he was mayor of Toronto in the 1970s called the NSRA "the most impressive and intelligent lobby I have ever known."

Don Lewis, a sometime ally of Mahood, heads the Ottawa-based Canadian Council on Smoking and Health. Given his own work on the issue, Lewis naturally wishes Mahood would stop acting as though he personally comprises the entire anti-smoking vanguard. Still, Lewis is a Mahood fan. "Gar is a frontal-assault guy," Lewis says. "Maybe his battering-ram approach doesn't always work, but his militancy is just what this issue needs if it's to get the attention it deserves." Norm McDonald of the Canadian Tobacco Manufacturers' Council acknowledges the industry's reluctance to confront Mahood. "Arguing with him," McDonald says, "is like getting into a pissing match with a skunk." Indeed, Mahood's notoriety extends beyond the borders of Canada. In 1986, the *Tobacco Reporter*, a U.S. industry journal, described the NSRA as a "vociferous anti-tobacco lobby — one of the fiercest in the world. The NSRA has had the ear of successive health ministers."

This is certainly true of the NSRA's dealings with Jake Epp, a Mennonite and pastor's son who was predisposed to the NSRA's position before he arrived at the health ministry. Epp began a meeting with Mahood in Ottawa in the spring of 1986 by telling the NSRA director, "I just want to thank you for what you've done. For whatever reason, others have been or are unable to put pressure on the government. Keep it up." Mahood expects Ottawa will require continued external pressure to maintain the commitment it now has apparently made to the anti-tobacco cause. Citing the Califano experience, Mahood worries the tobacco lobby may try to have Epp transferred to another ministry, or stir up fears that the ban on tobacco ads is a mere crack in the dike and that makers of everything from alcohol to sugar will someday suffer the same treatment. "Getting the government to announce this program was just a skirmish," says Mahood. "Now comes the battle of ensuring this thing doesn't lose its momentum."

In fact, though, there are many signs the anti-tobacco lobby's day of irrefutable victory is at hand. In early 1987, the U.S. federal government imposed restrictions against smoking in all 6,800 of its buildings, a move that effects 890,000 federal employees and is part of the most widespread attempt since Prohibition to alter people's personal habits through regulation. Some forty states now restrict smoking in public places, and there are more than eight hundred local ordinances against tobacco use. About 42 per cent of private businesses in the United States have some kind of smoking policy, up from 16 per cent in 1980. The reason? "Tobacco is a dangerous substance," says John Pinney, director of the Institute for the Study of Smoking Behaviour and Policy at Harvard's Kennedy School of Government. "An employer who doesn't do anything is likely to be sued." Already the decline in tobacco consumption is exacting a financial toll on farmers. In Ontario, where most Canadian tobacco is grown, land devoted to tobacco cultivation has dropped from 100,000 hectares in the late 1970s to 30,000 hectares today. As for tobacco executives, they now must suffer abuse from new critics sometimes even more outspoken than Mahood. Among these is Relatives and Friends of Dead and Dying Smokers, an advocacy group launched in Toronto in early 1987. The RODD is calling on governments to prosecute tobacco executives for misleading the public about the dangers of smoking. At its inaugural press conference RODD advisor Robert Aaron, a Toronto commercial lawyer, declared, "We want the executives of the tobacco industry behind bars."

Yet for all the progress to date, Mahood is impatient for much more. You can sense his frustration in the copy he writes for the NSRA's own ads. "This week tobacco products will kill an esti-mated 550 Canadians," Mahood wrote in a NSRA ad placed in *The London Free Press* that pleaded with the paper to stop accepting tobacco ads.[3] "Five hundred grieving families will bury their dead, no less torn apart by the death of a loved one on a cancer or cardiac ward than if he or she had died on a rainslick highway." Promising to escalate the battle, Mahood says the next front is lawsuits against tobacco firms by families of victims of tobacco-

---

3 In 1987, prior to the federal government's announced intention to ban tobacco ads, only *The Toronto Star*, *The Globe and Mail*, *The Kingston Whig-Standard*, and *The Brockville Recorder and Times* among Canada's 110 or so daily newspapers had dropped tobacco ads.

related diseases who seek redress on the grounds of product liability. And there will be, he says, more high-profile NSRA sniping at the industry's marketing practices. In order to strike as close to home as possible, the NSRA bought stock in Imasco and Rothmans Benson & Hedges Inc. in 1986, which entitles Mahood and his staff to speak at the companies' annual meetings. "If we really believe the death-rate statistics," says Mahood, "we have to abandon little ways of applying pressure. We have to figure out which buttons to push to make the pressure increase exponentially."

Despite constant temptations to give up his work for the NSRA in order to join, say, the nuclear-disarmament forces, Mahood will likely extend his tour of duty against the tobacco industry until that particular Goliath is truly vanquished. "I couldn't pick an issue more tailor-made for the type of work I like to do," Mahood says. "The health-care arguments are clearly on our side. Where else could you find an issue with so much going for it? I mean, suppose we're wrong about the thirty-two thousand deaths per year? What are the buggers gonna do, try to tell us it's only twenty-five thousand?"

Not Rust Away

Phil Edmonston, consumer car activist
Phil Edmonston has made a career out of blowing his top. He hollers for justice on behalf of the one out of every ten car owners who is having trouble with his or her vehicle—that is, with a product that is usually its owner's biggest expense, save for a house. When he stormily condemns the unholy trinity of carmakers, dealers, and repair-shop operators for its "dishonesty", "incompetence", and "fraud" Edmonston can always count on winning a few more frustrated fans, whether his soapbox is a radio show, a witness stand in small-claims court, or even a disruptive appearance at a car company's gala showing of its latest offerings. His caustic indictments provide a vicarious thrill for every car owner who has ever felt betrayed by an industry with more than its share of slick marketers, glib salespeople, and predatory repairmen.

Unrelenting belligerence has its drawbacks, though. In 1976, Edmonston's Montreal-based Automobile Protection Association was about to score its biggest victory—a landmark settlement with Ford Motor Co. of Canada in which the automaker agreed to compensate owners of rusted-out Fords from the model years 1970 through 1974 and to vastly upgrade the anti-corrosion provisions of its warranties. Yet as the triumphal moment drew closer, Edmonston's cockiness became oppressive. Toronto lawyer Jeff Lyons, who is now a Tory power broker and is chairman of the Toronto Transit Commission, remembers well a last-minute falling out between himself and Edmonston during the "Rusty Ford Campaign".

"The more progress we made with Ford's executives the farther he tried to push them," Lyons says. "He was full of himself to the point of being obnoxious, ordering everyone around — including me." When Edmonston continued to rant at Lyons while the lawyer was driving him back to Toronto from an especially rancourous session at Ford's Oakville headquarters, Lyons stopped the car. "That's it, I've had enough abuse," Lyons told his colleague, and ordered Edmonston out of the car. "I drove only a little ways down the road before coming back for him," Lyons says. "But I told him, 'If you start up again, you're walking.'"

Yet seldom has an apparent character flaw suited someone so well. Edmonston, forty-three, has literally shouted his way to the head of the line of Canada's consumer advocates: his name is synonymous with the cause of everyone who is determined to get a fair shake from the businesspeople who make, sell, and repair cars. Every year the APA receives more than 100,000 complaints through the mails or over the telephone. Edmonston deals with some of these personally. Often the 6'4" advocate looming behind a disgruntled customer is enough to force a cowering car mechanic to trim $100 or more off an excessive repair bill. "One of the things that gives him an edge over his adversaries," says Lyons, "is the plain fact that he's physically intimidating."

But the APA has more weapons in its arsenal than the bombast and imposing stature of its president, whose sandy brown hair and beard soften only a little the wary, unforgiving set of his eyes. In its often successful drives to extract compensation for shoddy workmanship from the likes of General Motors, Ford, Chrysler, and other large automakers, the APA has deployed elaborate campaigns. Its high-pressure tactics include generating negative publicity for the offending company, picketing plants and dealerships, organizing consumer boycotts, lobbying various levels of government to apply disciplinary measures, and launching multimillion-dollar class-action suits against auto firms. The backbone of this continuing crusade for safer and higher-quality cars is the APA's fearsome network of spies—whistleblowers within the car companies and malcontents in the civil service dismayed by their political masters' lack of conviction.

In its eighteen-year history, the APA has racked up several impressive victories that benefit not only its own twenty-four thousand members but all car owners. In the early 1970s Edmonston assailed makers of unsafe car seats for children, which at the time, Edmonston said, often provided no protection "and may be nothing more than high-priced, overrated frauds". These shoddy car seats soon disappeared from the market, to be replaced by much better products that were required to meet exacting quality standards. High-profile APA campaigns forced General Motors to withdraw its Firenza, Vega, and Astre models, which were plagued with defects; Volkswagen pulled its 1975 Rabbits off the market largely in response to APA pressure.

It was the rusty Ford débâcle, however, that secured national prominence for the APA. For three years in the mid-1970s the APA pressed its case that the auto-maker's products rusted prematurely. It was a two-pronged attack: Lyons led a class-action suit against Ford on behalf of 371,000 Ford owners in Ontario, while Edmonston whipped up anti-Ford sentiment among the public through relentless attacks delivered on radio and TV programs and in his nationally syndicated newspaper column. The APA's first big break came in the spring of 1976, when the federal consumer minister Bryce Mackasey offered his services as a mediator in the dispute, giving the APA campaign a tremendous credibility boost by signalling the government's concern over the issue. A much bigger break, coming at about the same time, was the revelation that Ford had slipped into third place in Canadian car sales, behind Chrysler—a ranking it had not suffered for almost forty years and one that was brought about mostly by the negative publicity generated by the rusty Ford campaign. Succumbing to the pressure, Ford unveiled a reparations scheme that fall in which it paid $3 million to compensate owners of Fords from the model years 1970 through 1974. A much more important concession, however, was Ford's decision to overhaul its warranties. It discarded its one-year or 20,000 kilometre warranty, which had been the industry standard, in favour of a three-year warranty against rusting. Ford has since committed itself to an even higher standard of corrosion resistance by offering six-year or 160,000 kilometre protection against rust.

The assault on Ford was well timed. The APA campaign coincided with the emergence of dozens of other consumer groups, which in turn attracted the attention of new consumer-affairs branches of government. And the press, keen to explore the new field, was suddenly very receptive to the issues raised by consumer activists. Meanwhile, the influx of Japanese imports, with their claims of higher quality and fuel efficiency, was beginning to have a significant impact. Ford hotly denied its cars rusted out at a faster rate than other companies' makes. But anyone who doubted the APA's charges had only to stand on any street corner and watch the rusty Fords go by; and few observers saw wisdom in attempting to go after the entire industry when one company's ultimate compliance would likely lead the other companies to fall into line.

"Edmonston had a hot issue on his hands," admits Ford public-affairs director Tony Fredo, "and he went all the way with it." When Ford capitulated, it became an uplifting example of how billion-dollar enterprises could be made to bend to the will of consumer activists, to whom Edmonston, naturally enough, became an overnight hero. "Phil should be grateful to us," says Fredo. "We gave him his place in the sun."

Edmonston arrived at that juncture in the most roundabout way. Indeed, up until the moment he founded the APA in 1969, Edmonston's life lacked direction and was guided mostly by sheer happenstance. Edmonston was born in Washington, D.C., the son of a refrigerator repairman who died when Phil was five years old. A bout with polio set his public-school education back a couple of years, and in the eighth grade Edmonston dropped out altogether. Despairing of formal education, he opted to earn his high-school equivalency with a stint in the U.S. Army. But his four-year tour of duty, beginning at the age of seventeen, exposed him less to the rigours of military discipline than to the deprivations endured by residents of Central America. Edmonston helped run a medical-aid station in Panama's U.S.-occupied Canal Zone. Located deep in the bush, close to the Costa Rican border, the station was seldom visited by U.S. servicemen. Edmonston spent most of his time attending to the needs of local villagers, helping to set up fishing co-ops and even acting as a liaison with local-government officials. Yet, while he found the work rewarding, Edmonston eventually became homesick.

Back in the United States, Edmonston waited on tables in Greenwich Village, ran YMCA dances, wrapped Christmas presents at Macy's, and worked as a department-store private eye on guard against employee pilferage. He hitch-hiked to California and spent some time in Acapulco. When his interest in education reawakened, Edmonston sweet-talked the president of a black college outside Washington, D.C., into granting him admission. During his three years at Bowie State College, Edmonston distinguished himself not only by being the only white on campus, but by becoming editor of the campus paper. Edmonston used the paper as a platform for a protest against inadequate facilities that culminated in the ousting of the same president but for whose graces Edmonston would have had to obtain his education elsewhere.

Edmonston hoped to follow up his studies at Bowie State with a stint in the Peace Corps, but during a trip to Mexico he met and fell in love with a French-speaking woman who ran a hairdressing salon in Montreal. Thinking he could find a teaching job there, Edmonston came to Canada and married the Montrealer. And while he was not caught up in the Vietnam protests in his native land — "the waves of social reform lapped over me, I wasn't carried away by them," he says — Edmonston quickly fell in with the community of U.S. draft dodgers in Montreal. Their defiant frame of mind and a nasty scene over a car gave rise to the APA. One day in 1969, Edmonston's mother-in-law came home with a car-repair bill which Edmonston deemed excessive. The two of them returned to the garage, where Edmonston succeeded in yelling the bill down by $100. But he didn't think he should have to yell: it seemed like begging to him. While at Bowie State, Edmonston had worked briefly for one of Ralph Nader's consumer research groups, and came away from a meeting with Nader greatly impressed by the man. Montreal at the end of the 1960s seemed like a fertile ground for protest movements, and when Edmonston discovered that no organizations existed to handle consumer car complaints, he decided to set one up.

Edmonston began by going after repair shops. He soon became a familiar face to the staff at Montreal's small-claims court, where he was quietly cheered from the sidelines as he argued on behalf of car owners who had been victimized by mechanics, rust-proofers, and dealers. Surprised at his own success, and gratified by the mailbags bursting with correspondence from distressed consumers that arrived regularly at the fledgling APA's head-quarters, Edmonston became more ambitious and audacious. It was not long before he was targeting the auto-makers them-selves, as well as insurers, whom he accused of charging exorbi-tant premiums and of stalling on claims payments.

Unlike so many other consumer-advocacy groups that sprang up in the late 1960s and early 1970s — a band of activists fighting outrageous price hikes that called itself Women Against Rising Prices (WARP) comes to mind — the APA did not fade into oblivion, and instead has gone from strength to strength. "Many groups proved unable to rally consumers or put pressure on companies because they weren't street fighters," says Lyons. "Phil has al-ways realized you have to sell your case to the public, and there-by hurt the companies you're after in the marketplace."

"The first thing I had to overcome was a Canadian fear of con-frontation," says Edmonston. "The advocacy groups that have been most effective have been those that are most provocative. The APA's power stems from its audacity. We try to appear as though we're ready to confront anyone, anywhere, anytime."

Inflammatory tactics have not, however, always served the APA well. Edmonston's first campaign was directed against Allstate Insurance Co., which he accused of delaying claim payments. Some of the zealous APA members who picketed the firm's offices bore aloft placards that showed the company's hallowed cupped-hands logo dripping with blood. Edmonston, his wife, and his mother-in-law were sued. Edmonston's allegations were wrong, and Allstate won a permanent injunction that threatens Edmon-ston with a fine or jail term if he unfairly criticizes Allstate in the future. Edmonston has been fined by the Quebec Bar Association for dispensing legal advice; and when he labelled a Japanese sports car — which was alleged to have brake-system problems — a "kamikaze car", Edmonston not only drew a lawsuit from the manufacturer but earned a rebuke from Nader, who complained to the APA chief about the racist overtones of the attack.

And while his noble intentions have won Edmonston the occasional praise of industry officials and government regulators, often he has gotten their backs up unnecessarily. The counterproductive side of Edmonston's aggressiveness showed itself most clearly during the rusty Ford campaign. "He was trying to push Ford too far," Lyons says. "If we'd stuck with his approach of just continually raising hell with no thought of the outcome we wanted, the APA would never had resolved that dispute." Indeed, the Ford campaign marked the high point of Edmonston's egotistical flights. During this period he delighted in demanding that Ford dispatch a limousine from its Oakville head office to pick him up at Toronto's Pearson International Airport "as if he were some kind of Maharajah," says Lyons. "There was a time," says APA treasurer Marc Clapp, a twelve-year APA veteran who is also a native of Washington, D.C., "when Phil was such a whirlwind he seemed to suck up all the oxygen in the room. You sometimes felt crushed."

Edmonston openly admits he's hard to please. "I have a tendency to be hyper," he says. "I want to get things done very quickly. But now I'm trying to encourage people to contest my views. I want to nurture the people I work with, and have them see me as just a fellow doing a job." Because it usually is recognized as a tool for advancing the cause, Edmonston's abrasiveness has not cost him as dearly as might be expected. Staff turnover at the APA is low by the standards of advocacy groups, most of which pay their workers poorly, if at all, and function as training grounds for young zealots who invariably move on to the more lucrative fields of government service and the business sector. Yet about one-third of the APA staff of twenty-seven has been with the organization for five years or more.

As well, in its outward appearances the APA is at pains not to seem, as so many other advocacy groups do, to be a one-note whiner. In its newsletters and its popular new- and used-car buying guides (entitled *Lemon-Aid*), the APA singles out a few cars for praise, thereby demonstrating it has *some* faith in the industry. "Lemons & Laurels", Edmonston's annual awards to industry executives who have been notable for either their responsive or callous treatment of consumer issues, is another expression of the APA's constructive approach. And in 1986, when Edmonston launched a boycott against Petro-Canada aimed at forcing the state-owned oil giant to drop gas prices in tandem with the drastic fall in world oil prices, he was careful to point out that consumers should not include the repair operations of Petrocan stations in the boycott, as these are autonomous small businesses operating independently of Petrocan.

If anything, Edmonston worries now that he has become *too* reasonable. "When people and companies we find fault with readily accede to our demands, I wonder if it's them being more understanding or me not doing my job," Edmonston says. "I worry about not being as sharp as I used to be, of becoming blasé and content."

To be sure, Edmonston now spends only about one day a month in small-claims court. And after putting in years of eighteen-hour days he is spending less time than ever at the APA's creaking Victorian duplex on St. Joseph Boulevard West at the foot of Mount Royal, where three counsellors are on duty to handle complaints of people who walk in off the street and another five staffers advise people over the phone. Edmonston spends a great deal of time on the road: he gives about five hundred media interviews a year, many of them during two annual cross-country tours to promote the *Lemon-Aid* guides, which are snapped up at the rate of more than forty-five thousand copies a year. (The interviews are a lucrative sideline: Edmonston is paid only $27,000 in salary by the APA, but he keeps the stipends he earns from interviews. He also splits the royalties from *Lemon Aid* with the APA, which uses its share — along with annual membership fees — to keep government funding of the APA's budget to a modest 10 to 15 per cent.) Edmonston is also finding more time as the years go by for diversions such as his passion for deep-sea fishing off Fort Lauderdale, Florida. "He can still be dictatorial," says APA treasurer Clapp. Then Clapp laughs. "But when you disappear as often as Edmonston does, how do you enforce it?"

Edmonston occasionally flirts with the idea of leaving the APA. He says there's a novel he wants to write, and "I find myself becoming more selfish about the time I spend on myself versus righting the wrongs out there." But then, Edmonston made similar noises in the early 1980s, and abruptly decided to stay on. He also is unlikely to be lured away by the siren song of politics, having failed once already as an NDP candidate to wrest the riding of Verdun away from the Liberals in a 1977 federal by-election. Edmonston, who is fluently bilingual, toured the riding in a rusted out '66 Caddy. Unfortunately for him, his vow to fight against a "rusty" Liberal government whose members were "lemons" moved some, but hardly enough, voters: he came in second, with about one-third of the vote. Edmonston gave some thought to running provincially in the 1985 Quebec election as a Liberal. Even in the aftermath of the Liberals' landslide — one that likely would have swept Edmonston into office — the auto advocate insists he's happy he stayed out of the race, convinced that he is too much of a lone wolf for a game that requires team players.

More to the point, Edmonston holds government in low regard. Its very slothfulness is powerful proof of the need for outside agitators like the APA. In 1975, the APA warned the federal transport department that some of Chrysler Canada's most popular 1975–77 models had chronic stalling problems, some of which were cited as the cause in auto accidents, but the government arm persistently reported it could find no evidence to warrant taking action. In early 1978, Chrysler recalled 180,000 of the cars in Canada (the U.S. government had earlier demanded a recall of models sold south of the border) in order to correct what it admitted was a serious design flaw in the carburetor. Federal authorities in Canada also failed to alert consumers to Ford Pintos and Mercury Bobcats whose fuel tanks were easily crushed and ruptured in even minor rear-end collisions, resulting in fires and — in some cases — the deaths of the cars' occupants. Ford, again after a U.S. safety agency put pressure on the parent company, recalled 111,000 Pintos and Bobcats in Canada.

Yet Edmonston can claim credit for exacting a handful of legislative reforms on behalf of car consumers. Working outside the system, rather than as a politician obliged to defend a government record of inactivity, Edmonston pressured Ottawa to develop an anti-corrosion code which is administered by the consumer-affairs ministry and which, when it was introduced in the late 1970s, called for new cars to last at least three years without rusting. More recently, the Ontario government unveiled an arbitration plan in which independent referees have the power to settle, quickly and amicably, disputes between consumers and car companies over alleged manufacturing defects. And only a year after the APA began lobbying for a province-run no-fault insurance system in Ontario, the proposal became a hot issue and was adopted as a central plank in the provincial NDP's election platform. In order to take the wind out of the NDP's sails, Ontario's Liberal government announced a freeze on most car-insurance premiums in April 1987 and proposed setting up an auto-insurance review board to regulate profits made by auto insurers. The government also unveiled plans for legislation to protect consumers from unscrupulous mechanics by forcing repair shops to provide written estimates, itemized invoices, and a warranty on all parts and labour, and boosted by $2 million its budget for monitoring Ontario's sixteen thousand car-repair outlets.

The pace of reform within the auto industry itself has also picked up. "Car companies are much more responsive now to customer complaints," says Edmonston. "And at the APA, we find we can now talk directly to the presidents of the companies and often get compensation for car owners before resorting to court action." In fact, the big Canadian auto companies are hardly resentful over the APA's relentless crusade for higher-quality cars: to the extent that auto-makers have addressed the APA's concerns, they have met the challenge presented by imports and the new widespread demand by the public that car manufacturers clean up their act.

"Our attitude is different from what it was at the height of the APA's rusty Ford campaign," says Fredo. "We have a real dialogue now. And by addressing the quality issue head on, we've been able to turn an overwhelming negative into a positive." Ford, whose slogan these days is "Quality Is Job 1", has indeed recovered: in 1986, its parent, Ford Motor Co., overtook Detroit-based General Motors Corp. in profits despite having a much smaller sales base than GM.

Lyons, for all his misgivings about Edmonston's personal style, credits him with having a big hand in changing the attitude both of the auto-makers and of consumers. "Phil brought consumer car advocacy to this country, and he really got the auto giants' attention," Lyons says. "And now he's keeping them honest."

If reform still comes too slowly for Edmonston's taste, he can take as a signal achievement the most important point the APA has made through the years: that through organized opposition — and even by taking a stand as an individual consumer — people don't have to suffer the abuse of insensitive industrial leviathans.

In many cases—more often than most consumers realize—justice is only a complaint away.

"The thing we've fought all along," says Edmonston, "is the 'home-economics' type of consumer advocacy I encountered when I first arrived in Canada. Nobody was bothering to attack the perpetrator, the manufacturer. The idea then was to educate people to be more careful consumers. For me, that amounted to a victimization of the complainers. We were shooting at ourselves instead of the real perpetrators, and failing to realize that consumer rights is nothing more than human rights applied to the marketplace."

Minority Rules

Stephen Jarislowsky, minority-shareholders' advocate
Little about the man or his surroundings suggests power. His shirt hangs loosely on his short, slight frame. Above his head, some of the yellowed ceiling tiles don't quite meet the wall, and two rows of fluorescent light boxes throw off a dusty, milk-store glow. Behind his desk (a modest secretarial model that spans almost the entire width of his office), a magnificent view of downtown Montreal is obscured by a windowsill cluttered with cactus plants, which invite inevitable comparisons to his own prickly disposition.

It is only as Stephen Jarislowsky dons his half-spectacles and begins to read aloud from an address he is to give in a few weeks that one senses the threat he poses to Canada's corporate hierarchy. "We will not invest with fast-buck artists," he begins, his German accent growing steadily more pronounced as he warms to his favourite topic. "We must deal with managements that value integrity and morality. Anything that smacks of greenmail or abuse of minority shareholders goes against the grain, or anything exclusively in the benefit of a select group of shareholders.

"Dirty deals must be overturned. In Canada, too many things that should be illegal are not. Too often, managers and their high-priced consultants put manipulation of the law ahead of morality. . . . "

When he finishes the reading Jarislowsky slumps back in his chair, which is wedged between two unruly rubber plants whose branches form a crown above his head. "Well, that's what I'm going to tell them," he says. A faint smile crosses his lips as he adds, a bit tauntingly, "Who knows what they'll think of it." What Jarislowsky *expects* is that his audience at the Conference Board of Canada luncheon, where business cheerleaders are more commonly heard than critics, will find his commentary more indigestible than the rubber-chicken dinner that precedes it.

If only he were a crank, Jarislowsky's warning shot could be dismissed as the untutored raving of a dedicated anti-capitalist. No such luck. Jarislowsky, sixty-one, is a pillar of capitalism. Indeed, he is the most powerful money manager in Canada: his investment counselling firm, Jarislowsky, Fraser & Co., administers more than $9 billion — about one-eighth of all the assets in trusteed pension funds in the country. He not only invests his clients' money in other people's businesses, but has run several himself. In fact, having been the president of five companies, the chairman of two, and a director of twenty others, he probably has learned more about running a business than many of the executives he criticizes have forgotten.

If there's a lesson he'd like to pass on to the CEOs of firms he invests in it's that if they don't play by ethical rules he's prepared to make their lives miserable. And as the largest, second-largest, or third-largest shareholder in some twenty-five big Canadian companies the man in the tiny Montreal office is in a position to do so. Already he has crossed swords with major corporations and made many titans of finance back down. On perhaps two dozen occasions Jarislowsky has thwarted the insensitive designs of giant corporations such as Dome Petroleum, Seagram Co. Ltd., and Canadian Tire, and on each of those occasions his indignation was rooted in his own experience as an ethical player who finishes first. "During the past thirty-two years, we've built Jarislowsky, Fraser into the biggest pension-fund management concern in Canada," says Jarislowsky, "and I can't think of a time during that period when we've taken a moral shortcut."

Jarislowsky has gotten ahead by putting his clients first. He lavishes corporate funds on research, not fancy premises: Jarislowsky's employees toil in offices as austere as his; and there is no reception area at head office, which ensures that clients are seen right away rather than being kept waiting in a posh holding pattern at the front door. But the principal means by which Jarislowsky has attracted new business lately has been his outspoken championing of his clients' rights as minority shareholders. And his clout as a shareholders' advocate is growing, because, far from leading a one-man crusade in this field, Jarislowsky is only the most outspoken of a new breed of professional money managers who have concluded that in order to obtain the highest possible return on their clients' investments they have no choice but to take a hard line against companies whose top executives and controlling shareholders seek to enrich themselves at the expense of pensioners and other small, minority shareholders they represent. "Traditionally, we've tended not to use our clout," says William Allen, president of Allenvest Group Ltd., a Toronto-based investment-counselling firm that has worked with Jarislowsky to make companies scrap proposals that might have harmed minority shareholders. "We used to just go along with these things, but the divine-right-of-kings attitude among the people who run corporations simply doesn't fly with us anymore."

Institutional investors have an enormous club to wield over the heads of recalcitrant company executives. The value of pension-fund assets in Canada has roughly quadrupled in the past decade, to more than $120 billion. Naturally, the institutions — be they banks, trust companies, life insurers or independent specialists — that do the best job for their clients stand the best chance of winning new business. Lately the contest has been going to the specialists: pension-fund clients have been plucking their money from the dark recesses of banks and trusts, where it languished, and planting it in hothouses operated by the likes of Jarislowsky, Fraser and Allenvest — firms that have strenuously opposed corporate flimflammery.

Money managers once were a uniformly passive lot, and there's no mystery why: often as not, they were spawned by the same blueblood families and attended the same private schools as their peers who run large corporations. These old-school investors were loathe to confront rogue companies, to complain about unscrupulous practices. Instead they preferred merely to "vote with their feet" — that is, simply sell an offending stock. But these days timidity is going out of fashion. "You still don't want to rock the boat," says Andrew Sarlos, a prominent Toronto independent investor. "But when it becomes obvious that a corporation is trying to screw around with its shareholders' property, you have to have the guts to say enough is enough." It's either that, or risk losing business to professional advisers who do have the stomach for opposing corporations that put their own interests ahead of their shareholders'. "We're obliged to inspect what's going on behind the smoke and mirrors," says Allen. "The old-boy ties don't count for much anymore, because we're fast approaching the day when fiduciaries who fail to fight will be sued out of their pants for improper fulfilment of their duty to clients."

Jarislowsky is one of the few senior people in his profession who does not need to recondition himself for the times, for he has always been an unorthodox player in what has until recently been a staid calling. He was born in Berlin, the son of an industrialist and merchant banker who died when Jarislowsky was five. He attended private schools in Holland, France, and North Carolina, switching schools each time his step-father, a French bureaucrat and engineer, was transferred. At Cornell University in upstate New York Jarislowsky obtained a degree in mechanical engineering, then served with the U.S. Army in post-war Japan, where he worked for nine months as a counterintelligence officer on the lookout for saboteurs and black-market racketeers. Fascinated by Asian culture, Jarislowsky followed up his tour of duty with studies at the University of Chicago, where he earned a master's degree in Far Eastern Studies.

Jarislowsky emerged from the University of Chicago with a yearning to teach; indeed, he taught a course there in Asiatic religion. But a conviction that he should first make some serious money propelled him to Harvard, where he obtained his third degree, an MBA. Now his career sights were more sharply focused. "I figured I'd get a job in international business," says Jarislowsky, "and when I was rich enough, say by the age of forty, I could afford to become an ambassador with the state department."

Unfortunately, his plans went awry soon after he was recruited in 1949 by Alcan Aluminium Ltd. The huge multinational company seemed to be the perfect ticket to a career in international business, but after a three-year stint at the firm's Kingston, Ontario, plant and Montreal head office, he quit out of boredom. He spent the next three years running his in-laws' New York-based art-book publishing house (which he sold), and started a mutual fund and a packaging company. In 1955 he and a partner,

Jack Brown, established the precursor to Jarislowsky, Fraser. Jarislowsky bought out Brown's share of the investment-counselling business in the 1950s, and second partner A. Scott Fraser's stake in 1978.

In the early days, Jarislowsky built his firm on a foundation of solid research and astute calls of the market's direction. But soon he found this wasn't enough. On many occasions, particularly during takeovers, he and other minority shareholders in large enterprises were being cut out of lucrative deals in which control of companies passed from one party to another without all of the shareholders being granted the opportunity to cash in, or even be consulted about the new order. Jarislowsky wasn't content to do the "Wall Street Walk", the time-honoured tradition of expressing displeasure with a corporation's conduct by simply selling one's shares. He decided to stay and fight.

Jarislowsky's early sniping attacks were modest forays. And his first was a complete rout: he got nowhere with his opposition in 1960 to a preferred-share issue by Metropolitan Gas (now Gaz Metropolitain, Inc.). He fared better in a 1966 court case over British Petroleum's takeover of Supertest, in which he extracted the then sizeable sum of $18 million from the stingy bidder. By the early 1980s, Jarislowsky had perfected his brand of dissident opposition. In 1980, he worked with fellow institutional investors at Royal Trustco and Sun Life to prepare a court case against Domglas Inc.; the outcome of the proceedings, in which Jarislowsky was the main witness, was a Quebec Superior Court decision that bumped an original $14-a-share offer to minority shareholders up to $36. A year later, he insisted his clients holding Hudson's Bay Oil and Gas Co. Ltd. stock be paid in cash rather than shares in suitor Dome Petroleum, a demand that nearly put Dome into bankruptcy. And, in one of his most prolonged disputes, Jarislowsky held up Conrad Black's 1983 reorganization of his Argus Corp. empire by complaining that Black's offer to buy additional shares of Argus affiliate Labrador Mining & Exploration was not generous enough. After several months of negotiations, and with only days remaining before the deal was to be brought before a Newfoundland court for approval, Black dug deeper into his pocket and came up with an offer Jarislowsky found acceptable.

By this time the issue of minority shareholders' rights had

come into its own. At Campbell Chibougamau Mines Ltd. (in 1979) and United Canso Oil & Gas (1980), dissident minority shareholders had taken the extraordinary step of seizing control from managements deemed to be mediocre. And at Mascan Ltd. (1983), the property company that created modern-day Mississauga, Ontario, prolonged minority agitation for an offer to buy their shares had the ultimate effect of driving CEO S. Bruce McLaughlin out of the company he founded. These bitter and highly publicized struggles were hardly unblemished victories for the minority shareholders, however. Under new management, Campbell and United Canso became bogged down in debt accumulated during ill-advised acquisition sprees; and the Mascan dissidents' actions served merely to add to the already beleaguered firm's misfortunes. But some important lessons were learned. No matter how formidable they might appear, entrenched managements could be dislodged even at the largest companies. And if the Mascan case proved anything, it was that institutional investors would have been better advised to rein McLaughlin in much earlier, before the firm self-destructed through overexpansion.

Corporate managers, for their part, have become paranoid at the sight of these developments. Particularly with the rise of takeover "raiders" such as T. Boone Pickens, Carl Icahn, and Irwin Jacobs in the United States, Britain's Sir James Goldsmith, and the Belzberg brothers of Vancouver, managements of most widely held companies have more reason than they ever have to fear losing their independence—and, indeed, their jobs. Since executives don't readily warm to the prospect of their companies being swallowed up and themselves spit out, many major companies throughout North America have gone to elaborate lengths to make themselves unattractive to potential buyers. There is the "poison pill" defence, in which the company fearing a takeover goes on a takeover binge itself, acquiring assets a takeover artist would not want to swallow, and accumulating a great deal of debt in the process. The opposite tactic is to shed the "crown jewels", that is, to abruptly dispose of the most profitable chunks of the business, thereby reducing one's allure in the eyes of likely acquisitors. Whether the decision is to grow or shrink, the executives erecting these defences can be counted on—usually as a first step—to arrange generous severance payments for themselves should the barricades ultimately be breached.

This activity impresses the money managers rather like a marriage without sex. They've committed themselves to the stock, and they'd like to see a little action. But their ostensible partners, managers of the firms in which they've bought shares, are set on forestalling consummation: the receipt of a takeover bid. While most institutional investors would agree that the takeover boom has gotten out of hand, they don't take kindly to being deprived of the maximum return on their investment, which generally can be achieved during a takeover. The takeover target, and its shares, will never be more valuable than at this moment. The average shareholder tendering stock in a takeover is paid 40 per cent to 50 per cent more for the shares than their current market value.

"A takeover represents the only moment when the shareholder realizes the full value of his or her investment," says Allen. Managements at besieged companies that are determined to turn away suitors invariably argue that they are doing so in the interests of all shareholders, but Allen and his peers are not easily convinced. To be sure, many well-run companies would not benefit from a disruptive takeover. But in some cases, management resistance is just a screen for the entrenched executives' incompetence, which will surely be exposed when a new, post-takeover team of managers transforms a laggard company into a star performer. "If a company is slovenly and run by perk-oriented, non-creative people, it deserves to be taken over and perhaps broken up," says Allen. "When a company is broken up, the pieces don't disappear: they're probably destined to be better, more efficiently managed under new owners."

What the institutional investors particularly object to is the sight of a small group of privileged investors tightening their control over a company without putting up much, if any, of their own money. The most popular device with which to accomplish this in recent years has been the creation of a class of non-voting shares. These securities are proliferating despite their long tradition of abuse.

Way back in 1926, Harvard political scientist William Z. Ripley warned that through the creation of a class of non-voting preferred shares, hired hands were usurping control over companies from their ostensible bosses, the shareholders. "And the amazing thing," Ripley wrote at the time, "is that this final deathblow to the exercise of voting rights by the general public has brought no voice of protest. Yet the plan bears every appearance of a bald and outrageous theft of the last tittle of responsibility for management of the actual owners by those who are setting up these latest financial erections."

Ripley rebelled against the opinion, which still enjoys a wide following today, that small investors weren't sufficiently interested in the affairs of companies they had stock in anyway, and would not be unduly troubled over losing powers they seldom exercised. "It will be objected that no real change is involved in these recent tendencies: that stockholders never did, and never will, exercise their voting rights. In fact the great trouble, oftentimes, is to secure enough proxies in widely owned corporations to validate the acts of their directors. But the fact remains that the power, even if rarely exercised, and then only under extreme provocation, was there; and every once in a blue moon some resolute individual or stockholder could rise in his place and organize a protective committee or dissenting group—and, if nothing else happened, at least there was a thorough ventilation of what sometimes proved to be a musty or unsafe tenement."

Like Ripley more than two generations ago, Jarislowsky is troubled by the implications of non-voting stock. In one of his greatest victories, he spearheaded a campaign among institutional investors to stymie plans by Seagram Co. Ltd., the world's largest distiller, to create a new class of multiple-voting shares—which would have had the effect of reducing the common stock to non-voting status. Charles and Edgar Bronfman, who control the Montreal-based company, unveiled the proposed share reorganization in 1983 in a bid to solidify their grip on the company. What the Bronfmans asked Jarislowsky and every other Seagram shareholder to approve at that year's regular annual meeting was a plan that would have allowed Seagram to create Class B shares carrying ten votes each; ordinary common shares would still have only one vote each, but as a sweetener would now be guaranteed an additional 15 cents (U.S.) in dividends. Thus the Bronfmans figured they would be the only ones interested in converting their common stock into Class B shares—a move that would instantly turn their 37 million votes into 370 million.

Jarislowsky amassed close to 15 million votes in opposition to the move, which likely would have resulted in a drop in the value of Seagram common stock, since non-voting shares trade at about

10 per cent less than voting shares. The Bronfmans backed off when it seemed clear the controversial scheme would be rejected at the annual meeting in New York. They have since chosen a more elaborate but fairer means of accomplishing their goal: the family has sold off its holdings in Cadillac Fairview Corp. Ltd., Bow Valley Resources, and other companies in order to free up cash with which to buy Seagram common shares.

Even though they most often are a device intended to block unwanted takeovers, non-voting shares are frequently deemed palatable enough to find a place in money managers' portfolios. Sometimes they represent the only way to invest in an attractive company. When fast-growing Four Seasons Hotels Inc. went public in 1985, founder Isadore Sharp emerged with ownership of an entire class of multiple-voting shares with twelve votes each, while the public was offered only common shares with one vote each. Thus Sharp ended up with 83 per cent of the votes even though he put up only 20 per cent of the equity. But that was the only method by which Sharp was prepared to go public. As he said at the time, "It was a condition of going public that I not give up control. I wanted to avoid even the thought of a takeover threat."

In other cases, families eager to keep control of the companies they founded but who wanted to raise funds through the stock market won favour with institutional investors by attaching sweeteners to new non-voting classes of stock through which they raised necessary expansion capital. Sporting goods maker Cooper Canada Ltd. overcame institutional resistance to its 1985 creation of a class of non-voting shares by way of additional dividends and the unusual concession of board representation. At about the same time, Canadian Tire adopted a measure designed to protect its non-voting shareholders known as a "coat-tail" provision. A coat-tail provides that if an offer is made for all the voting shares, and a majority are tendered, the non-voting shares become voting equity. Thus anyone bidding for the company would be encouraged to make an equal offer to all shareholders.

The Canadian Tire move appeared to be an enlightened bow to the concept of corporate democracy until the fall of 1986, when, as one Toronto stockbroker put it, the company's founding family "transformed the image of this erstwhile fine company from bicycle heaven to shareholder hell". In October of that year,

Alfred, David, and Martha Gardiner Billes, the children of company co-founder A.J. Billes, announced they would entertain offers for their 60.9 per cent interest in Canadian Tire voting shares. Among the four bids received, the Billes's accepted one made by 348 of the company's 361 dealers (owner-coperators of Canadian Tire's retail stores). The dealer group was prepared to pay a stunning $160.24 per share, four times the market value, but intended to purchase only 49 per cent of the common stock. In this way, they hoped to get control of Canadian Tire without triggering the coat-tail provision at 50 per cent.

The deal was outrageous. Only two years earlier, tobacco giant Imasco Ltd. of Montreal had been spurned by the Billeses when it offered a reputed $1.1 billion for all of the common and non-voting shares of the company — a price it was willing to pay because Canadian Tire, founded in 1922, has been one of the most consistently profitable retailing concerns in Canadian history. Now the dealers appeared set to obtain control of the prized company for a mere $272 million in a deal that would ignore 13,819 non-voting shareholders who had been expressly assured that control of the company would not change without their being offered a chance to cash in their holdings.

Jarislowsky and Allen wasted no time mounting a campaign to stop the deal. Within days of its having been announced in December, a posse of institutional investors had been assembled; so sure were they of their cause that they placed large ads in the financial press to trumpet it. Jarislowsky, whose clients owned 6 per cent of Canadian Tire's non-voting stock, publicly called the dealers' offer "crap", and the stock market seemed to agree: non-voting shares plunged in value, and by January 1987 were worth only 17 per cent of the value of voting shares. But the cynicism of the market traders was premature. After nine days of highly publicized hearings, an unprecedented joint decision of the Ontario and Quebec securities commissions ruled against the deal, and that decision was upheld by the Supreme Court of Ontario.

The saga was far from over — a falling out occurred among the three offspring of A.J. Billes in the spring of 1987, and the ultimate disposition of their control bloc is still in question — but the dissidents secured a dramatic victory. Whoever ends up buying out the Billeses will have to include the non-voting shareholders in the deal.

Some people become mellow with victory. But every time Jarislowsky jousts with corporate titans his verbal attacks become more extreme and his analogies faintly ridiculous. His conviction that someone out there is always ready to pull a fast one is evident from the parallel he draws between his present calling and the work he did as a counterintelligence officer in Japan. "Part of my job involved de-Nazifying Germans in Japan, getting declarations out of them renouncing Nazism," he says. "It was investigative work, and that fits in with what I do today. I have to find out if these guys at companies I invest in are honest." Jarislowsky pauses and places his hands together as in prayer. "You know, most of the Nazis in Japan were nice people, family men and all that. But they were still Nazis. It all fits in."

Not surprisingly, Jarislowsky has won the respect of his peers. "Steve is tremendously admired for his courage and imagination," says Allen. "He seems outrageous, but the situation demands people who are outspoken, if only to make the public know that there's someone in their corner fighting for them. And that the world isn't dominated by fat guys in pinstripes with cigars plugged in their mouths."

What does come as a surprise is the degree to which Jarislowsky gets along with his adversaries. He took on Seagram only after "exhaustive talks with my friend Charles [Bronfman]" had come to nothing. After the Labrador Mining débâcle, Black joined Jarislowsky and John Turner, Jarislowsky's lawyer for the negotiations, in a round of drinks and jovial conversation. "And," says Jarislowsky, "we've been friends ever since. I stay friends with the Establishment because I don't mind them making an honest profit. I just don't want them to be pigs. Sometimes they *have* been pigs, and they know it."

T. Boone Pickens has struggled mightily to tart up his image as a "greenmailer", someone who buys a company's stock and makes menacing noises about a complete takeover until his stock is bought back by that company at a huge premium. But he has failed utterly to explain how his crusade for "corporate reform" has made managers more efficient, or indeed had any effect other than to deplete shareholders' treasuries and stampede paranoid managements into implementing anti-takeover devices that are anathema to minority shareholders.

Jarislowsky, by contrast, represents a positive influence in business. He and his peers have real and enduring power because they do not seek to run companies or extort payoffs from them. Their goal is to work with management, not against it; and, if it comes to that, to obtain justice for every class of shareholders, even if it means going to court. "I don't pose a spectre to managers," says Jarislowsky. "I don't propose, I merely oppose." He does so in the name of honest and efficient capital markets that ordinary investors can believe in, and with the credibility that comes of acting on behalf of tens of thousands of pensioners and not merely himself.

Jarislowsky is heard to complain these days that he is too front-and-centre in the minority-shareholders' movement. "I've been quarterbacking too many of these disputes," he says. "We can't have this looking like a one-man crusade, some crazy guy carrying out a vendetta. Managements might get the idea I enjoy doing this." But having made that clear, Jarislowsky is off to the Conference Board to loudly decry "unfair management ploys" that proliferate in corporate Canada these days, and take credit for the fact that "All those who want to perpetuate shams have been given pause."

It has not escaped the notice of his friends that in the process of becoming Canada's largest independent pension-fund manager Jarislowsky has become a man of more than comfortable means. Indeed, his original $100 equity stake in Jarislowsky, Fraser, of which he is sole owner, now has a book value of $30 million; the firm would command far more than that were Jarislowsky to entertain bids for it. He would be sure to hold out for the highest price — in fairness to the sole shareholder, himself — and then he could finally become an ambassador. But, of course, he has become something of an ambassador already, albeit one rarely described as diplomatic.

"Managers have to go along not because of me, but because it's simply the right thing to do," you hear him say, and you almost believe the system might not need him. But then he adds, "Canada is ahead of the U.S., the U.K., and most other world markets in the quality of [stock-market] activity. And institutional managers are responsible for much of that. Why, we're almost to the point of having markets we can be proud of."

CHAPTER NINE
NEW WORLD INVESTING:
PUTTING YOUR MONEY
WHERE YOUR MORALS ARE

There is no such thing to my mind as an innocent stockholder. He may be innocent in fact, but socially he cannot be innocent. He accepts the benefits of the system. It is his business and his obligation to see that those who represent him carry out a policy which is consistent with the public welfare.
—Louis Dembitz Brandeis, Associate Justice of the
   U.S. Supreme Court (1926)

It is 11:15 A.M. in the opulent ballroom of a fashionable big-city hotel. The chairman and directors of Consolidated Tongue and Groove Inc. (CTG) having concluded a masterful summation of the company's noble past endeavours and bright prospects for the future, graciously throw the annual meeting of shareholders open to questions from the floor. Microphone stands are erected, two to an aisle. The house lights go up. The chairman of CTG takes a half-step back from the podium, ostensibly to adjust his company tie with its motif of gold tongues and grooves on a royal-blue field, and furtively surveys the sea of potential inquisitors in the seats below him. In theory, this is their moment to probe into the byzantine and, by some accounts, dubious ways and means of the company they own.

In practice, however, no one is eager to match wits with the managers of their multibillion-dollar enterprise. Some shareholders are cynical enough to believe the top CTG executives have spent several weeks of the company's time preparing an obfuscatory response to any question they might ask; others are numbed into silence by the grandeur of CTG depicted a few moments earlier in a slick, $50,000 audio-visual presentation, funded out of the shareholders' treasury. Others still, for whom the proceedings are a mere side-trip from a visit to Aunt Mildred or Canada's

Wonderland, don't care how their firm is run and are eagerly awaiting the lavish luncheon that will be served the moment this tedious Q&A session is over. And so the meeting is brought to a close without any genuine calling to account, save for a gentle rebuke from a wizened crank who insists CTG is ignoring a potentially lucrative sideline by failing to diversify into the chimney-repair business.

These days, however, the people who run large publicly held companies can no longer take such placid relations with their shareholders for granted. A new generation of investors weaned on 1960s idealism is infiltrating the shareholder ranks. Unlike most of their older peers, they are likely to make the connection between their ownership of Union Carbide shares and the deaths of thousands of people when a poorly maintained Carbide plant explodes. Nor do they feel comfortable reading in the papers that a company they own shares in is being accused of upholding the racist apartheid system in South Africa, destroying a river with its pollutants, or taking a miserly approach to charitable giving. To these shareholders, children of a rebellious era, it seems passing strange that while people make obscene gestures and hurl over-ripe fruit at heads of state, the petty potentates of corporations escape censure for even their most obvious failings, and rarely have their power checked. This is about to change.

By whatever name, "ethical investing" or "socially responsible investing" is a potent new force challenging the hegemony of corporate executives. Its most obvious tools are the ethical mutual funds, which have attracted billions of dollars in savings from institutional investors and ordinary people in Canada, the United States, and Europe. Less visible but potentially more significant, however, is the infrastructure of consultants, newsletter publishers, and ethical-data-gathering bureaus that has sprung up to support the funds, which must sort "good" firms from "bad" in order to decide where to invest their money. Far from merely advising the funds, the small but rapidly growing ethical-information industry is constantly searching for new markets. As it accumulates more information on the ethical conduct of companies, and disseminates this data to an ever larger and more varied audience, the social-investing movement's power to enhance standards of corporate social responsibility grows exponentially.

Of course, there always have been people who avoided "sin"

stocks, such as liquor and tobacco. But ethical mutual funds are still something of a novelty on the investment scene. They trace their roots back to 1968 when the U.S. ethical-investing pioneer Alice Tepper Marlin founded the Peace Fund, an informal program of ethical investing options she devised for socially aware clients of her brokerage firm. A few more funds — notably Dreyfus Third Century (the largest ethical fund) and the Pax World Fund — got their start in the early 1970s, when a foreign war (Vietnam) and pollution at home ignited widespread protests over the role of corporations as arms suppliers and bespoilers of the environment.

However, it took a near-disaster at a nuclear facility in Pennsylvania in 1979 to transform ethical investing from being the bailliwick of an enlightened few into a widespread movement that now finds adherents among hard-headed financial analysts. The mishap at Three Mile Island (TMI) was an early, dramatic sign of the common interests of idealistic activists and practical, profit-conscious investors. For, quite apart from the alarums that went out about the safety of nuclear power, TMI has been a horrific investment for its owners — as have shareholder-owned utility companies throughout the United States that have committed themselves to nuclear power.

TMI awakened investors to the consequence of liability, to the idea that they had something to lose financially if their company operated an unsafe plant or made a product that hurt people. Meanwhile, the ironic upshot of fiscally conservative governments coming to power in Britain, the United States, and Canada has been the demand, publicly stated by the highest government officials, that the private sector pick up some of the slack in social-program spending that has resulted from federal cutbacks in health, culture, and education. And, companies are now expected not only to be exemplary, philanthropic citizens at home, but to play a role in curbing infamy abroad. In the past few years, 15 states, 36 U.S. cities (including New York, Los Angeles, and San Francisco), and 120 colleges and universities have dumped their stock in companies with South African operations and in some cases banned purchases from companies doing business there. A handful of cities and counties in the United States have passed similar edicts against companies engaged in nuclear-arms production.

Exploiting the popular sentiment that underlies such acts, dozens of mutual funds have sprung up to cater to the socially conscious investor. A fund in Colorado invests only in employee-owned firms. The Amana Fund avoids anything offensive to Moslems. And a San Francisco-based fund started by a women's group screens potential investments for sexist advertising, fair hiring, and equal-pay practices. Indeed, there are so many ethical funds now that they have their own trade association, the Boston-based Social Investment Forum. By the SIF's reckoning, assets of the six largest ethical funds—which apply a general prohibition against nuclear power, bad labour relations, weapons suppliers, South African exposure, and abuse of the environment—have soared from $102 million in 1982 to $450 million in 1986. The SIF estimates that the total amount of money that has been redeployed because of some ethical consideration—by a university pulling out of companies with South African operations, for example—but not necessarily invested in ethical funds jumped from $40 billion in 1984 to $350 billion in 1986.

And with every new innovation, the concept of social investing comes closer to everyday life. A Boston bank, working in partnership with the Working Assets ethical fund, has introduced an ethical credit card that donates 5 cents to charitable causes with each use of the card. And the Council on Economic Priorities, a corporate social-reform agency presided over by Tepper Marlin, recently produced a highly publicized guide to ethical shopping. The CEP's *Rating America's Corporate Conscience* allows readers to select brands of detergent, gasoline, peanut butter, and dozens of other commonplace products on the basis of whether the firms that make them are good corporate citizens.

Rating may never match the awesome popularity of business books such as *Iacocca* or *In Search of Excellence,* but it has managed in the few months since its appearance in the fall of 1986 to find its way into the hands of tens of thousands of consumers, professional money managers, ethical-fund administrators, and casual investors. For Tepper Marlin believes the impact of ethical shopping will eventually outstrip that of socially conscious investing. "Unlike investing, shopping is something that everyone does, and it brings ordinary investors into the corporate social-responsibility movement," says Tepper Marlin. "Consumers have a tremendous influence with their economic ballots. Companies battle furiously to capture a quarter of a percentage point in market share for their products. Meanwhile, a concerted campaign directed against an irresponsible company can reasonably be expected to discourage 5 per cent or even 10 per cent of the public to stop buying that company's products." The most notable example of an effective boycott was the drive, led by church groups, to pressure Swiss food giant Nestlé into reforming the sales techniques it employed in peddling infant formula in the Third World. After several years of resisting the pressure applied by the boycotters — whose worldwide campaign had a small but measurable impact on sales of everything from Nestlé's Quik to Libby's beans — the firm gave into protesters and agreed to abide by stern directives on the proper marketing of formula drafted by the World Health Organization.[1]

Ethical investing was late arriving in Canada. But in the short space of two years the movement has sprung full-blown onto the Canadian investment scene. As recently as 1985 there were no ethical funds in Canada; now there are six. The oldest is the Ethical Growth Fund, launched by the Vancouver City Savings Credit Union in February 1986. VanCity was a natural sponsor for Canada's first ethical fund: as a co-op, it has always prided itself on a heightened awareness of community concerns and the welfare of its member-owners. More surprising was the decision of Winnipeg-based Investors Group, Canada's largest mutual-fund vendor, to launch a similar ethical fund (the Summa Fund) early in 1987. Investors is a conservative firm, and its commitment to ethical investing has been interpreted as a sign that this type of investing has truly arrived as a credible option. It became more difficult to dismiss ethical funds as a passion limited to granola-crunchers after the spring of 1987, when Investors was the sole sponsor of a performance of the Canadian Opera Company in Toronto. That evening, Investors touted only its Summa Fund,

---

1 One of the earliest successful boycotts against business occurred during the 1930s, when the Southern Pacific Co. — then the largest employer in California and owner of the ferries that plied the waters of San Francisco Bay — attempted to block construction of the Golden Gate Bridge. The 2,694-metre-long orange-coloured landmark was eventually completed in 1937 after Southern Pacific abandoned its obstructionist legal tactics in the face of a massive boycott of the company by local residents.

and none of its other products, in program inserts received by the well-heeled opera patrons.

Summa's arrival was followed a few months later by the introduction of the two Environmental Investment funds (one invests only in Canadian securities, the other in global issues) by Energy Probe, an advocacy group affiliated with Toronto's Pollution Probe. While these four funds attract money from ordinary investors, two other new funds are tapping the institutional market of pension, endowment,and foundation funds: the Crown Commitment Fund, operated by Crown Life Insurance Co., one of Canada's largest insurers; and the C.E.D.A.R. Balanced Fund, administered by C.E.D.A.R. Investment Services Ltd. of Vancouver and Edmonton. Remarkably, no fewer than three information-gathering networks have sprung up to serve the funds and other ethical investors: the Canadian Social Investment Study Group, based in Ottawa; the Canadian Network for Ethical Investment, headquartered in Vancouver; and EthicScan Canada Ltd., a corporate-ethics databank based in Toronto.

The Canadian funds have caught on very quickly with investors. VanCity, for instance, expected its Ethical Growth Fund to attract $3 million in its first year: the fund lured that much from investors in a matter of weeks, and ended the year with assets of $11.4 million. The Summa Fund's growth has also far outstripped projections. Partly this is the result of the funds' respectable performance. Far from exacting a financial penalty from socially aware investors who opt for them, ethical funds almost without exception outperform stock-market indices and mutual-fund averages. With a 15.1 per cent rate of return in 1986, the Ethical Growth Fund outperformed the Toronto Stock Exchange composite index, the average return on treasury bills and guaranteed investment certificates, and several much larger mutual funds.

Another factor behind the funds' popularity is the careful manner in which they've been marketed. The funds are designed to appeal to baby boomers who now are rising in the corporate ranks and constitute a huge market of consumers and investors. The trick in selling to these people is to awaken in them the romance of their past efforts to challenge the establishment without reminding them of how ultimately futile and frustrating that campaign of idealism was. Ted Jackson, head of the Canadian Social Investment Study Group, identifies this market as "'new-collar

Canadians' and people with high incomes and a desire to protect them but also concerned about issues like global peace, the environment, and South Africa, as all the polls indicate." Roger Laing, vice-president of C.E.D.A.R. Investment Services, says the attitude of the typical investor in an ethical fund would in many ways be like his own. "The seeds of my concern about how my money was being used were sown in the 1960s," Laing says. "Eventually, economic reality dictated that I had to earn a living, to play their game. But I didn't lose the idealism of that time."

Yet while the funds have grown quickly, at a total of 10,000 investors they have nabbed only 0.03 per cent of the 3.2 million Canadians who have investments in stocks and mutual funds. To continue their exponential growth, the fund operators pitch their products with hard-nosed financial analysis, not the balmy, altruistic rhetoric that typically issues from the mouths of social reformers. "There are no rainbows or endangered whales or redwood trees printed on our sales material," says David Mather, the Crown Life vice-president who oversees the Crown Commitment Fund. "We don't want to be perceived as being on the fringe."

At the same time, the implicit message is that investors have a responsibility not to get involved in disagreeable corporate behaviour, and should not pass up this realistic opportunity to change things for the better. By and large, this new crowd of investment advisors speak the language of power, not hope. "If money is power, then it follows that the investment of money is the exercise of power," says Amy Domini, vice-president of a Boston investment firm (Franklin Research and Development Corp.) that specializes in ethical investing. "If goods and services are produced that are not useful to society, society — not the corporations — pays the bill. We pay it though tax dollars, through medical bills, through the higher cost of products. With ethical investments we minimize these costs." The obligation to be a standard-bearer in the corporate social-responsibility revolution is all the more pressing for pension-fund managers, who are surrogates for thousands of unseen investors. "Trustees of pension plans for unions, church groups, and universities not only have a fiduciary obligation to be prudent," says Mather of Crown Life. "They now must also possess a heightened sense of social awareness on behalf of the people whose money they're in control of."

Naturally, the funds have attempted to avoid controversy in

order to widen their popularity. But sitting in moral judgment of companies is not easy. As Ted Jackson says, "This drive is still new. It starts messy."

Picking "clean" companies is a risky business. In the fall of 1985, Alix Granger, a stock analyst with Pemberton Houston Willoughby Bell Gouinlock Inc. in Vancouver and possibly the first Canadian analyst to champion ethical investing, singled out several stocks that were ethically attractive and which *Investors Digest* described as "a portfolio of sound stocks, socially responsible". Alas, within a few months five of the eleven stocks Granger had selected became items to avoid: Bank of British Columbia was merged out of existence, a victim of too-liberal lending practices; Chateau Stores, a one-time glamour stock, took a downturn after its flamboyant founder presided over an exodus of top management; both Crownx (parent of Crown Life) and Torstar (publisher of *The Toronto Star*) became enmeshed in separate cases of alleged abuse of minority shareholders' rights; and food producer Nabisco Brands was suddenly transformed into a food and *tobacco* producer after being acquired by cigarette giant R.J.R. Industries, making the stock a no-no for some ethical funds on health grounds. The Crown Commitment Fund, which screens out companies with bad labour-relations records, had a similar experience when, at the very moment it released its list of preferred investments in the fall of 1986, one of its angels (Spar Aerospace Ltd.) was not only struck by its workers but accused of maintaining unsafe work conditions.

A more fundamental problem is the clash in principles that is sometimes apparent among the funds. VanCity's Ethical Growth Fund, because of its co-op heritage, likes to invest close to home, which means investing in the forest-products companies that dominate the B.C. economy. Many of these firms are high on everyone's list of notorious polluters, but the fund conveniently has no environmental screen. VanCity services division manager Bob Quart explains that "it is difficult to obtain data on the environment and it isn't easy to reach a consensus on what is truly damaging. Airplanes damage the environment; are we going to stop flying?" Strangely, VanCity does draw the line, however arbitrarily, when it comes to defence contractors, of which there are few in B.C. Bombardier Inc., of Montreal for instance, is definitely on the don't buy list because of its contract to maintain jet fighter aircraft. Never mind that defence work constitutes a small part of Bombardier's business; that the firm is a rare Canadian-owned entry in the overwhelmingly foreign-owned heavy-manufacturing field; and that, equally rare, it generates a lot of foreign exchange for Canada by building, among other things, subway cars for New York City.

Granger is not a fan of the VanCity fund. "VanCity's decision not to include an environmental screen makes the whole thing a wash-out," she says. Granger, who is an advisor to the Crown Commitment Fund, places such a heavy emphasis on environmental issues that few forest-products, mining, or other resource-based firms pass her muster. Ditto for the two Environmental Investment funds. That policy not only rules out the largest single portion of the Canadian economy, but drives the environment-conscious funds into the arms of the financial-service and communications sectors, which have their own set of problems: The banks and trusts have fought off unionizing efforts with a passion that has often bordered on illegal harassment; and the financial institutions are the source of funding for all manner of companies — including clients in the resource sector. As for communications firms, few radio- and TV-station operators in Canada observe the spirit — or often even the letter — of federal regulations designed to promote Canadian content.

Philosophical differences over what constitutes an ethical investment are never far from the surface. At the Financial Forum, a convention of financial service-product providers held in Toronto in early 1987, Larry Trunkey was promoting his Vancouver-based Canadian Network for Ethical Investment. Kenneth Rumak, who, like Trunkey, is a professional stock analyst, was also in attendance. An active Christian, Rumak gives seminars that interpret the "biblical position on personal financial planning". The two men, ostensibly allies, engaged in a lengthy argument in front of potential clients over the propriety of defence-related investments. Rumak objects to excluding defence stocks; he favours a strong national defence and feels he can justify that position on religious grounds. Trunkey attempted, without much success, to convince Rumak that the ethical funds have been created to give investors the option of being selective about which moral values they want to apply to their investment portfolios, and are not in the business of telling people what their values should be.

The funds must get their act together if only to overcome resistance from otherwise natural allies, such as organized labour and church groups. "I've had labour spokespeople worry that a bad survey result from me might hurt his union's workers at a particular company," says David Nitkin, who runs the EthicScan corporate-ethics databank in Toronto. "The bad result might reduce the share price of the company or its sales volume. That could hurt employees, not only through potential layoffs, but through a drop in personal assets since they often own some of the company's stock themselves."

At the opposite pole, some labour leaders could be counted upon to want an ethical fund to drop stocks in any firm that suddenly adopted a hostile stance against a unionized workforce. In order to avoid such disruptive suggestions—which have the potential to pile up since organized labour is responsible for about half of the boycotts called against companies each year—Crown Life's David Mather tries to inject some pragmatism into the process. "In our discussions with labour officials, we've explained that when a company runs into trouble, the market immediately discounts the value of its stock," he says. "I asked the union officials if they wanted us to sell that stock right away, to blow those securities out of the portfolio. But these guys understand the difference between street theatre and fiduciary management. They said wait until the stock recovers. Then sell, and don't buy any more."

Mather argues that there should not be absolutes when assessing a company's ethical character. "You have to be reasonable," he says. "You can't run a pulp mill and expect to be able to drink the effluent. What you can do is invest in companies that best exploit the available pollution-control technology, and avoid the ones that don't care and just kill the river. It's the same with companies like Inco and Falconbridge. If these companies can be made to meet a reasonable target for pollution reduction, we're satisfied that a genuine effort is being made. If we put them out of business right now because of the current shameful pollution levels, we'd also have destroyed the local economy. You have to keep things in perspective."

Oddly, church groups are among the prospective ethical-investing clients having the hardest time developing a unified perspective. Churches have been in the vanguard of corporate ethical reform: the oldest continuing ethical fund, Pax World

Fund, was created in 1971 by members of the United Methodist Church; and clerics blazed the trail for others when they first called executives to account at shareholders' meetings in the 1970s over corporate complicity in apartheid and Third World issues such as the sale of infant formula in underdeveloped countries. Pope John Paul II reinforced that crusading spirit during his 1984 tour of Canadian cities, when he declared, "The needs of the poor must take priority over the desires of the rich, and the rights of workers over the maximization of profits."

Yet there is a curious dichotomy in the practices adopted by church leaders. Many religious organizations have proved to be as conservative as the most hidebound investor, and won't place their money with ethical funds for fear of earning a subpar return. As he travels across Canada promoting the concept of ethical investing, Larry Trunkey says "preachers have been acting as though what I'm talking about is fresh water in the desert. They're so enthusiastic. I've been blessed by ministers of every denomination, as if I was running some kind of ministry myself. Yet they're surprised when I turn it around on them, and point out the tremendous disparity between what the church preaches and how it invests its own money."

Then there are the church groups that take the exact opposite tack. Some religious organizations are so dedicated to economic reform and the campaign to empower the poor they have side-stepped the stock market altogether. The Toronto-based Canadian Alternative Investment Cooperative channels its $2 million worth of funds into group homes, co-op housing, and financing the sale of Nicaraguan produce in Canada. The CAIC, which was created a few years ago by a group of religious orders, disdains traditional stock-market investments "because there are no clean companies," says CAIC treasurer Father Joseph Horrigan. "CAIC is an alternative for church and other investor groups that feel they don't know what will be done with their funds if placed in the market, and who want a safe haven in which to invest and do some social good."

This approach dismays Moira Hutchison, co-ordinator of the Task Force on Churches and Corporate Responsibility, an advocacy group that tries to raise the level of corporate awareness of Third World issues. Hutchison worries that the funds pose a threat: ordinary investors and institutions may opt to throw in with the funds, rather than keep their stock in misguided companies and use it as a lever to work for change from within. "By abdicating social concerns to the funds," says Hutchison, "investors are ceasing to exercise power or question policies for themselves."

The task force, which is entitled to much of the credit for the current exodus of Canadian companies from South Africa, intends to build upon that triumph by continuing to hold stocks in wayward firms in order to agitate for reform at shareholders' meetings and through shareholder resolutions. "We have already pushed companies into broadening their sense of responsibility," says Hutchison, "and by continuing to apply pressure we hope to expand from South Africa to other issues, such as more complete disclosure practices."

Shareholder resolutions are often dismissed as a futile tactic since, like private members' bills in the House of Commons, very few are passed. In fact, however, many issues raised as *prospective* resolutions are speedily resolved by reformers working quietly with executives behind the scenes, before the resolutions are printed up on proxy statements dispatched to the shareholders. And many resolutions that do end up on proxy statements and don't win passage are successful none the less, as a response of 5 per cent in favour of a resolution is usually enough to prod executives to address the issue. And where 5 per cent was until recently the threshold activists aimed to cross, corporate reformers now have reason to be more ambitious. In the spring of 1987, the average shareholder resolution against doing business in South Africa garnered 17 per cent of the votes cast among U.S. corporations. "The fact that this was brought to a vote means that management has to be more responsive to shareholders," says Don Carter, head of the Carter Organization, a large U.S. proxy solicitation firm. Of course, some firms continue to resist the will of dissident shareholders. Toronto-based Varity Corp., formerly Massey-Ferguson Ltd., generates only 1.8 per cent of its sales in South Africa. Yet in the spring of 1987 it decided to directly confront the activists who have been hounding it for years to get out of that country. It responded to a looming shareholders' resolution on the South African question by bringing two black South Africans — a seventy-one-year-old medical doctor and a thirty-eight-year-old machine operator employed by Varity — to the annual meeting, where they pleaded for the defeat of the motion to divest. The motion nevertheless won an impressive 14.7 per cent of the votes cast, in part because large stakes in Varity held by the federal and Ontario government were voted in favour of the resolution. Still, Varity chairman Victor Rice adamantly stuck to the company's policy of staying in South Africa, and while asserting that "all of us agree that apartheid is wrong" also challenged the motion's backers to say that they had visited South Africa.

Despite the many setbacks that reformers have suffered, Moira Hutchinson's faith in shareholder activism is merited, given the record. In probably the most famous example, General Motors rejected a shareholder request in 1970 that it substantially escalate minority and outside representation on its board of directors, but shortly thereafter appointed Leon Sullivan, a black Baptist minister from Philadelphia, to its board. Sullivan failed in his effort to get GM to shut down its substantial South African operations, but his 1977 draft of a fair labour-practices guide in South Africa (the Sullivan Code) — designed to assure that companies with South African operations eliminate racial discrimination in the workplace — was adopted not only by GM but by most major U.S. corporations, as well as many in Canada.[2] In 1980, several

---

2   In 1985, Sullivan reverted to his original stance and called on U.S. companies to withdraw from South Africa if the apartheid system was not dismantled within two years. In the spring of 1987, Sullivan announced he was disgusted with the intransigence of the racist South African government and no longer believed U.S. and other Western corporations could realistically hope by their presence — no matter how enlightened — to effect significant change in the condition of blacks. Sullivan downplayed his own influence in how the code is administered, but *Fortune* said "the code probably can't work without him. Corporations would be suspect if they judged compliance with it themselves, and they will be hard pressed to find a replacement as respected and dedicated as the man who wrote the rulebook." By this point, however, the issue was of only passing interest to most major U.S. corporations: In the two years that followed Sullivan's 1985 warning, more than seventy big U.S. firms — many of which had funded career training, housing, educational programs, and legal clinics in South Africa — pulled out of the country. In just one week in October 1986, GM, IBM, Warner Communications, and Honeywell announced plans to leave — an event of great symbolic importance, since GM, in particular, had insisted for more than a decade that anti-apartheid activists underestimated the beneficial impact of the firm's presence. At about the same time, Canadian hold-outs gave into pressure to withdraw from South Africa: by early 1987, Alcan Aluminium, Falconbridge, Dominion Textile, and Bata Shoe — the largest single foreign employer to give in to the pressure — had announced their plans to quit South Africa.

years after an incident in which chemical giant American Cyanamid Co. required female workers in its pigments division to be sterilized because exposure to lead is potentially damaging to the fetus, the company reached an out-of-court settlement with five women who had allowed themselves to be sterilized, and responded to a union- and church-sponsored resolution by setting up a board-level Public Responsibility Committee to oversee health, safety and environmental issues. And after initially denouncing church groups as "enemies of the free-enterprise system" who used annual meetings as a battleground for "divisive and abrasive" political issues, Castle & Cooke, Inc. (maker of Dole brand canned fruit and vegetables) eventually consented to create and abide by new guidelines for humane labour practices in the United States, the Philippines, Honduras, and other countries in which it operates.

Hutchison views the proper role of the funds to be only one element in a multi-pronged campaign to raise standards of corporate morality. In order for the campaign to succeed, the various corporate-ethics professionals — fund managers, consultants, and activists — must co-ordinate their efforts. "This movement is an emerging paradigm," says C.E.D.A.R.'s Roger Laing. "It's still a small enough field that we all know each other, but there's great value in creating networks in which we all keep in constant touch."

The most ambitious of the three networks already operating in Canada is EthicScan Canada Ltd., which was launched in the spring of 1987 by Toronto strategic planner David Nitkin. The foundation of Nitkin's company is a database that contains ethics-related information on 1,300 Canadian companies. From this database, which is constantly updated, Nitkin hopes to spin off newsletters, special reports, and books that report on trends such as the number of women in senior management, daycare services, and enhanced pollution-abatement techniques. Ultimately, EthicScan will function as a clearinghouse for investors and companies themselves, which can subscribe to EthicScan's publications as a means of learning how to implement social-awareness programs that other firms have already experimented with and perfected. Already EthicScan has established a link with Van-City's Ethical Growth Fund, which it will advise, but Nitkin is aiming to develop a substantial clientele among Canada's major corporations, as well. "There's a breed of managers who have a sense of Canada's new economy, and who are proud to lead it in a progressive way," Nitkin says. This, he believes, will make them candidates for his seminars and consulting services advising companies on how to set up internal ethics committees, and handle layoffs and plant relocations in the most humane way possible. Eventually, EthicScan could even be called upon to help assess the moral character of prospective merger and acquisition targets.

Obviously, if taken to extremes the plans of Nitkin and other ambitious ethics professionals could make the lives of corporate executives miserable. In its highly refined state somewhere down the road, Nitkin's screening process may accumulate inappropriate criteria. Already Nitkin muses about asking companies if products they make "are essential needs or desirable wants of society." Questions of that nature would, of course, open a Pandora's box of vague and contentious ethical questions — starting with whether anyone should have the right in a free society to determine what is an essential need or desirable want. "It becomes a loaded question over the value of pace-makers versus hula-hoops," Nitkin admits.

It is the fear of this prospect that has aroused animosity. "Many executives and financial professionals are totally outraged at the presumptuousness of funds like ours to be saying who's a good guy and who's a bad guy," says John Guffey, executive vice-president of the Calvert Social Investment Fund, one of the largest ethical funds in the U.S. "We've been called everything in the book: unAmerican, pinkos, you name it. But it's a free economy — companies are free to carry on as they do, and we're free to assess that conduct."

There are two extremes in determining the proper role of shareholders in either condoning or actively opposing unethical corporate conduct. At the turn of the century, the corporation was held to be an artificial, soulless construction whose shareholders could not hope to impose any sense of morality on it. "There is nothing like distance to disinfect dividends," American sociologist Edward A. Ross wrote in *Sin and Society: An Analysis of Latter-Day Iniquity* (1907). "Therefore the moral character of the stockholders makes little difference in the conduct of the affairs of the corporation. . . . The corporation is not in dread of hell-fire.

You cannot Christianize it. You may convert its stockholders, animate them with patriotism or public spirit or love of social service; but this will have no effect on the tenor of the corporation. In short, it is an entity that transmits the greed of investors, but not their conscience; that returns their profits, but not unpopularity."

Unfortunately, the other extreme—of finding virtually all corporate profit-making pursuits repugnant and demanding that business take upon itself a commanding role in ameliorating the whole gamut of social problems—is as simplistic as the earlier mood of resignation and passivity. Indeed, the sort of hate psychology that was inflamed by the anti-business rhetoric of the 1960s and early 1970s did much to impede the progress of corporate reformers. Today that rhetoric is being replaced by facts, which provide a sound basis on which to judge companies. This explains why companies are more willing than even the most hopeful people in the ethical-investing movement expected to provide data about themselves. "People with left-wing political persuasions and those working for social reform used to have a knee-jerk reaction to government solutions, such as nationalization," says Ted Jackson of the Canadian Social Investment Study Group. "Now we're seeing that government solutions are no panacea. But under direct pressure from the ethical-investment movement corporations can be more responsive than we thought."

Indeed, it seems likely the funds and the infrastructure of consultants, newsletters and databanks that support them will function to strengthen business, and indeed become a partner to it. "The essential thing is to approach this as an exercise in building bridges between companies and their stakeholders—investors, employees and customers," says Larry Trunkey. "What we're aiming for is best described as 'responsive capitalism', something that is not purely critical or antagonistic but genuinely positive and constructive."

From the perspective of corporations themselves, the movement already functioning as a mechanism that alerts them to emerging social issues, to which companies can respond before the heavy hand of government imposes an arbitrary and perhaps unworkable solution. "We have four million customers, and as they and our investors become more vocal in expressing their concerns we pay more attention to those concerns," says Jeff Roach, vice-president of public relations at the Canadian Imperial Bank of Commerce. "We think of ourselves now as an entity within the larger society, and don't make decisions without going beyond the mere dollars and cents of the issues we confront. That has resulted partly from meeting with special-interest groups to deal with issues in an open, straightforward way."

Few people in the social-investing field exaggerate how far the movement has come. "It may be too early even to call it a movement," says Jackson. "It may still be just the seeds of a movement." Still, the ethical investors have made more progress than they thought possible. "Ten years ago most companies didn't care about South Africa, pollution, or weapons manufacturing — they just weren't aware of them," says Tom Grauman, an Edmonton social planner and member of the C.E.D.A.R. fund's national advisory board. "Already the social criteria used in boardroom decision-making have broadened to a degree that would have seemed inconceivable a decade ago."

Late in arriving, the new approach is now taking on an air of inevitability. "Social investing is a democratizing process," says Grauman. "As consumers and investors we have been uneasy for years. Without being bad people ourselves, we were contributing to bad things. In the 1960s, we made a somewhat naive effort to go back to nature, to gain some measure of control over the world by making sure our food and fuel wasn't coming from some black-hearted corporation. Now we have more realistic channels with which to be selective about what we buy and invest in." Indeed, ordinary investors have found that the way to gain control is to take responsibility. "We've come to realize corporations don't go wrong out of evil, it's just ignorance," says Larry Trunkey. "As consumers and shareholders, we've been pointing our fingers at big business and big government for years, instead of taking responsibility ourselves and working with people in government and business to educate them about our concerns. We're all in this together."

Investing, because it is principally a means of preparing for the future, is ideally suited to the reforms social-investment advocates are bringing to it. "A pension-fund manager, for instance, has a responsibility to invest in things that will ensure the well being of a pensioner in his retirement years," says Laing of C.E.D.A.R. Investment Services. "Nothing could be more short-sighted than taking the bottom line as one's only goal. The bottom line isn't profits, it's the future of the planet. If we don't invest in such a way as to ensure that corporations act responsibly on issues like weapons, nuclear power, and pollution, this won't be a safe world to live in. *That's* the new bottom line."

Ethical mutual funds performance

	Assets (millions of dollars) 1986	Return on investment (per cent) 1986	1985
U.S. funds			
Dreyfus Third Century	US$153.5	4.6	30.16
Calvert Social Investment Funds: Managed Growth Portfolio (stocks and bonds)	121.5	18.1	26.97
Money Market Portfolio	59.8	6.2	7.77
Working Assets Money Fund	96.6	5.38	7.59
Pax World Fund	53.8	8.5	25.89
New Alternatives Fund Inc.	2.4	22.2	24.06
Parnassus Fund	1.3	2.6	18.06
Canada (for period ending February 1987)			
Ethical Growth Fund	Cdn$11.4	15.1	—

For purposes of comparison, the Standard & Poors 500 Composite Index, a leading indicator of average U.S. stock performance, increased 15.8 per cent during 1986. The Toronto Stock Exchange 300 composite index rose 5.7 per cent during 1986.

Note: Because the five other Canadian ethical funds in operation during 1987 have been in existence for less than one year, no figures for them were available at time of publication.

CHAPTER 10
THE CORPORATE
GOOD SAMARITAN

Addressing a group of Salvation Army officials at a 1986 luncheon, Allan Taylor was at pains to jolly up his sober audience. These battle-weary veterans of countless corporate fund-raising drives had recently encountered heightened resistance to their pleas for assistance from company donations officers. And Taylor, who is chief executive of the Royal Bank of Canada, was there to say that while some companies are sympathetic to the pressing needs of charities, many more likely will continue to turn a deaf ear to the call without a great deal of persuasion. However, not wanting to start off on a pessimistic note, Taylor began with a joke that hinted there was cause for hope.

An executive was shipwrecked and wound up stranded on a deserted island with a college student who had been a crew member on the boat.

"The businessman took it calmly," said Taylor. "But the young man worked himself up into a panic."

"'How can you just sit there?' he cried. 'Don't you realize we're marooned on this godforsaken rock, hundreds of miles from anywhere? No one even knows we're alive! If you aren't worried, you must be crazy!'"

"'No, son. I'm not worried,' the executive replied. 'Let me tell you why. A few years ago, my company started doing fairly well for itself. At the end of our first really good year, I decided to raise our corporate donations to match. We gave $50,000 to the Salvation Army; another $50,000 to the United Way; and the same again to my old university.

"'Since then, my company has done even better. And every time we've doubled our revenues, I've doubled our donations. Last year, I gave one million dollars to the Salvation Army; the same to the United Way; and another million to the university.

"'Well, son, now it's 1986. And I KNOW they're going to find me!'"

Unwittingly or not, Taylor hit a raw nerve. Charitable organizations are, indeed, more persistent than ever these days. They have to be. Their number has multiplied, partly in response to the significant retreat from social-services spending by conservative political regimes in Canada and the United States. There are now fifty-five thousand hospitals, educational institutions, arts groups, churches, and community organizations hustling for funds in Canada; some two-thirds of the worthy causes in the United States didn't exist in 1960. Fiscally tight government agencies are giving charities the cold shoulder. The rise of the two-income family has thinned the ranks of volunteers from which the non-profit sector has traditionally drawn the bulk of its workers. And, unfortunately, when worthy causes turn to corporations for succour they often have doors slammed in their faces.

Some 90 per cent of Canadian companies make no contributions to charity, while about 75 per cent of individual Canadians *do*. Always tight-fisted, Canadian firms actually have been giving proportionately *less* to charitable causes during the past few years, just as the demand for services provided by the non-profit sector has skyrocketed. "Companies say they can't give to charity because the recession hurt them so badly," says Allan Arlett, executive director of the Canadian Centre for Philanthropy, which provides administrative assistance to more than one thousand non-profit organizations. "But it's hard to see how they can cry the blues. Profits have long since recovered, but charitable giving has not." Indeed, it has fallen sharply, from an average of 1.5 per cent of pretax profits in the halcyon late 1950s to between 0.4 per cent and 0.6 per cent today.

In 1987, charitable organizations in Canada planned to hit up the private sector for $1.7 billion, an 11 per cent increase over the previous year. Not many observers expected that goal to be met. In the field of corporate giving, which is acutely sensitive to peer pressure, a reduced commitment by one industry or even one company can be calamitous. In 1987, fund-raisers watched anxiously to see if major companies would follow the example of the oil industry, traditionally one of the most generous business sectors. The petroleum industry, devastated by low world oil prices, has trimmed charitable spending; Imperial Oil Ltd., one of Canada's biggest corporate donors, projected a 7 per cent decline in 1987 donations, to $6.8 million. It hardly matters that the oil sector is something of an anomaly, and that many other industries are enjoying record profits. "I warn charities that if they concentrate their fund-raising efforts on companies they're headed for trouble," says Ken Wyman, a Toronto fund-raising consultant. "I don't see much leadership among companies. The money just isn't there."

The irony, so far undetected by the bulk of Canadian businesses, is that companies with a serious, sophisticated approach to charitable giving extract rewards that go beyond the warm glow of feeling themselves benevolent. Which explains why the oil companies have been as gentle as possible in administering cuts, which have been in the order of 10 per cent to 20 per cent even though in some cases oil revenues have dropped by more than 50 per cent. A well-co-ordinated giving program of cash donations, payments in kind (free use of company premises and equipment, for instance), and employee time can pay hefty dividends in the form of higher morale and lower turnover, a better trained workforce, a widening network of contacts among potential clients and management recruits, an enhanced corporate image, and ultimately higher sales and profits. Companies that have embraced charitable giving as a worthwhile corporate strategy have discovered that altruism is only one of the many motives for the socially responsible corporate citizen.

Unfortunately, though, the notion that business people have an obligation to share the burden of remedying society's ills has caught on slowly, and is far from evolving into a serious management discipline. Andrew Carnegie, who rose from cotton-mill bobbin boy to steel magnate, set a fine early example. In his famous essay, "The Gospel of Wealth", Carnegie argues that rich men should give away their great fortunes, and in so doing, create "an ideal state in which the surplus wealth of the few will become, in the best sense, the property of the many." True to his beliefs, when Carnegie retired in 1901 he funnelled his enormous wealth into endowments and foundations for education and science, and embarked on a multitude of philanthropic campaigns, including the gift of funds to build public libraries in the United States, Canada, and English-speaking countries throughout the world. Oil baron John D. Rockefeller and two successive generations of his progeny were equally consumed with a sense of social obligation: to date the Rockefeller family has given away more than $1.5 billion to universities, medical schools, and dozens of other worthy institutions and causes.

For most of Carnegie's and Rockefeller Sr.'s contemporaries, however, the philanthropic impulse was a sometime thing, the product, more often than not, of a capricious and idiosyncratic mind. Liquor baron Hiram Walker, who was born in New England but based his distilling empire in the company town of Walkerville (now a suburb of Windsor, Ontario), built churches in both Detroit and Walkerville, but closed the latter chapel for two years after discovering its pastor preached temperance.

The mercurial auto pioneer Henry Ford, who was by turns tender and tempestuous with factory hands and family members alike, was a pacifist when the First World War broke out. Ford was horrified by the carnage in Europe. Fearful that the United States would soon be drawn into the hostilities, he vowed to "give all my money—and my life—to stop it". Ford publicly opposed military preparedness, and chartered an ocean liner to transport a bizarre contingent of writers, teachers, clergymen, and activists to Europe, where the pacifists were to bombard the combatants with peace proposals until a ceasefire was reached. But soon after Germany announced an all-out submarine war in the Atlantic, Ford renounced his pacifistic stance: he cut off funding to the peace mission, upon which he had lavished $520,000, and assured President Woodrow Wilson that Ford Motor Co. stood ready to build arms if needed.

Donald Smith (a.k.a. Lord Strathcona), the Canadian Pacific Railway financier who drove the CPR's last spike, was a munificent but quixotic philanthropist. Smith gave away $12 million during his lifetime, and another $20 million in his will. Among his most outstanding gifts were the donation in 1900 of an entire mounted regiment to British forces fighting the Boer War, and a $1 million donation to found Montreal's famed Royal Victoria Hospital. Still, Smith's generous legacy was marked by personal biases: unable to forgive Winnipeg voters for their failure to re-elect him to his House of Commons seat, Smith withheld his charitable donations from schools and hospitals in that city; and his upper-class pretensions were betrayed in his will, which stipulated that some of his money be used to set up a leper colony —but that only Englishmen of good social standing be allowed to stay there.

The image of business philanthropy has been tainted over the years by acts of opportunism disguised as charity. Among the most outrageous of these was Charles Tyson Yerkes's offer to build an astronomical observatory at the University of Chicago in 1892. The truth was that Yerkes couldn't finance his own business operations in Chicago, most notably the city's streetcar system. His apparent benevolence was merely a clever ploy designed to bolster his credit rating. Yerkes's offer to the university stipulated that it announce his gift immediately, but wait a few months for the money. When the announcement was made, Yerkes was presumed by potential bankers to be a good credit risk, since he appeared able to give away a million dollars. Yerkes got the lines of credit he so desperately needed. And the Yerkes Observatory, which boasts the largest refracting telescope in the world, still stands in Lake Geneva, Wisconsin, where it attests to the convenient public-spiritedness of a man who once allowed that "the secret of my business is to buy old junk, fix it up a little, and unload it on the next fellow."

Often the philanthropic urge is awakened by an aching desire for respectability. The Rockefellers' image has been well and truly cleansed, to the point where even the most thorough encyclopedia accounts often do not trouble to mention how paterfamilias John D. Rockefeller employed a vast network of spies to sabotage competing oil refineries and pipelines. But invariably they *do* carefully record the inventory of his good works, which include the financial backing that ensured the rise to pre-eminence of the University of Chicago — founded by John D. in 1890 (and which ironically enough is now home to economist Milton Friedman, the most outspoken critic of corporate gift-giving). Unfortunately, devotion to good works is no assurance of underlying morals, as witness the generosity of disgraced insider trader Ivan Boesky, who sought admittance to high social echelons by making liberal donations to Harvard and Princeton.

Because it functioned so often as a cover for chicanery, George Bernard Shaw scorned charity in the preface to his play *Major Barbara* (1905). "Cain took care not to commit another murder, unlike our railway shareholders (I am one) who kill and maim shunters by hundreds to save the cost of automatic couplings, and make atonement by annual subscriptions to deserving charities. Had Cain been allowed to pay off his score, he might possibly have killed Adam and Eve for the mere sake of a second luxurious reconciliation with God afterwards." In our time, CEOS who make time for charitable work sometimes seem to do so only as a cover for their usual wheeling and dealing. "The business leaders are all fulfilling their social responsibilities by being on the right museum boards," says Toronto professional investor Andrew Sarlos, who has himself been a trustee for Dalhousie University's endowment fund. "But when they manage money, their job is to maximize profit." With some dismay Sarlos notes that their community work "is totally separate and divorced from their responsibilities to shareholders."

Finally, corporate charity has always invited suspicion because of the pained selectiveness of its virtue. Ever since the fateful evening of March 13, 1893, when Mrs. William K. Vanderbilt organized a grand ball at the Waldorf in New York to benefit St. Mary's Free Hospital—thereby inventing the charity fund-raiser—businesspeople have strived to be associated with "correct" charities. To this day, a disproportionate amount of corporate giving is funnelled into "establishment" hospitals, art galleries, and opera halls, and very little finds its way to, for instance, rape-crisis centres and half-way houses for refugees from oppresive foreign regimes. Indeed, as recently as 1985, *Toronto Life* magazine could report on the greater and lesser cachet of diseases vying for corporate dollars. "The more fatal the disease the more glittery the function," a high-society observer told the magazine, which concluded that, "Certain diseases attract more social clout than others. Colitis is trying, but unfortunately hasn't yet made it. A ranking by prestige: cancer; heart; multiple sclerosis; diabetes; pregnancy, which may not be exactly a disease, but is a popular cause anyway (see Planned Parenthood); and almost any hospital, but Women's College is particularly good."

As well, the fund-raising extravaganzas are an end in themselves for many participants, often diverting attention from the causes they purport to assist. In 1986, the powerful New York investment banker Felix Rohatyn, who with his wife, Elizabeth, is a member of several proper charities himself, publicly scorned the lavish charity dinners and balls for their excess, and argued that the vast wealth of New York's affluent citizens should no longer be concentrated on a narrow band of prestigious charities and instead be directed as well at the social problems of the city's poor. "People in our world are swimming in money," said

Rohatyn, "But in order to get the city's rich to give a lousy thousand dollars to the poor who are drowning in front of their eyes you have to . . . give them party favors. I've read Dickens and most of Edith Wharton, but I can't recall . . . anything quite so monstrous." Predictably, Rohatyn was promptly condemned for his temerity. "Let's forget for the moment that Snow White [Elizabeth Rohatyn] had Bill Blass whip up a special number for her appearance at the Carnegie Hall benefit last year," sniped one socialite. Rohatyn probably had taken on too revered a tradition, concluded *Newsweek*: "He was striking at one of the most central prerogatives of wealth in New York: the right to dance on the same floor as William and Pat Buckley, Jackie Onassis, or the grand dame of New York society and philanthropy, Brooke Astor — and, if fortune should smile, to be mentioned in the account of the event in the next day's *Times*, perhaps even in the same paragraph as a duchess."

Still, as it has become more professionally administered, and less a function of an entrepreneur's personal whim, corporate philanthropy has become more credible than Shaw could have imagined. The trend has, however, been agonizingly slow to develop. Concerted and co-ordinated corporate giving didn't emerge until the First World War, when local businesses throughout North America began giving cash and gifts-in-kind to national and international service agencies such as the Red Cross and the Young Men's Christian Association. And not until the 1930s was it even clear whether companies could legally give funds to charity without abusing the rights of shareholders, from whom those funds were diverted. It was in those dark days of the Depression that the Bank of Montreal was challenged in court by a group of shareholders who challenged the bank's policy of providing financial aid to hospitals in Montreal. The bank won its case, and thereafter it and other large corporations became an attractive target for fund-raisers. Similarly, in the United States a 1935 ruling by the Securities and Exchange Commission established that companies were permitted to give up to 5 per cent of pretax earnings to non-profit organizations on a tax-deductible basis; in 1981, this figure was raised to 10 per cent. Yet these developments only set the stage for the institutionalization of corporate giving; they did not bring about its widespread acceptance. The first matching-grant program didn't come about until

1955, when General Electric Co. offered to match employee contributions to institutes of higher education; and this method of giving — very effective because of its high degree of employee involvement — has yet to be adopted by more than a few of North America's biggest and most conscientious corporate donors. A measure of how slow Canadian companies were to commit themselves to a serious charitable-funding program is that in 1971, only 3 of 393 firms surveyed by the then newly formed Institute of Donations and Public Affairs Research in Montreal had a full-time officer in charge of donations.

Today, the vast majority of companies — particularly those outside the Top 500 firms in the United States and Canada — continue to reject the Good Samaritan ethic. The owners and executives of these firms find comfort in two theories. The first is that business has no mandate to meddle in social issues. Indeed, so this argument goes, business could become a menace to society if it so chose, given its tremendous resources. Harvard economist Theodore Levitt, in a famous 1958 essay in the *Harvard Business Review*, sounded this alarm when he held up the spectre of an "encircling business ministry" which, given the invitation to do so, would take control of the state and bring about nothing short of a fascist regime.

The second and more widely circulated theory is that which was expounded by Milton Friedman. In his 1962 book *Capitalism and Freedom*, the conservative economist argued that society's welfare rests in part on the ability of businesspeople to do what they do best — generate profits, which enhance the general prosperity — free of government interference and such distractions as social causes. Since then Friedman has preached that business has "one and only one social responsibility — to use its resources and engage in activities designed to increase its profits so long as it stays within the rules of the game, which is to say, engages in open and free competition, without deception or fraud." Spending the shareholders' money to rectify even the most obvious and abusive social ills is a "fundamentally subversive doctrine", a breach of the executive's fiduciary duties as guardian of funds entrusted to him or her by the owners of the business. What is more, unlike politicians or social-service administrators, businesspeople are simply not qualified to look beyond their own bottom lines to the problems of the larger society. Indeed, how, Friedman wonders, "can self-selected private individuals decide what the social interest is?"

As attractive as they are to executives keen to shirk social obligations, the Levitt and Friedman arguments haven't withstood the test of time. In the generation since the two professors first postulated their theories, North Americans have witnessed a surge in government spending and regulatory intervention, unparalleled in history, which nevertheless failed to eradicate any number of intractable problems. In fact, business leaders are among the first to argue that by consigning all the responsibility to government, the undoubtedly useful input of business and other groups was not put to use in the fight against poverty, unemployment, urban decay, and other ills. As for business do-goodism getting out of control, the same checks and balances — the regulatory framework, a strong press, and the weight of popular opinion — that keep government and other institutions in check would surely restrain ill-informed business initiatives, as indeed they already do.

The fact is that business is already very "socially involved", whether by choice or not. Few business ventures proceed without the consent, and more often, active assistance of government and other social institutions. As a beneficiary of the societal infrastructure of roads, sewers, safe neighbourhoods, workforces trained for the most part at public expense, and tax concessions, among other assistance, business is wedded to society. It may choose not to play an active role in ameliorating social problems, but is often an active contributor to those problems. And it is usually the taxpayer who picks up the tab for cleaning polluted rivers, compensating the victims of unsafe products and workplaces, and assisting those who have been displaced from their jobs by automation. As a taxpayer itself, business has not only an obligation but the *right* to be part of solutions to these and other ills, not merely part of the problems.

"Traditionally, there has been a curious double standard applied to ordinary citizens and corporations," says Harvard University ethics professor Kenneth Goodpaster. "We expect a higher standard of ethical behaviour from individuals than companies, as if companies and not individuals were entitled to single-mindedly pursue only their own self-interest. That attitude has been unacceptable for individuals for some time, and I think it will prove unsatisfactory for the capitalism of the twenty-first century, as well."

Goodpaster concedes that corporations, vested with the rights and responsibilities of helping reshape society in ways outside of their own business environment, might somehow go awry. "You have to ask if it really is a wonderful idea or whether we may be creating a Frankenstein monster," Goodpaster says. "If we change the social contract and expect companies to not be self-interested profit-seekers, we have to do it carefully. Otherwise when we zap this thing on the table it may go off and muck up the village. Somehow, though, with all of the societal constraints in place to protect us from institutions that get out of hand, I don't think there will be a problem. I think we have to throw the switch, and see what a socially conscious business community will do."

Without much prompting, some executives with an eye to their firms' long-term interests already have come to view their social standing as an asset or liability — depending on whether they are regarded fondly or with scorn by the community. As the examples in this chapter illustrate, firms that build walls around themselves or view the public with contempt tend to fare badly when, in a crisis, they call upon the community for assistance. A corporation that has forged strong links with the communities in which it operates will have an easier time convincing legislators of the need, say, for import restrictions against marauding overseas competitors, protection from hostile takeover "raiders", or understanding and aid should a major accident occur at one of its facilities. To cite only a couple recent examples, the reputation for product quality and the lengthy, commendable public service record of New Jersey drugmaker Johnson & Johnson served it well when it was discovered that a batch of its Tylenol painkillers had been laced with cyanide by a psychopath. Aided by co-operative legislators and a sympathetic press — both of whom widely publicized the fact J&J was known as a good corporate citizen — J&J was able to quickly regain its big share of the pain-killer market after briefly withdrawing the product. Similarly, the citizens of tiny Bartlesville, Oklahoma, rallied around hometown Phillips Petroleum Co. when it was under siege by takeover raider T. Boone Pickens in the early 1980s. The prospect of losing the benevolent employer to an out-of-town upstart prompted

Bartlesville to prevail on legislators to stall the pending take-over — a delaying tactic that enabled Phillips to survive as an independent company.

Apart from the obvious benefits that a good reputation can bring, Toronto mining executive Martin Connell argues that business "simply must share a portion of the burden of remedying social ills". Connell, who is chairman of Conwest Exploration Co. Ltd. and has devoted time to close to a dozen charitable organizations in recent years, insists "corporations have a social responsibility to their communities, quite apart from the obvious marketing advantages that are to be gained for assisting non-profit groups. The recent erosion in charitable funding is a crisis, but also an opportunity for companies to take a leadership role in improving the quality of life in Canada." Connell himself presides over the fledgling Calmeadow Foundation, which, with a $1 million endowment from the Connell family's mining fortune, is working with other international aid groups to assist native Canadian and Third World entrepreneurs by providing them with credit to finance expansion of their businesses.

Samaritanism can take many forms. At its most passive, it consists merely of extending a helping hand in a crisis. During Expo '86 in Vancouver, for instance, Toni Bolton, manager of the American Express Travel Service Office at the site, sheltered in her home for two days a couple of German travellers who had been robbed of their funds and belongings. For this she was recognized by AmEx with $4,000 in travellers' cheques and a three-day, expenses paid trip to New York. Since 1978, Exxon Corp.'s tankers in the South China Sea have rescued more than four hundred "boat people" fleeing communist regimes in Indo-China, and another sixty thousand refugees have sought aid at Exxon's offshore drilling platforms in the region. Exxon could not deny aid, as that would be a breach of maritime law. However, Exxon did choose to publicize the stories of its employees in the South China Sea in internal publications as a means of encouraging similar behaviour in other parts of the company.

Sometimes corporate Good Samaritanism takes the form of a bid to generate international goodwill. In the summer of 1986, brothers Harrison and Wallace McCain were appalled by news reports that farmers across the southern United States were suffering the worst drought in a century. The brothers, whose

McCain Foods Ltd. is one of the world's largest frozen French-fry producers, organized a relief program whereby McCain itself and hundreds of growers who sell produce to the Florenceville, N.B., company sent more than two thousand tons of hay to the stricken farmers free of charge. The bales of hay, each bearing the message, "Gift of the farmers and citizens of New Brunswick, Canada", began arriving while U.S. farmers still awaited proposed drought-relief legislation from their own government, and made unnecessary a choice by farmers to let their livestock die or sell the animals at below-market prices. After the nuclear accident at Chernobyl in the U.S.S.R. in 1986, the Americare Foundation—a non-sectarian relief agency set up by paper-products magnate Robert Macauley of Connecticut, made overnight requests to drug companies who responded with $970,000 of dried milk, vitamins, and potassium iodide to protect thyroid functions. The supplies were airlifted to Eastern Europe several weeks before the U.S. Congress approved a much smaller sum for the same purpose.

Closer to home local businesses in several U.S. cities have banded together and made a mutual commitment to each devote between 2 per cent and 5 per cent of pretax earnings to charitable activities. There are "Five Percent Clubs" in Minneapolis (Dayton-Hudson, First St. Paul Bank), Baltimore (Black & Decker, Noxell), and "Two Percent Clubs" in Minneapolis (General Mills, Honeywell), Kansas City (Hallmark Cards, H&R Block), San Francisco (Bank of America, Levi Strauss), and Seattle (Safeway Stores, Weyerhaeuser). In Boston, area businesses have created a $5.5 million endowment program called ACCESS to ensure that all public high-school graduates who make it into college are provided with sufficient funds to go, and those who complete their college courses can count on job offers from local employers.

Corporations can also become agents for significant change by battling chronic scourges such as urban decay and unemployment among minorities and the disabled. One of the most ambitious and risky efforts of this sort has been the campaign by a handful of large U.S. firms to build factories in ghettos, in the belief that unemployment is the root of most minority problems. Lockheed Corp. was the first company to adopt this idea; it opened a fuselage plant in Watts shortly after the predominantly black Los Angeles neighbourhood erupted in riots in 1965. Unfortunately, of the fifteen inner-city factories built by social pioneers such as Control Data, Digital Equipment, General Electric, IBM, Xerox, and Westinghouse in the mid-1960s, nine have either been sold or closed (Lockheed's Watts facility survives). The task the companies set for themselves may have proved too daunting. The plants were plagued with high rates of absenteeism, and did not solve but merely highlighted the problem of untrained work-forces in their communities. Managers of ghetto factories still in operation are now working with government agencies to set up job-training programs in order to create a pool of recruits capable of working in the plants.

Of course, it is this very scenario of becoming mired in a prob-lem that appears to defy solution that scares off many would-be corporate philanthropists. Yet between the two extremes of pas-sive and highly ambitious responses to social problems lies a wide middle ground in which business can make a significant contribution without compromising its basic profit-making mission.

As a first step, philanthropic activities must be soundly admin-istered if a corporation and its employees — to say nothing of the intended beneficiaries — are to take them seriously. "The key to effective philanthropy programs is treating them exactly like any other corporate endeavour," say Joseph Berman and Ed Waitzer, authors of "The Bottom Line for Corporate Philanthropy", a guide to corporate giving prepared under the auspices of the Canadian Centre for Philanthropy and the Agora Foundation in 1982. "A dollar is a dollar, whether it is spent on the production line, management salaries, or social concerns."

In the early 1970s, only a handful of large Canadian companies had sophisticated mechanisms for dispensing charitable dollars, employee time, and gifts-in-kind. Today most major companies have institutionalized the giving process in a number of ways. These include establishing charitable activity as a corporate goal, and enshrining that goal in the company's formal mission statement or code of social conduct. Some firms create a standing committee of the board of directors to monitor the corporation's social performance, including donations policies, on the premise that the full board does not have the time or skills to devote as much attention as is required by this area. And many companies set up a department of full-time staff to administer the company's donations program and ensure that the department has direct reporting links with senior management and the board of directors' standing committee on social affairs. (As a general rule, one full-time donations officer—or "philanthropoid", as they are known in the trade—is required for every $1 million in donations distributed.)

For a charitable program to be effective, it is essential that senior managers participate, thereby lending their own credibility to the cause. "Employees get the signal that becoming involved in community activities is highly regarded at the top levels of the company if the CEO plays a role," says Peter Brophey, vice-president of corporate affairs at Xerox Canada. "You're working uphill when the top people aren't involved." As well, donations officers must be kept fully informed of corporate developments in order to adjust giving programs accordingly. Christine Lee, manager of corporate affairs at Suncor Inc., participates in a monthly meeting of senior management that discusses Suncor's financial affairs. "In that way, I know immediately about when and where in the company cutbacks are planned,"says Lee. "Lights go off in my head about communities in which we're located that are going to need extra help."

It is also vital that as many employees as possible become involved in the decisions about where charitable dollars and gifts will be directed. Molson Companies Ltd. has eight provincial donations committees across Canada and a national committee at head office; in all, some forty people are involved, providing input according to geographic region and business unit. In order to fully integrate giving programs into the firm's everyday business, Xerox appends its "Team Xerox" slogan—the same tagline used in its advertising—to internal charitable operations. "The teamwork approach appeals to people," says Brophey, "reinforcing the company's financial objectives and its external non-profit activities at the same time." And operations such as SUPPORT, a Xerox program in which the company contributes funds to volunteer organizations in which employees are involved, "have the effect of putting every employee on the contributions committee." Great Northern Apparel, the Canadian division of giant U.S. clothing manufacturer Levi Strauss & Co., similarly appeals to its 1,700 employees for help; as a consequence of heeding their suggestions, a large portion of Great Northern's

$500,000 in annual donations is channelled into low-profile but worthy causes that cannot muster the fund-raising field force of big-city symphonies and hospitals.

As they make the transformation to becoming more professionally run, charitable giving programs at major corporations tend to be more focused with their donations. As Berman and Waitzer point out, "Corporate social responsibility is not best served by writing cheques to the most persuasive fundraisers." In order to be effective, a large portion of charitable giving should be directed to causes and spent in communities in which the companies have a special interest, or in which its own expertise can be put to maximum use. Partly this is a function of economics. Floralove Katz, director of public-affairs programs at Molson, says the company's $1 million charitable budget "can only make its mark if it's administered on a carefully selected basis. One million dollars doesn't go very far when you're getting requests from seven thousand organizations." Molson put special emphasis on health and education research, particularly worthy projects that have been put on hold for lack of funds. Some projects that Molson helps finance, such as research on multiple sclerosis at the University of British Columbia and on advanced prostheses for children and adults at the University of New Brunswick, are not directly related to the company's business. But many others are, such as research on lung disease in farmers caused by inhalation of grain dust (grain being a principal ingredient in beer).

Hard times in the oil patch have made Shell Canada equally selective. "We used to cover the waterfront," says Elaine Proulx, manager of community affairs at Shell. "When the crunch came, we began to focus on universities from which we are most likely to recruit or which are doing research allied with our industry. Instead of giving small amounts to many hospitals, we've begun to devote more substantial amounts to hospitals closest to where our employees live." The Canada Life Assurance Co. could not have chosen a more selective approach than when it set out to save the white pelican. The huge bird, which has a wingspan of more than two metres, has been Canada Life's corporate symbol for 140 years. But it was no friend to boaters in Western Canada who mistakenly thought it competed with fishermen for sports fish. Harassed by boaters, the birds abandoned their nests and faced extinction. Thanks largely to a $30,000 research and public-information program sponsored by the insurer, the number of breeding pairs of white pelicans has climbed from a 1970s low of fewer than fifteen thousand to an estimated fifty thousand pairs, and in 1987 the World Wildlife Fund Canada announced the bird had come off its endangered list—the first time a species has been removed from the list.

Traditionally, corporate donors have been conservative in their choice of charities. Wary of controversy, most firms shy away from "risky" causes and simply hand over the bulk of their donations budgets to the United Way and other "safe" umbrella groups, which redistribute the funds to needy causes. Companies usually benefit, however, by adopting a more ambitious approach. "There's no question the United Way does good works," says professional fund-raiser Ken Wyman. "But many worthy organizations—universities, for instance—don't belong to the United Way. For many companies just wanting to pat themselves on the back for doing their bit for charity, the United Way is an easy answer. But they should be going beyond that, or they'll miss the opportunity to do useful and interesting things for their communities."

An obvious advantage of this approach is that it provides employees at all levels of the company with an insight into problems and issues in the world around them. At Shell, which has funded half-way houses for battered women and ex-prostitutes and has underwritten scholarships at the Ontario College of Art for ex-convicts, community-affairs manager Proulx says, "Our charitable efforts have given us links to the community enabling us to know what's going on out there." At Xerox, Peter Brophey equates the company's sprawling network of connections to non-profit organizations with the Distant Early Warning line. "By being involved with these groups, our managers and employees see early evidence of societal trends, many of which will effect our business and our own employees," he says.

The church-basement image of the volunteer sector belies its power as an economic force. Volunteer work in Canada contributes an estimated $5 billion to the economy and accounts for about four hundred million hours of work each year. And, according to a 1984 Gallup poll, managers and professionals are more likely to be attracted to volunteer work than any other group, including that old standby, housewives. The appeal of volunteer work to rank-and-file businesspeople is the opportunity it offers of doing some good, making new friends, and brushing up on people-handling and problem-solving skills. A 1986 Conference Board of Canada study showed a majority of Canada's largest firms are promoting the volunteerism trend. Almost 70 per cent of the firms surveyed by the Conference Board encourage employee volunteerism through a variety of methods, including lending employees to volunteer organizations, providing charitable groups with the use of company facilities and equipment, and making donations to non-profit groups that employees become involved with.

Xerox Canada's parent, Stamford, Connecticut-based Xerox Corp., has a Social Service Leave program, created in 1971, that pays employees for a month to a year to work for non-profit community organizations. The program, which costs Xerox about $350,000 a year, pays dividends: employees return with better interpersonal and problem-solving skills. England's National Westminister Bank uses a variation on that approach to solve the problem of what to do with employees who are near retirement and are blocking the way for younger people seeking advancement. NatWest "lends" willing older employees to the voluntary sector. While allowing that the program has a cost (as the bank continues to pay their salaries), NatWest's personnel director points out the many benefits: "Any alternative is expensive too. Redundancy costs money anyway and early retirement is usually bad for the man as well. It is damaging to his pride and leaves a need to supplement his income. This way, hopefully, we help everybody. We help the man, we help others farther down the ladder who are eligible for promotion, and can often give deserving causes not only money but human assistance."

Participation in external causes is often also useful in sending internal signals through a company. By sponsoring the production of *The Disability Myth*, a film series broadcast on TV that was critical of government and corporate practices that discriminate against the handicapped, Suncor Inc. "was able to develop good training material for ourselves," says Suncor's Christine Lee, "and send a signal to our own managers that hiring and equitable treatment of the disabled is a major priority of Suncor." Tackling the problem of underrepresentation of women in non-traditional jobs at the firm also spurred Suncor to work with outside groups.

Suncor sends its executives into high schools in communities where the company has operations. The message they spread is that teenage girls should reconsider dropping out of maths and sciences before high school is over, and that guidance counsellors are ill-advised to keep steering women away from engineering into fields such as industrial nursing.

Another obvious benefit from community involvement is the networking possibilities its affords. The long association of Mobil, Texaco, and Philip Morris with various arts organizations has made the names of the prestigious arts groups almost interchangeable with the companies. IBM Canada's longstanding support of the National Ballet has earned the latter the sobriquet "IBM National Ballet". A similar fusion of identities is likely for the famous Harbourfront Literary Reading Series in Toronto, which has enjoyed a great deal of support from Imasco Ltd.'s du Maurier cigarette division.

And major sponsors can be counted upon to try to benefit from their own largesse. In 1980, the Bank of Montreal pretty well adopted the Montreal Symphony: every year since, the bank has funded the symphony's ambitious schedule of appearances in U.S., European, and Canadian cities. Happily for the bank, its alliance with the symphony coincided with a maturation of the symphony's performing standards and a heightened international profile. The fruits of this symbiotic relationship are impressive: the Montreal Symphony's fortunes have improved in part through the support of its generous sponsor, and the bank's own profile in Europe and the United States has been greatly enhanced by its association with a classy arts institution. At a function at New York's Plaza Hotel in conjunction with an appearance by the Montreal Symphony in the city in early 1986, the bank's guest list included the presidents of RCA Corp., American Express, J.C. Penney Co., British Petroleum, McGraw-Hill, Inc., and Jos. E. Seagram & Sons Inc., complete with a supporting cast of high-powered Manhattan lawyers and investment bankers. Bank chairman William Mulholland revels in the cultivated audience the symphony link helps him attract (and with which it does a little pre-performance business), and maintains that the symphony's foreign appearances help alter Canada's image abroad as a cultural wasteland.

Corporations have traditionally used charitable works as an

image-enhancement tool. In the mid-1970s, when oil companies were widely scorned for booking enormous profits during the energy crisis, some oil giants attempted to blunt the full force of those accusations by engaging in acts of conspicuous goodwill. Atlantic Richfield Co. (ARCO) bailed out the financially troubled U.K. daily *The Observer*, and *Harper's*, a liberal American journal. Imperial Oil Ltd., which is controlled by New York-based Exxon, came up with $100,000 in the mid-1970s to prevent the ailing nationalist magazine *Saturday Night* from slipping away. Of course, when such efforts are intended to overcome a legacy of ill-will developed by a company or an entire industry, these shallow bows to charity can appear to be mere afterthoughts. Between 1968 and 1975, forest products giant MacMillan Bloedel (MB) — which stood accused of mismanaging the forest resource — bought twenty-two J. Fenwick Lansdowne paintings. An MB vice-president later explained that there was "a love-hate relationship between people and the forest industry. We tear down trees and people love trees." MB felt that the paintings purchase demonstrated that forest companies "care about the flora and fauna. That we're responsible custodians of the forest." For similar reasons, Consolidated-Bathurst uses part of its donations budget to highlight its role in making products that carry the printed word: it underwrites the cost of hiring well-known writers to lecture at McGill University.

But there are ways of ensuring that charitable efforts do not appear to be isolated acts of contrition. In its most highly refined form, charitable giving can be a very sophisticated form of marketing. This new, calculated approach to donations was heralded in a remarkable essay published in the 1984 annual report of Continental Bank of Canada (now Lloyds Bank Canada). Continental, which was dwarfed in size by the Big Six banks, had few resources compared with its huge competitors. Its donations budget was not big enough to have much of an impact for social good, and its marketing budget, while much bigger, was still embarrassingly small compared with those of the Big Six. The solution Continental hit upon in the early 1980s was to create an alliance between the donations and marketing operations, with the result that in helping non-profit organizations the bank candidly promoted itself, and vice versa.

In 1984, Continental described its new tactic, which it held out as an example worthy of emulation, in its annual report essay, entitled "The Corporate Gift Horse":

> We believe that the division between [the donations and marketing] funds should not be as sharply defined as in the past; that philanthropy does not always have to be totally altruistic, and that marketing does not always have to be a mechanistic process of placing commercial messages before the public.
>
> There will always be a portion of each philanthropic dollar dedicated to those worthy causes whose nature makes commercial exploitation inapproriate. But as many other companies are now discovering, that leaves the lion's share available for other things, and in these areas we consciously work to achieve a level of recognition that will help us meet specific goals in no uncertain terms.

Continental's compelling argument was that charitable sponsorships are cheaper than conventional TV and print ads and reach a more demographically attractive audience. Sponsorship of one appearance by a major theatre company cost about $3,000 in 1984, a sum far lower than the price of placing a full-page ad in a major newspaper. A major dance company tour, and the nationwide publicity it generates, could be had for $100,000; a TV ad costs anywhere from $80,000 to $250,000 to produce, exclusive of air time. Of course, the audience for cultural events is generally much smaller than the number of people exposed to ads, but it's an attractive audience. Cultural events attract well-educated and affluent patrons, and their number is growing. In 1961, the arts could draw audiences from just 12 per cent of the Canadian population; by 1981, that number had increased to 28 per cent, and by the turn of the century it is expected to reached about 40 per cent.

In recent years, this new approach to charity has been accepted as gospel by several major corporations. Probably its most ardent advocate in the United States is American Express Co., whose president, Louis Gerstner Jr., says, "American Express's philanthropy is guided by the same market-driven strategy that serves the company's businesses." The concept of "cause-related marketing", as it has come to be known, is attractive because it produces great impact for the sponsor at minimal cost. In 1986, the Hands Across America drive hoped to collect between $50 million and $100 million for the hungry and homeless by getting some 5.4 million Americans to join hands in a human chain spread across the continent. Corporations were invited to sponsor miles anywhere along the Hands Across America line. Rather than opt for a section passing through a densely populated district, AmEx paid $33,000 for a one-mile stretch of desert between Phoenix, Arizona, and Albequerque, New Mexico, that was billed by the drive's promoters as "the toughest mile in America". In the process of rounding up the 1,320 hand holders needed to cover the remote section of the chain, AmEx generated press attention worth several times its contribution to Hands Across America which, incidentally, turned out to be something of a fund-raising flop.

AmEx had similar success in 1983 when it initiated a fund-raising drive for the Statue of Liberty refurbishing. It raised $1.7 million in three months by agreeing to donate a penny for each charge on an AmEx card, a penny for every purchase of travellers' cheques, $1 for each new card issued, and $1 for every vacation worth more than $500 purchased at an AmEx travel agency. The popularity of the drive translated into billions of dollars in AmEx card charges. But of the sixty or so cause-related marketing efforts AmEx has launched around the world in the past few years, the most startlingly effective probably was its campaign to thwart a group of British hotels and restaurants that was balking at the high fees AmEx charges for credit-card transactions. AmEx responded not with lower rates, but instead offered to contribute to the Duke of Edinburgh Award (a charity for young people named for Prince Philip) when people used the AmEx card. In newspaper ads for the charity, the Duke of Edinburgh's name was juxtaposed with the AmEx logo, and shortly thereafter the British Hotels, Restaurants and Caterers Association's placards calling for an AmEx card boycott were removed from hotel lobbies and restaurant windows.

This quid pro quo approach is taking hold with a wide variety of companies. Beecham Canada began sponsoring curling bonspiels after discovering that curlers have the same demographic profile as one of its rarely advertised products, a liniment called Minards. General Foods promised to give 10¢ to Mothers Against Drunk Drivers for every Tang orange drink proof-of-purchase they sent in. The firm also reversed a market-share decline in its

Post Raisin Bran cereal by reformulating it as Post *Natural* Raisin Bran, and offering to contribute 50 cents to upgrade nature trails in national parks for every proof-of-purchase submitted.

McDonald's is preferred seven to one over Burger King by Hispanics in the United States these days almost entirely because McDonald's has assiduously participated in Hispanic-related events—the Puerto Rican Day parade, the Miss Colombia pageant, and Peruvian independence day celebrations, among others. It also donated $100,000 to victims of the 1986 Mexican earthquake. Burger King by contrast, has made little headway in cracking the Hispanic market; not coincidentally it has shied away from specifically targeting its ads and community involvement at ethnic groups. McDonald's was only following the example of Coors beer, which by acknowledging cultural differences in its promotional efforts enjoyed an 80 per cent increase in sales to Hispanics in the short space of two years.[1]

Sometimes, of course, these well-targeted goodwill gestures backfire. Late in 1986, some Ontario universities rejected brewery sponsorship of athletic events out of concern about over-indulgence in drinking, and a conviction that athletic heroes on campus shouldn't be used to promote alcohol. A similar outcry accompanied RJR-MacDonald's sponsorship of the Canadian Ski Team a few years ago; ski champion Steve Podborski publicly expressed his dismay at the prospect of participating in events in which RJR was attempting to associate cigarettes with a healthy athletic pursuit.

By an overwhelming margin, however, corporate sponsors of charitable events are pleased with the results—even if many charities are alarmed at the degree to which some companies are

---

1   This image-building campaign was undermined in May 1987, when brewery magnate Joseph Coors enthusiastically explained to joint hearings of the House of Representatives and the Senate into the Iran-contra affair that he had participated in the White House's covert drive to overthrow the left-wing Sandinista government in Nicaragua. Coors testified he had donated $65,000 to the contras for the purpose of replacing their one aging DC-3 with a fleet of new small planes.

   Many Hispanics in America are refugees from repressive right-wing governments in Latin America and are sympathetic to the Sandinistas, who deposed the corrupt government of Anastasio Somoza-Debayle in 1979.

intent on milking their goodwill for all its commercial worth. Indeed, the slavish attention to commercial gain evidenced in some ostensible acts of corporate charity brings to mind H.L. Mencken's dour observation that "Doing good has come to be, like patriotism, a favorite device of persons with something to sell."

These concerns were brought into focus in early 1987 during the last days of wheelchair athlete Rick Hansen's Man in Motion tour, with which the disabled B.C. hero sought to publicize the need for better conditions for the disabled. Corporate involvement helped push Hansen's fund over the $5 million mark—a remarkable fund-raising achievement—and his good name helped corporate sponsors such as Imperial Oil, Canadian Pacific, Nabob Foods, and McDonald's win a wider appeal for their products. In order to ensure that outcome, Nabob Foods, for one, spent two and one-half times more to publicize its support of the Man in Motion than it did on direct donations to the fund. And McDonald's was literally everywhere Rick Hansen was: the burger chain's logo was a prominent fixture on almost all Hansen's garments, and he made publicized stops at its restaurants along his route. McDonald's prepared print and TV ads promoting the event and its role in it, some of which ran free of charge as public-service messages, and offered to donate $1 to the cause for every Big Mac sold in a city on the day the Man in Motion wheeled through. In the aftermath, says fund-raising consultant Ken Wyman, "some groups raising money for the disabled worry that the handicapped will have to hop, skip, or crawl across the country to raise money. And charities with less marketable causes now are becoming reluctant to attempt to raise money from corporations." Even some corporate donors were put off by certain aspects of the Man in Motion campaign. "I think there was some overkill," says one corporate donations officer. "At times, it turned into a bit of a circus."

To some extent, this depiction of the insidious side of corporate charitable giving is overdrawn. Wyman himself insists that "appearances aside, most companies are not that set on getting a huge bang for their charitable buck. And the attendant publicity that sometimes overtakes a corporate sponsor's assistance to a cause usually produces more good than harm. It attracts the attention of a large audience of potential individual donors—and individual donors account for 90 per cent of the charitable dollars generated in Canada." And as unseemly as cause-related charity sometimes appears to be, it won't often stray across the line between good and bad taste because, after all, the marketing effectiveness of a corporate sponsorship is surely diminished once that line is perceived to have been crossed.

Most importantly, though, the Continental Bank's essay correctly predicted that raiding corporate marketing budgets for donations dollars would create a new pool of funds available for charity. This is the "corporate gift horse" Continental advised charities not to look in the mouth, and that seems a reasonable suggestion considering the miserly sentiments that prevail in most parts of the corporate world. A lot of cost-conscious executive officers still think like R. Donald Fullerton, CEO of the Canadian Imperial Bank of Commerce: "I think it's only fair to warn those who fancy corporate cultural philanthropists as the new Medici that they are likely to be disappointed," Fullerton said in 1986. "We must be market-oriented to survive, and Lorenzo de Medici was a lousy banker." And while the search for a marketing payoff from charitable works strikes some as unseemly, the private sector is not alone in appending an ulterior motive to its charity: some two-thirds of Canada's foreign-aid payments are tied to purchases of Canadian goods and services.

Recently there have been signs that major corporations are loosening their purse strings. According to a survey by the Institute of Donations and Public Affairs Research, nearly half of the eighty firms polled said they would increase their total donations in 1987, while 55 per cent said they would increase their total donations to the United Way, specifically. In the future, fundraisers must concentrate less on big firms, which already are the most likely business enterprises to have a sense of social obligation, and instead try to convert the broad middle- and small-business wedges of the business spectrum to the belief that they too must contribute to the communities from which they draw their employees, raw materials, and profits. And it will not be easy to arouse the Samaritan urge among these firms. "Big corporations are carrying a disproportionate share of the burden in corporate philanthropy," says Martin Connell, who is spearheading a drive to publicize the degree to which non-profit organizations contribute to the quality of life in Canada. "Unfortunately, it takes a least a decade for a small, emerging company to develop an interest in philanthropy. Our job as fund-raisers is to get more of them into the act."

It will likely be some time before the majority of executives come to appreciate the many and varied means by which philanthropy can benefit them and the image of business generally. Corporate giving is a means by which business can demonstrate that it may not be the monolithic, wholly profit-obsessed institution its many critics perceive it to be. Engaging in acts of community goodwill forces businesspeople into the unfamiliar territory of people whose work cannot be measured with flow charts and spreadsheets, people whose values and aspirations are usually very different from, and sometimes contradictory to, the ones upheld in business itself. But business and businesspeople will be immeasurably strengthened as they absorb those new values, even if they do so with some trepidation. "To give away money is an easy matter, and in any man's power," said Aristotle. "But to decide to whom to give it, and how large and when, and for what purpose and how, is neither in every man's power — nor an easy matter. Hence it is that such excellence is rare, praiseworthy and noble."

Conclusion

The belief that business necessarily is accountable to a lower standard of ethical conduct than the rest of the community is deep-rooted and enduring. When corporations first emerged as the principal means by which business was conducted, the eighteenth-century English jurist Edward Thurlow asked, "Did you ever expect a corporation to have a conscience when it has no soul to be damned and no body to be kicked?" Some two hundred years later, the influential American philosopher John Ladd seemed unaware of the budding social-reform movement when he insisted in 1970, "It is improper to expect organizational conduct to conform to the ordinary principles of morality. We cannot and must not expect formal organizations, or their representatives acting in their official capacities, to be honest, courageous, considerate, sympathetic, or to have any kind of moral integrity. Such concepts are not in the vocabulary, so to speak, of the organizational language game." And today a new generation of business leaders, a seeming throwback to the robber-baron era of one hundred years earlier, is embracing a commercial strategy dubbed "ruthless management". "The new order," said *The New York Times* in 1987, "eschews loyalty to workers, products, corporate structure, businesses, factories, communities, even the nation. All such allegiances are expendable under the new rules. With survival at stake, only market leadership, strong profits and a high stock price can be allowed to matter."

Is this indeed what business is all about? Narrow self-interest, an abiding insensitivity to communal concerns, and a rapacious exploitation of workers, suppliers, and customers? If this be true we are all diminished, for the majority of workers in Western society spend the better part of their waking hours in the employ of the business system.

Yet the abysmal recent examples of Boesky and Bhopal, and the legacies of the Love Canal and the Dalkon Shield, do not define the norm. In fact, the process of social reform in business has not stalled. Most major companies are coming to realize that organizations, like ordinary people, can and must be made to distinguish between right and wrong, and that business has obligations well beyond the demands made of it by shareholders.

To be sure, the argument is still sometimes advanced that "artificial persons" such as corporations are "value-neutral" — that is, they cannot take it upon themselves to make moral judgments. The persuasive counterargument, however, is that if corporations can have all manner of other human motives imposed on them — namely to make things, convince people to buy them, and profit therefrom — what justifies the claim that they must remain morally inanimate? "Whether the issue be the health effects of sugared cereal or cigarettes, the safety of tires or tampons, civil liberties in the corporation or the community, an organization reveals its character as surely as a person does," insists Harvard business-ethics professor Kenneth Goodpaster.

Business leaders themselves are now to be heard acknowledging that the morality of corporations cannot be separated from that of the people who run them and work for them. "Through a legal fiction, a corporation is in fact a person at law, but in reality it is more than this abstract concept," says Arden Haynes, chief executive officer of Imperial Oil Ltd. "It has a human dimension and morality brought to it by its owners, management and employees. A corporation has an ethical reputation; it is judged by those it deals with — employees, shareholders, customers, sales associates, suppliers, and the community — against the same ethical standards as individuals."

Executives are also more willing now than ever before to openly recognize that they do have an impact far beyond the confines of their own operations. "'Social resonsibility' is not some extra added dimension, some additional 'frill' not integrally connected to the 'real' job itself," says David Grier, vice-president and chief advisor on public affairs at the Royal Bank of Canada. "Social responsibility *is* the real job, because *every* business decision made, every day, has ethical content and moral consequences." The New York-based Conference Board, a leading business think tank whose clientele consists mostly of *Fortune 500* corporations, recently stated: "Corporate decisions affect the relative prosperity of various regions of our nation, the development of foreign nations, submission or resistance to foreign boycott threats, discrimination or non-discrimination against blacks, women, Jews or other social groups, the future of cities, the quality of urban life, the retirement income of the aged, the development and conservation of energy, the state of the environment and even the viability of human life itself. There is virtually nothing a corporation does any more that can be considered exclusively 'its own business'."

The impression that a business is responsible only to its owners was effectively debunked in the 1970s by Harvard sociologist Daniel Bell, who argued that, "To the extent that the traditional sources of social support (the small town, church and family) have crumbled in society, new kinds of organizations, particularly the corporation, have taken their place; and these inevitably become the arenas in which the demands for security, justice and esteem are made. To think of the business corporation, then, simply as an economic instrument is to fail totally to understand the meaning of the social changes of the last half century."

More important, perhaps, was Bell's observation that in the past few decades, as sole proprietorships have been replaced by widespread ownership of shares in the modern, publicly traded corporation, the notion that the owner has sole claim to a commercial enterprise's resources is no longer valid. "Given the pattern of stock ownership today—particularly with the growth of mutual funds, pension funds and trust funds—the stockholder is often an 'in-and-out' person with little continuing interest in the enterprise. . . . True owners are involved directly and psychologically in the fate of an enterprise; and this description better fits the employees of the corporation, not its stockholders. For these employees, the corporation is a social institution which they inhabit. It is politically and morally unthinkable that their lives should be at the mercy of a financial speculator."

The final impediment to corporate social reform is the unease many businesspeople feel in assessing the ethical complexities of what otherwise would be a straight dollars-and-cents proposition, a feeling that without formal philosophical training a manager forced to cope with the moral dimensions of his or her activities will become afflicted with decision-making paralysis. Yet there are certain basic precepts and moral values that are more than adequate to guide managers through most ethical problems. Stopping to consider whether a decision can be explained candidly to one's family and friends is as good a place to start as any; so, too, is the golden rule, which requires simply that a person place a high priority on the interests of others when pursuing his or her own goals. "In vain do they talk of happiness who never subdued an impulse to a principle," said Horace Mann, the eminent nineteenth-century U.S. educator. "He who never sacrificed a present to a future good, or a personal one to a general one, can speak of happiness only as the blind do of colors." Such basic maxims as this are within everyone's grasp. "The ability to do ethical analysis is not a semi-rote skill which needs to be drilled into people," says Imperial's Arden Haynes. "To recognize right and wrong, to justify one's choices with reason, to feel the pangs of a guilty conscience and to think one's way through a hard case are widespread skills among ordinary adults, including line workers, middle managers, and executives."

There is a malignancy in business today: it is the widespread perception that unfettered capitalism inevitably gives rise to conduct unbecoming members of a civilized society, and that business will therefore have to be constrained through legislative fiat — if only in response to a growing outcry from the public over real and perceived transgressions by business. "There's something essential missing from an economic system propelled only by greed and by conspicuous consumption," says William Dimma, deputy chairman of Royal LePage Ltd., Canada's largest real-estate brokerage, "a system that rewards inordinately too many who are callously indifferent to craft and workmanship, to such basic things as producing superior quality and service at a competitive price. If there's no more to it than that, I fear for the survival of an economic system which spawns such parasitical behaviour and rewards it so extravagantly."

There is much more to business. It is, in fact, a noble calling. Business activity raises individuals and whole populations from idle penury to greatness. By attending to a society's basic needs for goods and services, it frees people for other pursuits. By generating wealth for workers, investors, and governments, it liberates individuals and countries from the enslavement of poverty and the tragedy of limited opportunities. The commercial vitality of a nation largely determines the degree to which other disciplines — art, medicine, and education — will flourish or falter. Indeed, in most parts of the world, business is the very underpinning of civility.

The time has come, at this juncture in the history of its social evolution, for business to make more than a purely monetary contribution to the civilization of man. It is time for business to make a priority of overtly demonstrating that virtue and profit are not antithetical concepts. And to live by and impart ethical standards that are as ambitious as those set by any other individuals and organizations in society. Indeed, with its remarkable efficiency and unequalled talent at marshalling financial, managerial, and technological resources, business is more favourably suited than most institutions in society to the challenge of harvesting truly just rewards.

APPENDIX I
Documents

Attention Must Be Paid

Judge Miles Lord and the Case Against the Makers of the Dalkon Shield

On February 29, 1984, Federal District Court Judge Miles W. Lord addressed A.H. Robins Co. executives E. Claiborne Robins, president; Carl D. Lunsford, senior vice-president for research and development; and William A. Forrest Jr., vice-president and general counsel. The following is an exerpt from the speech Lord made to the executives in his Minneapolis courtroom as he approved a $4.6 million product-liability suit against Robins, maker of the Dalkon Shield intra-uterine contraceptive device, which is alleged to have caused injury to thousands of its users.

Mr. Robins, Mr. Forrest, and Dr. Lunsford: After months of reflection, study, and cogitation—and no small amount of prayer—I have concluded that it is perfectly appropriate to make this statement, which will constitute my plea to you to seek new horizons in corporate consciousness and a new sense of personal responsibilty for the activities of those who work under you in the name of the A.H. Robins Co.

It is not enough to say, "I did not know," "It was not me," "Look elsewhere." Time and again, each of you have used this kind of argument in refusing to acknowledge your responsibility and in pretending to the world that the chief officers and directors of your gigantic multinational corporation have no responsibility for its acts and omissions.

Today as you sit here attempting once more to extricate yourselves from the legal consequences of your acts, none of you has faced up to the fact that more than 9,000 women claim they gave up part of their womanhood so that your company might prosper. It has been alleged that others gave their lives so that you might prosper. And there stand behind them legions more who have been injured but who have not sought relief in the courts of this land.

I dread to think what would have been the consequences if your victims had been men rather than women — women, who seem, through some quirk of our society's mores, to be expected to suffer pain, shame and humiliation.

If one poor young man were, without authority or consent, to inflict such damage upon one woman, he would be jailed for a good portion of the rest of his life. Yet your company, without warning to women, invaded their bodies by the millions and caused them injuries by the thousands. And when the time came for these women to make their claims against your company, you attacked their characters. You inquired into their sexual practices and into the identity of their sex partners. You ruined families and reputations and careers in order to intimidate those who would raise their voices against you. You introduced issues that had no relationship to the fact that you had planted in the bodies of these women instruments of death, of mutilation, of disease.

Gentlemen, you state that your company has suffered enough, that the infliction of further punishment in the form of punitive damages would cause harm to your business, would punish innocent shareholders, and could conceivably depress your profits to the point where you could not survive as a competitor in this industry. When the poor and downtrodden commit crimes, they too plead that these are crimes of survival and that they should be excused for illegal acts that helped them escape desperate economic straits. On a few occasions when these excuses are made and remorseful defendants promise to mend their ways, courts will give heed to such pleas. But no court will heed the plea when the individual denies the wrongful nature of his deeds and gives no indication that he will mend his ways. Your company, in the face of overwhelming evidence, denies its guilt and continues its monstrous mischief.

Mr. Forrest, you have told me that you are working with

members of the congress of the United States to find a way of forgiving you from punitive damages that might otherwise be imposed. Yet the profits of your company continue to mount. Your latest financial report boasts of new records for sales and earnings, with a profit of more than $58 million in 1983. And, insofar as this court has been able to determine, you three men and your company are still engaged in a course of wrongdoing. Until your company indicates that it is willing to cease and desist this deception and to seek out and advise the victims, your remonstrances to Congress and to the courts are indeed hollow and cynical. The company has not suffered, nor have you men personally. You are collectively being enriched by millions of dollars each year. There is no evidence that your company has suffered any penalty from these litigations. In fact, the evidence is to the contrary.

The case law suggests that the purpose of punitive damages is to make an award that will punish a defendant for his wrongdoing. Punishment has traditionally involved the principles of revenge, rehabilitation, and deterrence. There is no evidence I have been able to find in my review of these cases to indicate that any one of these objectives has been accomplished.

Mr. Robbins, Mr. Forrest, Dr. Lunsford: You have not been rehabilitated. Under your direction, your company has continued to allow women, tens of thousands of them, to wear this device — a deadly depth charge in their wombs, ready to explode at any time. Your attorney denies that tens of thousands of these devices are still in women's bodies. But I submit to you that he has no more basis for denying the accusation than the plaintiffs have for stating it as truth. We simply do not know how many women are still wearing these devices because your company is not willing to find out. The only conceivable reasons that you have not recalled this product are that it would hurt your balance sheet and alert women who have already been harmed that you may be liable for their injuries. You have taken the bottom line as your guiding beacon and the low road as your route. That is corporate irresponsibility at its meanest. Rehabilitation involves an admission of guilt, a certain contrition, an acknowledgment of wrongdoing, and a resolution to take a new course toward a better life. I find none of this in you or your corporation. Confession is good for the soul, gentlemen. Face up to your misdeeds. Acknowledge the personal responsibility you have for the activities of those who work under you. Rectify this evil situation. Warn the potential victims and recompense those who have already been harmed.

Mr. Robins, Mr. Forrest, Dr. Lunsford: I see little in the history of this case that would deter others. The policy of delay and obfuscation practiced by your lawyers in courts throughout this country has made it possible for you and your insurance company to put off the payment of these claims for such a long period that the interest you earned in the interim covers the cost of these cases. You, in essence, pay nothing out of your own pockets to settle these cases. What corporate officials could learn a lesson from this? The only lesson they might learn is that it pays to delay compensating victims and to intimidate, harass, and shame the injured parties.

Your company seeks to segment and fragment the litigation of these cases nationwide. The courts of this country are burdened with more than 3,000 Dalkon Shield cases. The sheer number of claims and the dilatory tactics used by your company's attorneys clog court calendars and consume vast amounts of judicial and jury time. Your company settles those cases out of court in which it finds itself in an uncomfortable position, a handy device for avoiding any proceeding that would give continuity or cohesiveness to this nationwide problem. The decision as to which cases are brought to trial rests almost solely at the whim and discretion of the A.H. Robins Co. In order to guarantee that no plaintiff or group of plaintiffs mounts a sustained assault upon your system of evasion and avoidance, you have time after time demanded that, as the price of settling a case, able lawyers agree not to bring a Dalkon Shield case again and not to help less experienced lawyers with cases against your company.

Another of your callous legal tactics is to force women of little means to withstand the onslaughts of your well-financed team of attorneys. You target your worst tactics at the meek and the poor.

If this court had the authority, it would order your company to make an effort to locate each and every woman who still wears this device and recall your product. But this court does not. I must therefore resort to moral persuasion and a personal appeal to each of you. Mr. Robins, Mr. Forrest, and Dr. Lunsford: You are the people with the power to recall. You are the corporate conscience.

Please, in the name of humanity, lift your eyes above the bottom line. You, the men in charge, must surely have hearts and souls and consciences.

Please, gentlemen, give consideration to tracing down the victims and sparing them the agony that will surely be theirs.

The immediate response of the Robins executives was to initiate legal proceedings to have Judge Lord censured. Lord was not censured, but his comments were stricken from the court record as having denied the defendant (A.H. Robins Co.) due process of law and fundamental fairness.

Glory Be to Wealth in the Highest

An excerpt from Shaw's **Major Barbara**

In his lifetime, playwright George Bernard Shaw (1856–1950) witnessed the blossoming of capitalism into the mightiest engine of wealth creation that man has ever known. Yet in the midst of unprecedented plenty there was also widespread abject poverty among those who could not, or would not, adjust to the new economic system. Soon after the turn of the century, Shaw, an ardent socialist, was deeply troubled by this emerging contradiction. Attempting in his uniquely irreverent style to reconcile the presence of so many beggars at the banquet, Shaw wrote the fatalistic *Major Barbara* (1905) in which he argues that it is proper — and inevitable — that people submit themselves to the evil of unprincipled business pursuits rather than to the only apparent alternative — namely, the greater evil of poverty. For all its intended Swiftian logic and malevolence, the spirit of the passages was heartily embraced by businesspeople and society as a whole at least until the Great Depression. Indeed, vestiges of the conviction stated here that laissez faire has great utility as a social tonic have yet to fade entirely from view.

In the preface to the 1907 edition of *Major Barbara*, Shaw explains how his contempt for poverty and its causes is so great that even a man engaged in manufacturing instruments of death — his heroic character, the arms merchant Andrew Undershaft — is to be considered as having a superior morality to the other players. Certainly his moral outlook is more clear-eyed than that of Barbara, a newly minted major in the Salvation Army — whose ineffective do-goodism, Shaws thinks, actually *institutionalizes* poverty and casts it in a false, sickly glow of noble humility and virtue.

"Security, the chief pretence of civilization, cannot exist where the worst of the dangers, the danger of poverty, hangs over everyone's head, and where the alleged protection of our persons from violence is only an accidental result of the existence of a police force whose real business is to force the poor man to see his children starve whilst idle people overfeed pet dogs with the money that might feed and clothe them," Shaw writes. "Undershaft, the hero of *Major Barbara,* is simply a man who having grasped the fact that poverty is a crime, knows that when society offered him the alternative of poverty or a lucrative trade in death and destruction, it offered him, not a choice between opulent villainy and humble virtue, but between energetic enterprise and cowardly infamy."

Exerpt from Act III:

CUSINS: Do you call poverty a crime?

UNDERSHAFT: The worst of crimes. All the other crimes are virtues beside it: all the other dishonors are chivalry itself by comparison. Poverty blights whole cities; spreads horrible pestilences; strikes dead the very souls of all who come within sight, sound or smell of it. What *you* call crime is nothing: a murder here and a theft there, a blow now and a curse then: what do they matter? They are only the accidents and illnesses of life: there are not fifty genuine professional criminals in London. But here are millions of poor people, abject people, dirty people, ill fed, ill clothed people. They poison us morally and physically: they kill the happiness of society: they force us to do away with our own liberties and to organize unnatural cruelties for fear they should rise against us and drag us down into their abyss. Only fools fear crime: we all fear poverty . . . . I had the strongest scruples about poverty and starvation. Your moralists are quite unscrupulous about both: they make virtues of them. I had rather be a thief than a pauper. I had rather be a murderer than a slave.

Dark Legacy

An excerpt from Upton Sinclair's **The Jungle**

The Jungle, published in 1906, is a novel. Yet, so compelling was this realistic study of social conditions among immigrant workers in the Chicago stockyards that the young Winston Churchill concluded that the book "disturbed . . . the digestions and perhaps the consciences of mankind". The public outcry that was sparked by Sinclair's description of the casual morality of turn-of-the-century capitalism — and its consequences — hastened the passage in Congress of the Pure Food and Drug Act of 1906.

The following is an excerpt from *The Jungle*.

There was never any inspection of meat at all after it left the killing-floor save by the packers themselves, and with meat intended for export. Jurgis asked why this was, and the men told him that there were some foreign countries in which the laws were enforced. For this reason all the best meat was sent abroad — it was impossible to get it in this country, not even the richest hotels and clubs could get it. The good went to France and England, and the very best to Germany, which was apparently the one country there was no deceiving. Germany had caused the packers no end of trouble — for which, with characteristic ingenuity, they had recouped themselves by putting out imitations of German meat for home markets! The great Anderson printing-plant made labels by the tens and hundreds of thousands, French, German, Italian, and what not; one of the men had some of them in his pocket and showed a whole set, for smoked and canned meats, labelled in brilliant colors: "August Bauer, Frankfurt am Main."

Jurgis heard of these things little by little, in the gossip of those who were obliged to perpetrate them. Every time you met a person from a new department, you heard of new swindles and new crimes. There was, for instance, a Lithuanian who was a cattle-butcher for the plant where Marija had worked, which killed meat for canning only; and to hear this man describe the animals which came to his killing-floor would have been worthwhile for a Dante or a Zola. It seemed that they must have agencies all over the country, to hunt out old and crippled and diseased cattle to be canned. On the prairies nearby, for instance, were hundreds of farms which supplied the city with milk; and all the cows that developed lumpy jaw, or fell sick, or dried up of old age — they kept them till they had a carload, which was twenty, and then shipped them to his place to be canned. Here came also cattle which had been fed on "whiskey-malt," the refuse of the breweries, and had become what the men called "steerly" — which means covered with boils that were full of matter. It was a nasty job killing these, for when you plunged your knife into them they would burst and splash foul-smelling stuff into your face; and when a man's sleeves were smeared with blood, and his hands steeped in it, how was he ever to wipe his face, or to clear his eyes so that he could see? It was enough to make anybody sick, to think people had to eat such meat as this; but they must be eating it — for the canners were going on preparing it, year after year! . . . No doubt it was stuff such as this that made the "embalmed beef" that had killed several times as many United States soldiers as all the bullets of the Spaniards; only the army beef, besides, was not freshly canned, it was old stuff that had been lying for years in the cellars . . . .

There is another interesting set of statistics that one might gather as his acquaintance broadened in Packington, and that is the afflictions of the workers. When Jurgis had first inspected the packing-plants with Szedvilas, he had marveled while he listened to the tale of all the things that were made out of the carcasses of animals, and of all the lesser industries that were maintained there; now he found that each one of these lesser industries was a separate little inferno, in its way as horrible as the killing-floor, the source and foundation of them all. The workers in each of them had their own peculiar diseases; and the wandering visitor might be skeptical about all the swindles, but he could not be skeptical about these, for the worker bore the evidence of them about on his own person — generally he had only to hold out his hand.

There were the men in the pickle-rooms, for instance, where old Antanas had gotten his death; scarce a one of these had not some spot of horror on his person. Let a man so much as scrape his finger pushing a truck in the pickle-rooms, and like as not he would have a sore that would put him out of the world; all the joints in this finger might be eaten by the acid, one by one.

Of the butchers and floormen, the beef-boners and trimmers, and all those who used knives, you could scarcely find a person who had the use of his thumb; time and time again the base of it had been slashed, till it was a mere lump of flesh against which the man pressed the knife to hold it. The hands of these men would be criss-crossed with cuts, until you could no longer pretend to count them or to trace them. They would have no nails — they had worn off pulling hides; their knuckles were swollen so that their fingers spread out like a fan. There were men who worked in the cooking-rooms, in the midst of steam and sickening odors, by artificial light; in these rooms the germs of tuberculosis might live for two years, but the supply is renewed every hour. There were the beef luggers, who carried two-hundred-pound quarters into the refrigerator-cars; this was a fearful kind of work, that began at four o'clock in the morning, and that wore out the most powerful men in a few years. There were those who worked in the chilling-rooms, and whose special disease was rheumatism; the time-limit that a man could work in the chilling-rooms was said to be five years. There were the wool-pluckers, whose hands went to pieces even sooner than the hands of the pickle-men; for the pelts of the sheep had to be painted with acid to loosen the wool, and then the pluckers had to pull out this wool with their bare hands, til the acid had eaten their fingers off. There were those who made the tins for the canned-meat; and their hands, too, were a maze of cuts, and any cut might cause blood-poisoning; some worked at the stamping machines, and it was very seldom that one could work long at these at the pace that was set, and not give out and forget himself, and have a part of his hand chopped off. There were the "hoisters," as they were called, whose task it was to press the lever which lifted the dead cattle off the floor. They ran along upon a rafter, peering down through the damp and the steam. Old man Anderson's architects had not built the killing-room for the convenience of the hoisters, and so every few feet they would have to stoop under a beam, say four feet above the one they ran on; this got them in the habit of stooping, so that in a few years they would be walking like chimpanzees. No man who worked as a hoister had ever been known to reach the age of fifty years. Worst of any, however, were the fertilizer-men and those who served in

the rendering rooms. These could not be shown to the visitor
— for the odor of the fertilizer-men would scare any ordinary
visitor at a hundred yards, and as for the other men, who
worked in tank-rooms full of steam, and in which there were
open vats upon the level of the floor, their peculiar trouble was
that they fell into the vats; and when they were fished out,
there was never enough of them left to be worth exhibiting.
Sometimes they would be overlooked for days, till all but the
bones of them had gone out to the world as Anderson's Pure
Leaf Lard!

Why Charity Should Begin at Home

B.C. Forbes on the travesty of hollow corporate goodwill
Forbes, which claims to have more millionaires among its readers
than any other magazine in America, first appeared in 1917, the
same year Lenin's communists seized power in Russia. The
magazine has always enjoyed playing up this coincidence; and
the smart-alecky sobriquet it has long employed, "Capitalist
Tool", shows how strong was founding editor B.C. Forbes's belief
that capitalism would prevail over communism as the dominant
economic and political system in the world.

Still, Forbes had serious misgivings about the inherent motives
and morals of capitalists, which he expressed in his first, remarkably prescient, editorial in the magazine's premier issue:

> Business was originated to produce happiness, not to pile up
> millions.
>
> Are we in danger of forgetting this?
>
> Too often in talking with so-called "successful" men I cannot
> but feel that they are making business an end aim in itself, that
> they regard the multiplying of their millions and the extension
> of their works as the be-all and end-all of life, life itself.
>
> Such men are sometimes happy in a feverish hustling sort of
> way, much as a fly placed in a tube of oxygen is furiously
> happy until its life burns out.
>
> But they have no time for the tranquil, finer, deeper joys of
> living. They are so obsessed with the material that they cannot
> enjoy the immaterial, the intangible, the ideal, the spiritual
> — quiet thought, self-communion, reflection, poise, inward

happiness, domestic felicity, an evening of conversation on the things that do not pass, sober self-analysis conducive to unselfish human service.

What profiteth it a man to gain uncounted riches if he thereby sacrifices his better self, his nobler qualities of manhood?

Mere getting is not living.

The man who depends upon his bank account to insure him a happy life reaps disappointment.

Success is, or should be, the ambition of each one of us.

But success need not necessarily be measured by dollars.

To the painter, success is to be acclaimed justly as a great artist. To the author, success is to be recognized as a great writer, a truthful interpreter of human nature.

To the business man, success heretofore too often has been merely to become rich.

That is not a high standard. It is a standard, happily, that is passing. I find as the years pass that more and more men of achievement and wealth are becoming increasingly concerned over their reputation, over the regard in which they are held by their fellowmen. They are more anxious to enhance their standing in public opinion than in Bradstreet's.

It's a healthy sign, a gratifying sign.

The trouble is, however, that this solicitude for the public's esteem very often comes only after a life of wholly self-centered, selfish, grasping endeavor, a life based on the devil-take-the-hindmost plane.

Take, by way of illustration, Bernard M. Baruch — and I cite his case solely because it is the latest conspicuous one.

He was all his life a stock market plunger. His creed may be deduced from the officially ferreted out fact that on a recent occasion when everything outside the United States was atremble, when men and business everywhere were fearful lest panic were to break loose, when international as well as national conditions were in parlous state, when President Wilson and the whole Government were beset with fate-laden perplexities — at such a critical moment in the nation's history this plunger jumped into the financial arena and began to pound and pound the pillars of the republic, for the more panicky he could make things the greater would be his profit — in dollars.

Some of his friends—and he has many staunch ones—have since sought to argue that he rendered a public service by puncturing an overinflated stock market; but Baruch's own testimony makes this claim ridiculous, for when asked what he would have done on a certain date if he had known the market was going to break the next day, he frankly replied, "I would have sold all day long."

His ill-timed activities netted him—he was dragged to the witness stand and had to confess it—no less than $476,168.47. This was several times the reported amount of his generous contributions to the Wilson presidential campaign.

Now, while short selling is perfectly legitimate and ought not to be stopped by law, as is sometimes threatened, that was not a patriotic thing to do at such a grave juncture. For a man of Baruch's professions of public-spiritedness, it was condemnable.

He would probably give half of all he possesses to undo that act, to blot it out of the record.

The idea of entrusting Bernard M. Baruch, a man utterly without constructive industrial experience, perhaps the most gigantic business task of the whole war, namely, headship of the purchase of ten or twelve billion dollars of war materials for the United States, England and France—such action passes comprehension, save, of course, on the basis of repaying political favors. No huge corporation would have dreamed of selecting such a man for such a task.

Barney Baruch, I am told, is a shining example of the type here being discussed, men engrossed in moneymaking on the devil-take-the-hindmost principle—or lack of principle—during the greater part of their lives but who "reform" and pine to become somebodies, figures of national prominence, accepted as public spirited, altruistic citizens, examples fit to be held up to the youth of the land.

Too few millionaires who aspire to win fame as philanthropists begin at home, among their own workers.

To grind employees and then donate a million dollars to perpetuate his name is not a particularly laudable record for any man to live or leave behind him. Of course, it is more spectacular, it makes more of a splash to do the grandiose act in sight of all men, where it will be read and talked of.

But it is rather a pitiable form of philanthropy.

I have often veered the conversation round to this subject when talking with very large employers and have cited what others were doing. Some have squirmed. Others have referred sarcastically to the efforts of other employers, who have worked wonders in looking after the health, happiness and well-being of their employees — as if a sneer would cover up their own deficiencies.

This subject of treating workers as human beings, as fellow-citizens, as co-equals is destined to come up after the war in a larger more forcible way than ever before.

Individuals like George Eastman and John N. Patterson, both employing thousands of men, who take deep personal interest in the happiness of their workers and spend money freely in furtherance of it, will by and by come into their own.

So, too, shall slave-driving corporations and individuals.

Latter-Day Saints

The Moral Transformation of the Rockefellers

The Rockefeller family exemplifies the family-business dynasty in transition. Paterfamilias John Davison Rockefeller rose from the humble station of bookkeeper at the age of sixteen to become, by the time of his retirement from active management of his enterprises at age seventy-two, one of the greatest capitalists of the modern era. Yet while ruthless in driving competitors to the wall and bending the will of suppliers to his own, Rockefeller was remarkably generous in the latter decades of his life, donating about half of his estimated $1 billion fortune to charity — the largest sum ever donated by a single individual.

John D. Rockefeller Jr. succeeded his father as president of Standard Oil in 1911, but eventually relinquished his business positions and dedicated himself almost entirely to the supervision of the family's four charitable foundations, established by his father. Third-generation Rockefellers, notably Nelson and David, have devoted much, and in some cases, all of their lives to public service and charitable endeavours. Most of the eighty-three heirs in the current fourth, fifth, and sixth generations have little interest in business or, alas, in propelling the family's remarkable century-old mission of unparalleled philanthropy. To date, however, the benevolent legacy of this family whose origins are inextricably linked to the Robber Baron era already totals $1.5 billion in charitable gifts.

The Rockefeller Center, a sprawling complex of twenty-one office buildings in mid-town Manhattan built during the depths of the Depression and whose construction was overseen by John D. Rockefeller Jr., is a startling expression of confidence in capitalism during its darkest hour. Rockefeller Jr.'s personal credo, cast in bronze on a plaque that overlooks the Center's renowned skating rink, embodies most of the elements of contemporary American corporate values. Its sententiousness is forgivable considering the strained circumstances of the Depression; indeed, Rockefeller's measured juxtaposition of traditional and progressive sentiments is an accurate reflection of the values that comprise most businesspeople's notion of corporate social responsibility even today:

> I BELIEVE in the supreme worth of the individual and in his right to life, liberty and the pursuit of happiness.
>
> I BELIEVE
> that every right implies a responsibility, every opportunity, an obligation, every possession, a duty.
>
> I BELIEVE
> that the law was made for man and not man for the law, that government is the servant of the people, and not their master.
>
> I BELIEVE
> in the dignity of labor, whether with head or hand, that the world owes no man a living, but that it owes every man the opportunity to make a living.
>
> I BELIEVE
> that thrift is essential to well-ordered living and that economy is a prime requisite of a sound financial structure, whether in government, business or personal affairs.
>
> I BELIEVE
> in the sacredness of a promise, that a man's word should be as good as his bond, that character not wealth or power or position is of supreme worth.

I BELIEVE

that the rendering of useful service is the common duty of mankind, and that only in the purveying fire of sacrifice is the dross of selfishness consumed and the greatness of the human soul set free.

I BELIEVE

in an all-wise and all-loving god, named by whatever name, and that the individual's high fulfillment, greatest happiness, and widest usefulness are to be found in living in harmony with His will.

I BELIEVE

that love is the greatest thing in the world, that it alone can overcome hatred, that right can and will triumph over might.
— John D. Rockefeller Jr.

To Thine Own Self-Interest Be True

Milton Friedman explains why business should mind its own business

About two decades ago, prominent economist Milton Friedman, a professor at the University of Chicago, became a self-professed prophet warning his business followers not to stray from the narrow path of the bottom line. As the issue of corporate social responsibility has gained momentum in recent years, Friedman's adherents and detractors alike have been trotting out his earliest writings on the subject, citing them either as articles of wisdom or as objects of scorn. The following excerpt is from Friedman's "The Social Responsibility of Business is to Increase Its Profits", an article that appeared in the September 13, 1970 issue of *The New York Times Magazine*:

> When I hear businessmen speak eloquently about the "social responsibilities of business in a free-enterprise system," I am reminded of the wonderful line about the Frenchman who discovered at the age of 70 that he had been speaking prose all his life. The businessmen believe that they are defending free enterprise when they declaim that business is not concerned "merely" with profit but also with promoting desirable "social" ends; that business has a "social conscience" and takes seriously its responsibilities for providing employment, eliminating

discrimination, avoiding pollution and whatever else may be the catchwords of the contemporary crop of reformers. In fact they are — or would be if they or anyone else took them seriously — preaching pure and unadulterated socialism. Businessmen who talk this way are unwitting puppets of the intellectual forces that have been undermining the basis of free society these past decades . . . .

What does it mean to say that the corporate executive has a "social responsibility" in his capacity as a businessman? If this statement is not pure rhetoric, it must mean that he is to act in some way that is not in the interest of his employers. For example, that he is to refrain from increasing the price of the product in order to contribute to the social objective of preventing inflation, even though a price increase would be in the best interests of the corporation. Or that he is to make expenditures on reducing pollution beyond the amount that is in the best interests of the corporation or that is required by law in order to contribute to the social objective of improving the environment. Or that, at the expense of corporate profits, he is to hire "hard-core" unemployed instead of better-qualified available workmen to contribute to the social objective of reducing poverty.

In each of these cases, the corporate executive would be spending someone else's money for a general social interest. Insofar as his actions in accord with his "social responsibility" reduce returns to stockholders, he is spending their money. Insofar as his actions raise the price to customers, he is spending the customers' money. Insofar as his actions lower the wages of some employees, he is spending their money. . . . If he does this, he is in effect imposing taxes, on the one hand, and deciding how the tax proceeds shall be spent, on the other . . . .

The short-sightedness is also exemplified in speeches by businessmen on social responsibility. This may gain them kudos in the short run. But it helps to strengthen the already too prevalent view that the pursuit of profits is wicked and immoral and must be curbed and controlled by external forces. Once this view is adopted, the external forces that curb the market will not be the social consciences, however highly developed, of the pontificating executives; it will be the iron fist of Government bureaucrats. Here, as with the price and wage controls, businessmen seem to me to reveal a suicidal impulse.

Be It Resolved: What's Ours Is Ours

At Exxon, a shareholder and the company tangle over charity
Among the resolutions received by shareholders of Exxon Corp. of New York, the world's largest oil company, in 1987 was this one, submitted by Evelyn Y. Davis:

> *Resolved*: That the shareholders recommend that the Board take the steps necessary to amend the Corporation's Certificate of Incorporation by adding thereto: 'No corporate funds of this Corporation shall be given to any charitable, educational or other similar organization, except for purposes in direct furtherance of the business interests of this Corporation and subject to the further provision that aggregate amount of such contributions shall be reported to the shareholders not later than the date of the annual meeting.'

> *Reasons*: Over the years your Company has given away millions of dollars of your money to charitable and educational institutions, money which belongs to you.

> Last year the total amount was $58 million.

> Last year the owners of 21.3 million shares voted FOR this proposal.

If you AGREE, please mark your proxy FOR this resolution.

This resolution, which appeared in Exxon's 1987 Notice of Annual Meeting and Proxy Statement, was followed by this advice to shareholders by Exxon management:

BOARD OF DIRECTORS RECOMMENDATION —
The Board recommends a vote AGAINST this proposal.

The vitality of the society in which the Corporation operates is directly relevant to its business interests. By supporting education, health care, civic and community services, the environment, and the arts, Exxon contributes not just to the needs of the communities in which it operates, but to its own success and future as well. The Board, therefore, believes these contributions benefit the Corporation and should continue to be made. The effect of the proposal would be to restrict significantly the ability of the Corporation and its managment to play its appropriate role in this area.

The grants the Corporation makes are carefully documented and information about them is made available to shareholders and others in annually published material.

A similar proposal was presented at Exxon's 1961, 1962, 1977, 1979, 1980, and 1986 annual meetings. In each of these cases, shareholders overwhelmingly rejected the proposal and supported the position that grants to charitable and educational institutions are in the Corporation's and shareholders' interest.

Exxon's contributions program is carried out within monetary levels and objectives established and regularly reviewed by the Board. The Board Advisory Committee on Contributions assists the Board in such reviews.

The Board of Directors remains convinced that Exxon's contributions policy is both responsible and in the shareholders' interest.
Accordingly, a vote AGAINST this proposal is recommended.

At Exxon's annual meeting on May 21, 1987, the proposal was defeated.

Social dividends

Corporate Good Samaritans discover the payoff is more than psychic
Continental Bank of Canada was the least deserving victim of the mid-1980s crisis of confidence in financial services institutions. Among the dozen or so banks and trusts in Canada that collapsed or were merged out of existence during that time, Continental was arguably the best managed. Despite its conservative lending policies, however, Continental was lumped in with other small financial institutions that had lent injudiciously to the oil patch and other recession-ravaged industrial sectors, and was deserted by institutional investors who feared it too would succumb as the Canadian Commercial Bank and the Northland Bank had in the fall of 1985. With no prospect of reviving its anemic deposit base, Continental sought refuge in a merger with a much larger institution, and survives today as the Canadian division of London, England-based Lloyds Bank.
Ironically, while Continental's small size relative to the Big Six

banks in Canada prompted the massive withdrawal of deposits that did it in, the bank's diminutive stature had in earlier, happier days made it one of the industry's most innovative players. This was especially apparent in the field of corporate philanthropy. Having a far smaller ad budget than its Big Six rivals, Continental sought in the early 1980s to distinguish itself from the rest of the pack by using a large portion of its charitable expenditures as a marketing device. In a twenty-one-page essay in its 1984 annual report, Continental argued convincingly that philanthropic activities, cleverly planned and executed, could bolster the bottom line *and* do society some good. The essay, entitled "The Corporate Gift Horse", accurately predicts the current trend towards marketing-oriented corporate giving, and is considered a seminal work by philanthropic professionals, whether they be benefactors or supplicants. The following is an excerpt from the essay:

At first glance, the timing seems incongruous. Across North America businesses have been cautiously emerging from the depths of a recession that has tightened corporate belts, slashed frills, curtailed payrolls and postponed expansion plans to more promising times. In the midst of this austerity, corporate treasurers have been scrutinizing all expenditures, including philanthropic activities, cultural sponsorships and other areas of community involvement; and at some very highly regarded companies they have reached a most unexpected conclusion.

Far from the unrequited drain on earnings that many have always assumed them to be, in companies where they have been strategically managed, philanthropic programs are paying their way through good times and bad. Activities once dismissed as unavoidable corporate obligations or a cost of doing business are now being tailored to meet specific company goals and are even having an impact on day-to-day sales. Applying the same discipline to the management of the corporate gift that is applied to other forms of spending is now producing a measurable benefit to the donor as well as the recipient . . . .

As a company that is active in all major cities across Canada, Continental Bank follows the debate on corporate support with keen interest. Like all banks, we recognize the value of maintaining a strong presence in the communities in which we do business. Our underlying motives are, frankly, rooted as much in good business as good will. Personal contacts help in generating new accounts and recruiting new staff. That's why we encourage our people to get involved and, as you'll see from a few examples on the following pages, their after-work activities represent a remarkable range of interests.

But we are also actively exploring new, less orthodox, ways to advance the bank's development. Traditionally, companies have maintained two separate funds for supporting community activities. The first, the donations budget, is dispensed with little regard for measurable return; it supports hospitals, education, social agencies and the like. The second fund, the marketing budget, is usually many times larger and is spent strictly to promote the corporation. At Continental Bank we believe that the division between these two funds should not be as sharply defined as in the past; that philanthropy does not always have to be totally altruistic, and that marketing does not always have to be a mechanistic process of placing commercial messages before the public.

There will always be a portion of each philanthropic dollar dedicated to those worthy causes whose nature makes commercial exploitation inappropriate. But as many other companies are now discovering, that leaves the lion's share available for other things, and in these areas we consciously work to achieve a level of recognition that will help us meet specific goals in no uncertain terms.

Our experience confirms that corporate philanthropy, efficiently and imaginatively administered, can be a powerful ally to other efforts in marketing, corporate relations and human resources. It is also a boon to the arts and social agencies who are desperate for support . . . .

Enlightened philanthropy can play a significant role in corporate development. Many companies now find that, relative to conventional advertising programs, community commitment—whether it's John Deere's hiring of the baritione Guillermo Silva-Marin to sing in its employee cafeteria and in neighbouring schools, or Noranda Mines' sending L'Orchestre Symphonique de Québec into the community halls of distant northern villages—can work as an effective marketing vehicle, one with the power to reach predetermined audiences with pinpoint accuracy. Many will not be surprised to discover that, for the time being at least, the corporate gift remains a very cost-effective vehicle.

Clarion Call

A CEO's plea for corporate social responsibility

No sooner had Control Data Corp. become a phenomenal success in the computer business shortly after its start-up in the 1950s than was CDC founder and chief executive William Norris promulgating a management strategy he calls "industrial statesmanship". Throughout the 1960s and 1970s, as CDC's business prospered, Norris funnelled a substantial portion of CDC profits into an extraordinary variety of social ventures designed to rehabilitate inner-city slums; train the chronically unemployed so that they could take their place in the workforce; and enhance the survival prospects of small business by granting it affordable access to state-of-the-art computer technology.

Unfortunately, by the mid-1980s, CDC's fortunes had faded; observers speculated whether the cause lay with the company's having simply lost its way in the fiercely competitive industry or with its having succumbed under the burden of its myriad do-good projects, most of which did not turn a profit. But even without a CDC financial comeback — which appears imminent at this writing — Norris, now seventy-five, has made his mark as a businessman whose unusually broad vision of business's role in society has inspired politicians, educators, community leaders, and other businesspeople.

In this excerpt from his 1983 book, *New Frontiers for Business Leadership*, Norris expounds on his notion of the social imperative for business:

> In the new business culture, corporate directors would foster innovation and leave it room to thrive. To assemble and effectively utilize the wide variety of resources required for major innovations, they would also institute policies to encourage cooperation.
>
> I have learned from experience that most executives do not at present think in these terms. To many, the idea of cooperation is anathema; they equate it with having to give away secrets or

relinquish some of their own power. They will need time to get used to the idea. A relatively easy first step might involve participating in at least a consortium engaged in urban revitalization or rural development. Membership would require a modest investment and entail a relatively small degree of risk, and the benefits would be substantial. To begin with, participation would generate sales leads for the company's own products, since both urban and rural renewal lead to increased economic activity over a wide front. And the company would be among the first to discover potential markets for new products and services, since a revitalization effort usually makes use of the most advanced existing and emerging technologies.

Participation in a consortium would yield indirect benefits as well. For one, top company executives would be exposed to the range of human problems that exist in poverty-stricken areas. The enormity of these problems is almost impossible to grasp unless one either experiences them or sees them with one's own eyes. We have all read or heard about the riots in Miami, Orlando, and Chattanooga; we all know about the persistent and shockingly high unemployment rates among disadvantaged youth; we are all cognizant of the mushrooming crime statistics and the fact that millions of people are living at or below the poverty line. Yet few of us have been personally affected by the problems and frustrations that go hand-in-hand with being poor. If we continue to ignore them, however, we will be affected sooner or later. Our silence will generate even greater social unrest and disorder. And the time will come when we, too, are touched by the devastating consequences of escalating crime rates and must fear for our own safety and security . . . .

We are at a crossroads: we can either choose to continue in our traditional mode of surveillance over the status quo, or we can provide the leadership needed to create a new business culture characterized by innovation and cooperation. We can sit back and wait and eventually find ourselves facing a hodgepodge of bureaucratically imposed national planning, or we can act like the industrial statesmen we are supposed to be. If we opt to behave as leaders, I am confident that together we will be able to revitalize American industry in an intelligent and democratic way.

Vows of Propriety

A selection of corporate good-conduct statements

J.C. Penney Co.   Codes of ethical conduct are a recent innovation at most of the companies that have them. Not so at this New York-based department store giant, where James Cash Penney and the firm's other co-founders framed "The Penney Idea" in 1913 — fifteen years after the company began operations:

The Penney Idea

To serve the public as nearly as we can to its complete satisfaction.

To expect for the service we render a fair remuneration, and not all the profit the traffic will bear.

To do all in our power to pack the customer's dollar full of value, quality and satisfaction.

To continue to train ourselves and our associates so that the service we give will be more and more intelligently performed.

To improve constantly the human factor in our business.

To reward the men and women in our organization through participation in what the business produces.

To test our every policy, method and act in this wise: "Does it square with what is right and just?"

Johnson & Johnson.   In the 1940s, long before the notion that corporations had multiple "stakeholders" besides the shareholders who owned the firm, Robert Wood Johnson first penned this health-care product company's avowed goal of respecting the interests of all of its constituencies, including employees, customers, and society as a whole. J&J, which is based in New Brunswick, N.J., has been guided by this statement (since updated) not only in goodwill efforts such as its leading role in revitalizing decaying districts of its hometown, but in the early 1980s crisis in which it promptly withdrew its single most important product, Tylenol, from the market after a still-unknown person (or persons) contaminated a batch of Tylenol tablets with cyanide.

Note the order of priority J&J accords each of its "stakeholders", which is exactly the reverse of conventional practice at many firms even today:

Our Credo

We believe our first responsibility is to the doctors, nurses and patients, to mothers and all others who use our products and services. In meeting their needs everything we do must be of high quality. We must constantly strive to reduce our costs in order to maintain reasonable prices. Customers' orders must be serviced promptly and accurately. Our suppliers and distributors must have an opportunity to make a fair profit.

We are responsible to our employees, the men and women who work with us throughout the world. Everyone must be considered as an individual. We must respect their dignity and recognize their merit. They must have a sense of security in their jobs. Compensation must be fair and adequate, and working conditions clean, orderly and safe. Employees must feel free to make suggestions and complaints. There must be equal opportunity for employment, development and advancement for those qualified. We must provide competent management, and their actions must be just and ethical.

We are responsible to the communities in which we live and work and to the world community as well.

We must be good citizens—support good works and charities and bear our fair share of taxes. We must encourage civic improvements and better health and education.

We must maintain in good order the property we are privileged to use, protecting the environment and natural resources.

Our final responsibility is to our stockholders. Business must make a sound profit. We must experiment with new ideas. Research must be carried on, innovative programs developed and mistakes paid for. New equipment must be purchased, new facilities provided and new products launched. Reserves must be created to provide for adverse times.

When we operate according to these principles, the stockholders should realize a fair return.

Conoco Inc. Formerly known as Continental Oil Co., this Stamford, Connecticut-based petroleum producer was an independent company until 1981, when it was acquired in a hostile takeover battle by E.I. du Pont de Nemours, which stepped into the bidding as a "white knight" to rescue Conoco. In 1976, Conoco published an in-house booklet on moral standards called *The Conoco Conscience*, which criticized the long-held belief that corporations have no souls and are thus not wholly responsible for their actions. What follows is an excerpt from the 1976 booklet:

> In the first part of the 17th century, Sir Edward Coke, one of Great Britain's most eminent jurists, concluded that a corporation was but an impersonal creation of the law — not a being, just a product of written rules and government fiat. But times have changed. Sir Edward could not have foreseen the results of the Industrial Revolution. He certainly did not foresee that 350 years after his pronouncements corporations would be the largest employers on earth, would generate the preponderance of the world's goods and services, and would be owned on a worldwide basis by millions of shareholders.
>
> Although it may be true that Conoco remains an inanimate being for legalistic purposes, the company has a very personal existence for its shareholders, employees, officers, and directors. The success or failure of Conoco affects most of them during their working lives, and may affect them during their retirement. And to the employees, officers, and directors, Conoco's reputation concerns their own reputation as well.
>
> No one can deny that in the public's mind a corporation can break the law and be guilty of unethical and amoral conduct. Events of the early 1970s, such as corporate violations of federal law and failure of full disclosure, confirmed that both our government and our citizenry expect *corporations* to act lawfully, ethically, and responsibly.
>
> Perhaps it is then appropriate in today's context to think of Conoco as a *living corporation*; a sentient being whose conduct and personality are the collective effort and responsibility of its employees, officers, directors, and shareholders . . . .

Imperial Oil Ltd. "Some time ago," Imperial Oil CEO Arden Haynes said in a January 1987 letter to employees, "a journalist asked me which of all the attributes of Imperial Oil Ltd. did I consider the most important. I replied that by far the most important was the ethical behavior of the company and all its employees.

"It still is.

"Our commitment to ethical behavior and integrity in all aspects of our business is the foundation of everything we have achieved in the past and stand for today. The Imperial Oil family of companies' high standard of ethics is among our most valued assets."

Haynes' letter to employees of Imperial, Canada's largest oil company, accompanied an updated edition of the firm's corporate-ethics booklet, which all Imperial employees are required to read and indicate, on an annual basis via a signed statement, that they understand and comply with. Following are two excerpts from the 1987 booklet, "Our Corporate Ethics":

Business ethics
(introduction)

It is the policy of the Imperial Oil family of companies to maintain the highest standard of ethics in relations with whomever it does business or is associated with — its employees, shareholders, customers, sales associates and suppliers, and with governments and the public. No one in the company, from the chief executive officer to the newest employee, is ever expected to commit an illegal or unethical act, or to instruct other employees to do so. Not in the name of business efficiency. Not to get results. Not for any reasons.

In addition to strict compliance with all the laws of Canada and those of other jurisdictions that apply to the company's business, the highest standards of integrity must be observed throughout the organization. These high standards require the accurate and open recording of all transactions, assets and liabilities on the company's books and records.

The company's reputation for ethical practices is one of its most valued assets. This reputation was achieved through the efforts of its employees and their avoidance of any activity or interest that might reflect unfavorably upon their own or the company's integrity or good name.

Employees

This company cares about how it gets results. And, because everything it does is a result of the decisions and activities of its employees, the company expects them to comply with its high standard of integrity in carrying out their day-to-day business transactions. At the same time, the company is committed to applying those same high standards in all of its relationships with its employees.

First of all, the company strives to maintain equality of opportunity for the employment, development and advancement of its employees. It compensates them through wages, salaries and benefits that are competitive with leading companies in its areas of business. It is committed to maintaining a safe working environment for its employees, and to communicating with them on matters that affect them.

Throughout the company, employees can be assured of regular performance evaluations with open discussions of appraisals that are based on reasonable standards for measuring the achievement of work objectives. The company strives to consider personal needs, values and aspirations of employees in plans for individual development. It maintains accurate employee records and safeguards their privacy.

The company seeks also to encourage and support employees in the development of their skills and abilities to meet the company's future needs for experienced people and to make the best of each employee's capabilities.

Finally, the company is committed to the policy that people will not be unlawfully discriminated against or harassed, on the basis of race, religion, creed, color, sex, marital or family status, sexual orientation, age, national or ethnic origin, ancestry, place of origin, political belief or handicap.

Royal Bank of Canada. The Royal, Canada's largest financial institution, distributes the following statement of "Purposes and Responsibilities" to all employees:

The Royal Bank of Canada has as its overall purpose to ensure survival as a progressive free enterprise, and continuity through short- and long-term profitability so that we may fulfill our responsibilities in society.

These responsibilities are to:

Provide potential and existing clients, throughout the world, with the broadest possible range and highest quality of banking and financial services;

Provide employees with opportunities for personal development and achievement, and equitable compensation;

Provide investors with an attractive and continuing return on their capital;

Act as a responsible corporate citizen, whose activities benefit the community, nation and society.

To attain this purpose and to meet these responsibilities, the bank considers it must:

Give good value—contributing rather than exploiting;

Deal with people and institutions fairly and honestly;

Recognize and respect each person's rights, individuality and human dignity;

Be a responsible citizen;

Be a leader, unceasingly striving for excellence in everything we do.

Dear Employees: We'll All Sink or Swim Together

A beleaguered CEO's call to moral arms

In mid-1986, Fred Joseph assumed the role of a moral fire-fighter. As CEO of Drexel Burnham Lambert Inc., Joseph had been privileged, until just a few months earlier, to preside over one of the most successful firms in Wall Street history. But with the arrest of a senior Drexel executive, Dennis Levine, in the spring of 1986—and the widespread expectation that the federal probe into insider trading that had caught up with Levine would touch other Drexel employees—Joseph suddenly found that his firm's vaunted reputation was slipping down the drain. For two weeks, Joseph agonized over the wording of a memo to his eight thousand employees, intended both to restore some sense of morale within the firm and assure outsiders that Drexel was not rotten at the core. As it happened, the memo's impact was diminished in the months that followed its distribution, particularly after the November revelation that leading Wall Street investor—and Drexel client—Ivan Boesky had confessed to illegal insider-trading activities. In light of the accurate prediction at the time of Levine's capture that Drexel would be in for a firestorm of bad publicity and client defections as several of its top traders were hauled away by lawmen, Joseph's memo from the late spring is poignant testimony to the consequences of unethical conduct, even if only on the part of a few rogue individuals:

MEMO TO ALL EMPLOYEES
FROM: FRED JOSEPH

During the past few weeks, several lawyers and Wall Street professionals, including three former Drexel Burnham professionals, have been accused, in separate incidents, of breaking the law or violating the standards of integrity in the conduct of a business traditionally based on trust and honor. For some reason these people placed in jeopardy — and may have destroyed — their reputations, careers and personal financial condition. Today they face possible jail sentences. Those of us in our firm, who have observed the standards and rules of the business, have opportunities that are exceptional. To squander these opportunities is incredibly foolish.

Because the integrity, *and* the *perceived* integrity, of our markets and our firm is the jugular vein of our business, we have never and must never tolerate any violations of the law or of the firm's and industry's rules. Indeed, even activities that are simply too close to the line and fail our "smell" test must be rejected as unacceptable. This has been, of course, our historic attitude and it served us well. Now, we will redouble our vigilance and efforts. For example, over the past year, we have utilized independent outside counsel and other special investigative consultants to help us strengthen our operating procedures and security measures. We are pursuing this vigorously and, while this intensification may be inconvenient, we know you will understand and cooperate. This effort will be a very serious priority for our senior management team. Please contact any senior officer if you have any information, thoughts, or suggestions, which you think might be helpful.

We can all take some comfort from the fact that our firm has not been accused of any wrongdoing. We have been the fastest growing and among the most successful firms in the history of our business by working hard and performing effectively for our clients. Now is the time for each of us to rededicate ourselves to those values on which we've built Drexel Burnham and concentrate all of our energies and resources on serving our clients' requirements.

FHJ:M   Fred Joseph

APPENDIX II
THE CORPORATE ETHICS
NETWORK

The following investment funds, advisory groups, and information agencies are all engaged in advancing the cause of corporate social responsibility.

Canada

ETHICAL MUTUAL FUNDS AVAILABLE TO THE PUBLIC
(write or call for a prospectus)

Ethical Growth Fund
Administered by VanCity Investment Services Ltd.
515 West 10th Ave.
Vancouver, B.C.
V5Z 4A8
(604) 873-0341

Launched in February 1986, this is the oldest ethical mutual fund in Canada. It was created by the 160,000-member Vancouver City Savings Credit Union, Canada's largest credit union. The Ethical Growth Fund is available in British Columbia at all VanCity branches, and elsewhere in Canada through stockbrokers and other investment advisors.

Summa Fund
Administered by Investors Group Inc.
280 Broadway
Winnipeg, Man.
R3C 3B6
(204) 943-0361

The Summa Fund was first offered to Canadian investors in early 1987 by the Investors Group, Canada's largest mutual fund vendor. Within a few weeks of its appearance, the Summa Fund had attracted seven thousand investors and $15 million in assets.

Environmental Investment Fund — Canada;
Environmental Investment Fund — Global
100 College St.
Toronto, Ont.
M5G 1O5
(416) 978-4397

These two funds, first offered in the spring of 1987, are an out-growth of a private investment club set up by thirty or so members and volunteers of Energy Probe, a non-profit research organization affiliated with Pollution Probe. The Canada fund invests strictly in Canada securities; the Global fund invests in securities throughout the world. Both funds restrict their investments to companies that exhibit a tangible respect for environmental and other social issues.

ETHICAL PENSION FUNDS

C.E.D.A.R. **Balanced Fund**
C.E.D.A.R. Investment Services Ltd.
Ste. 1, 10005-80th Avenue
Edmonton, Alta.
T6E 1T4
(403) 433-3413

The C.E.D.A.R. (Canadian Ethical Dynamic and Responsible) Fund is the first mutual fund in Canada designed specifically to encourage pension funds and other non-taxable organizations to invest according to socially responsible criteria.

Crown Commitment Fund
Administered by Crown Life Insurance Co.
120 Bloor St. E.
Toronto, Ont.
M4W 1B8
(416) 928-5722

The Commitment fund, introduced in the fall of 1986, was the first national ethical fund in Canada, and is offered by Crown Life, one of Canada's largest life insurers. The fund invests pension-plan and group-RRSP monies in the stock of companies deemed to be socially responsible.

ALTERNATIVE INVESTING
Canadian Alternative Investment Cooperative (CAIC)
P.O. Box 160
Postal Stn. V
Toronto, Ont.
M6R 3A5

Launched in November 1985 by a group of religious orders, CAIC offers four alternative investment funds to associations registered as charities. Non-religious organizations are also welcome to participate. By early 1987, nearly forty charitable organizations had invested a total of $2 million through CAIC, which has so far earned a respectable return on its investments in urban-renewal projects, non-profit housing, group homes, co-op business enterprises, and projects for the economically disadvantaged.

INFORMATION AND ADVOCACY ORGANIZATIONS
Canadian Network for Ethical Investment (CNEI)
Box 1615
Victoria, B.C.
V8W 2X7
(604) 381-5942

The CNEI, established in December 1985 by a group of socially concerned citizens led by stockbroker Larry Trunkey, is a non-profit organization that serves as a forum for those interested in monitoring and enhancing the ethical conduct of Canadian businesses. It publishes a newsletter that reports on trends in corporate social responsibility, and is loosely affiliated with the Social Investment Forum, a large Boston-based clearinghouse for data on socially responsible investing.

EthicScan Canada Ltd.
and the
Canadian Clearinghouse for Consumer and Corporate Ethics
P.O. Box 165
Postal Stn. S
Toronto, Ont. M5M 4L7
(416) 783-6776

Established in the spring of 1987, EthicScan and its sister ethics organization Clearinghouse are building a database on corporate ethical conduct in Canada. The data, in turn, will be the foundation of a for-profit business in ethical newsletters, consulting services, and seminars.

Canadian Social Investment Study Group (csisg)
Ste. 712
151 Slater St.
Ottawa, Ont.
K1P 5H3
(613) 230-5221

This non-profit research organization, created in 1985 by consultant Ted Jackson, examines the impact of socially responsible investing. csisg serves as a network for investors and brokers interested in ethical investing, and for people setting up ethical mutual funds and alternative investment schemes.

Taskforce on the Churches and Corporate Responsibility
129 St. Clair Ave. W.
Toronto, Ont.
M4V 1N5
(416) 923-1758

This national ecumenical coalition of major Christian churches in Canada, established in 1975, assists members and outside groups in implementing socially responsible investing goals. It has been a leader in agitating for corporate social reform. The Taskforce often makes headlines with its shareholder resolutions and public criticisms of corporate executives at annual meetings, but more often secures effective changes in corporate policies by working peaceably with executives behind the scenes.

Project Ploughshares
Conrad Grebel College
Waterloo, Ont.
N2L 3G6
(519) 888-6541

This church-sponsored advocacy group conducts research into the problems of disarmament and Third World underdevelopment. Ploughshares has a large and varied following among church groups, development agencies, and private individuals, and now is a consultant on corporate-ethics issues to groups advocating corporate social responsibility.

United States

ETHICAL MUTUAL FUNDS AVAILABLE TO THE PUBLIC
Dreyfus Third Century Fund
600 Madison Ave.
New York, N.Y. 10022
(212) 895-1206

Dreyfus is the largest and one of the oldest equity funds designed specifically to invest in socially responsible firms. In early 1987, it had assets of US$153.5 million.

Calvert Social Investment Fund
1700 Pennsylvania Ave. N.W.
Washington, D.C. 20006
(301) 951-4800

Calvert operates a socially responsible equity fund (assets in early 1987: US$121.5 million) and a sister money-market fund (assets: US$59.8 million).

Working Assets Money Fund
230 California St.
San Francisco, Ca. 94111
(415) 989-3200

Working Assets is a money-market fund with assets in early 1987 of US$96.6 million. In 1986, it began offering a "socially responsive" charge card, which pledges 5 cents to peace, hunger, and environmental groups with each use of the card.

Pax World Fund
224 State St.
Portsmouth, N.H. 03801
(603) 431-8022

Pax, one of the oldest ethical funds, invests heavily in both stocks and bonds, and had assets in early 1987 of US$53.8 million.

New Alternatives Fund Inc.
295 Northern Blvd.
Great Neck, N.Y. 11021
(516) 466-0808

This fund, founded in 1982, concentrates on investments in companies engaged in alternative energy, such as production of solar cells and operation of conservation systems, resource recovery plants, and co-generation facilities. New Alternatives avoids investments in nuclear energy, petroleum, atomic warfare material, and South Africa.

The Parnassus Fund
1427 Shrader St.
San Francisco, Ca. 94117
(415) 664-6812

Founded in 1984, The Parnassus Fund follows a "contrarian" policy of investing in stocks that are out of favour with the investment community but possess hidden growth potential. The fund also assesses companies on the basis of five "Renaissance Factors" the companies to be invested in should: (a) provide products and services of a high quality, (b) be market-oriented and stay close to their customers, (c) be sensitive to communities in which they operate, (d) treat their employees well, and (e) innovate and be responsive to change.

INFORMATION AND ADVOCACY ORGANIZATIONS
Council on Economic Priorities
30 Irving Place
New York, N.Y. 10003
(212) 420-1133

A leading and highly respected player in the corporate social-responsibility field, CEP was founded in 1969 by Alice Tepper Marlin (who created the first ethical mutual fund in 1968) and counts among its influential advisors economist Lester C. Thurow, pollster Daniel Yankelovich, and Paul Warnke, a former high-ranking arms-control diplomat and advisor to the U.S. government. The CEP conducts its own research into corporate ethical behaviour, and is a clearinghouse for the research of other agencies and individuals. It publishes the monthly CEP *Newsletter* and many special reports; and in 1986 produced *Rating America's Corporate Conscience*, a seminal analysis of the ethical standards of companies making toothpaste, detergents, peanut butter, and dozens of other everyday products.

Interfaith Center on Corporate Responsibility
475 Riverside Drive #566

New York, N.Y. 10115

(212) 870-2936

Interfaith, headed up by Tim Smith, a Canadian expatriate, co-ordinates the filing of shareholder resolutions on corporate social-responsibility issues lodged by churches; operates a clearinghouse on alternative investments for churches seeking to invest in projects that aid the poor; and publishes a monthly newsletter, *The Corporate Examiner.*

Ethics Resource Center

1025 Connecticut Ave. N.W.

Ste. 1003

Washington, D.C. 20036

(202) 223-3411

Highly respected by the business community almost to the point of being a pillar of the corporate establishment, the Ethics Resource Center is a sanctuary of solace and advice on corporate ethics that blue-chip corporations turn to in troubled times. In addition to conducting its own research and advocacy activities in the field of corporate social awareness, the Center often is called upon to dispatch one of its own advisors or an independent counsellor to companies that find themselves embroiled in ethics-related controversies.

National Boycott Newsletter

6506 28th Ave. N.E.

Seattle, Washington, 98115

(206) 523-0421

The *National Boycott Newsletter* tracks the scores of boycotts directed against U.S. companies at any given time. Todd Putnam, editor of the quarterly publication (annual subscription: US$5), tries not to take sides and dispassionately reports both sides of the disputes he covers. But Putnam is indelibly supportive of boycotts as a tactic for corporate reform, closing letters to his subscribers with the cheery salutation, "Happy Boycotting".

Investor Responsibility Research Center

1755 Massachusetts Ave. N.W.

Ste. 600

Washington, D.C. 20036

(202) 939-6500

The IRRC produces background research on issues related to shareholder resolutions for institutional investors, and publishes a monthly newsletter (*News for Investors*) and research reports on corporate responsibility issues.

Franklin Research & Development Corp.

711 Atlantic Ave.
Boston, Mass. 02111
(617) 423-6655

Franklin is an investment advisory firm specializing in socially-responsible investing. It publishes the newsletter *Insight* and generates published analyses of the social records of industries and individual companies.

Social Investment Forum

711 Atlantic Ave.
Boston, Mass. 02111
(617) 423-6655

This coalition of individual and institutional investors and corporate ethics advocates publishes a sellers' guide to socially responsible investment advisors and funds.

CORPORATE CHARITABLE NETWORK AGENCIES

The following organizations publish lists of charities that meet their standards, and also produce reports on about four hundred philanthropic institutions:

Philanthropic Advisory Service of the Council of Better Business Bureaus

1515 Wilson Blvd.
Arlington, Virginia 22209

National Charities Information Bureau

19 Union Square West
New York, N.Y. 10003

The following association consists of more than one hundred organizations offering aid to charities overseas:

InterAction

200 Park Avenue South
New York, N.Y.
10003

Bibliography

Aarsteinsen, Barbara. "Business giving outpaced by needs", *Globe and Mail*, Dec. 10, 1986.

Abley, Mark. "Mr. Right", *Canadian Business*, May 1987.

Baida, Peter. "Dreiser's fabulous tycoon", *Forbes*, Oct. 27, 1986.

Baldwin, William. "Morality plays", *Forbes*, July 29, 1985.

Bamford, Janet. "When do you blow the whistle?", *Forbes*, Oct. 21, 1985.

Bates, Thomas. "To buy or not to buy: whether 'tis nobler to invest for financial returns or social concerns", *Manhattan, Inc.*, February 1986.

Baum, Laurie. "The job nobody wants", *Business Week*, Sept. 8, 1986.

Beam, Alex. "Why few ghetto factories are making it", *Business Week*, Feb. 16, 1987.

Behar, Richard, and Mark Clifford. "Kibitzing from the boardroom", *Forbes*, Feb. 10, 1986.

Behr, Peter. "Insider trading probe worries Wall Street", *Washington Post*, June 7, 1986.

Benson, Gary L. *On the campus: how well do business schools prepare graduates for the business world?*, New York: American Management Associates, 1983.

Best, Dunnery. "Probing the new corporate morality", *Financial Post*, Feb. 15, 1986.

Best, Patricia, and Ann Shortell. *A Matter of Trust: Power and Privilege in Canada's Trust Companies*, Markham, Ont.: Penguin Books Canada, 1985.

Bianco, Anthony. "Wall Street's frantic push to clean up its act", *Business Week*, June 9, 1986.

Bianco, Anthony, and Vicky Cahan. "It's war on insider trading", *Business Week*, May 26, 1986.

Bianco, Anthony, and Gary Weiss. "Suddenly the fish get bigger", *Business Week*, Mar. 2, 1987.

Bird, Frederick, and James A. Waters. "The nature of managerial moral standards", *Journal of Business Ethics*, 1986.

Blackwell, Richard, and Renate Lerch. "Picking up the pieces when brokers go wrong", *Financial Post*, Nov. 10, 1986.

Bleecker, Samuel E. *The Politics of Architecture: A Perspective on Nelson A. Rockefeller*, New York: The Rutledge Press, 1981.

Bott, Robert. "The scourge of the oil barons: how Ida Tarbell helped bust the trusts", *Canadian Business*, August 1982.

Braybrooke, David. *Ethics in the World of Business*, Totowa, N.J.: Rowman & Allanhead, 1983.

Brimelow, Peter. "The man Gulf poured on its troubled waters", *Maclean's*, Apr. 4, 1977.

Brody, Michael. "When products turn into liabilities", *Fortune*, Mar. 3, 1986.

———. "Listen to your whistleblower", *Fortune*, Nov. 24, 1986.

Broome Jr., Taft H. "The slippery ethics of engineering", *Washington Post*, Dec. 28, 1986.

Brown, Michael H. "Love Canal and the poisoning of America", *Atlantic*, December 1979.

Brown, Warren. "Stiffer penalty for odometer-changing", *Washington Post*, Oct. 29, 1986.

Cahan, Vicky. "The markets keep outracing the SEC", *Business Week*, June 2, 1986.

Cannon, Margaret. "Doing well by doing good", *Canadian Business*, March 1987.

Climenhaga, David. "Varity shareholders vote to stay in South Africa", *Globe and Mail*, June 11, 1987.

Coll, Steve. "The puzzling Wall Street saga of Dennis Levine", *Washington Post*, May 22, 1986.

Corcoran, Terence. "Dog's breakfast for tippors, tippees in Canada", *Financial Times*, Nov. 24, 1986.

Crawford, Trish. "Is business hearing the voice of ethics?", *Toronto Star*, June 22, 1986.

DeLamarter, Richard Thomas. *Big Blue*, New York: Dodd, Mead, 1986.

Dentzer, Susan, Carolyn Friday, Doug Tsuruoka, and Elaine Shannon. "Greed on Wall Street", *Newsweek*, May 26, 1986.

Dickinson, Roger, Anthony Herbst, and John O'Shaughnessy. "What are business schools doing for business?", *Business Horizons*, November-December 1983.

Dreyfack, Kenneth, Judith H. Dobrzynski, and Seth Payne. "The Crown family empire", *Business Week*, Mar. 31, 1986.

Dunn, David J. "Directors aren't doing their jobs", *Fortune*, Mar. 16, 1987.

Dwyer, Paula. "Is Justice bungling the defense-fraud crackdown?" *Business Week*, Apr. 21, 1986.

———. "The phony leaks that can move markets", *Business Week*, Sept. 29, 1986.

Fallows, James. "The case against credentialism", *Atlantic*, December 1985.

Ferguson, Jock. "Kickbacks a way of life, drug executive says", *Globe and Mail*, June 10, 1986.

———. "Living it up before judge's gavel falls", *Globe and Mail*, July 26, 1986.

———. "Tax credits $200 million bonanza for pros", *Globe and Mail*, Dec. 29, 1986.

Finlay, J. Richard. "Big business unfettered: a lust for size and power", *Globe and Mail*, Mar. 18, 1985.

Flanigan, James. "SEC attack on insider trading deserves kudos", *Los Angeles Times*, June 3, 1986.

Fleming, James. *Merchants of Fear: An Investigation of Canada's Insurance Industry*, Markham, Ont.: Penguin Books Canada, 1986.

Fong, Diana. "Learning to do it their way", *Forbes*, Dec. 15, 1986.

Frank, Allan Dodds, and Ralph King Jr. "Greed Inc.", *Forbes*, Dec. 29, 1986.

Franklin, Stephen. *The Heroes: A Saga of Canadian Inspiration*, Toronto: McClelland and Stewart, 1967.

Fraser, Graham. "Time to take stock", *Globe and Mail*, Feb. 21, 1987.

Frederick, William C. "Toward CSR$_3$: why ethical analysis is indispensable and unavoidable in corporate affairs:, *California Management Review*, Winter 1986.

Freudberg, David. *The Corporate Conscience: Money, Power, and Responsible Business*, New York: Amacom, 1986.

Friedman, Milton. "The social responsibility of business is to increase its profits", *New York Times Magazine*, Sept. 13, 1970.

Friedrich, Otto, Robert Rjemian, and Anne Constable. "Where there's smoke", *Time*, Feb. 23, 1987.

Friedrich, Otto, D.L. Coutu, Frederick Ungeheuer, et al. "The money chase: business school solutions may be part of the U.S. problem", *Time*, May 4, 1981.

Frons, Marc. "All Richard Branson wanted to be was a magazine editor . . .", *Business Week*, June 30, 1986.

Geneen, Harold S. "Why directors can't protect the shareholders", *Fortune*, Sept. 17, 1984.

Gherson, Giles. "Boesky affair fueling push for tougher rules", *Financial Post*, Nov. 24, 1986.

Gibb-Clark, Margot. "Magna's main man", *Globe and Mail*, Oct. 31, 1986.

Glaberson, William B., Peter Engardio, Stan Crock, Scott Ticer, et al. "A question of integrity at blue-chip law firms", *Business Week*, Apr. 7, 1986.

Glaberson, William B., and Christopher Farrell. "The explosion in liability lawsuits is nothing but a myth", *Business Week*, Apr. 21, 1986.

Glazer, Myron Peretz, and Penina Migdal Glazer. "Whistleblowing", *Psychology Today*, August 1986.

Goleman, Daniel. "The strange agony of success", *New York Times*, Aug. 24, 1986.

Goodpaster, Kenneth, and John B. Matthews Jr. "Can a corporation have a conscience?", *Harvard Business Review*, Jan.-Feb. 1982.

Gordon, Sheldon. "Pricking corporate consciences", *Report on Business Magazine*, July/Aug. 1985.

Granger, Alix. "Socially responsible investing—a fad or wave of future?", *Investor's Digest*, Nov. 26, 1985.

Gray, Malcolm, Peter Lewis, et al. "Death in Europe's grandest river", *Maclean's*, Nov. 24, 1986.

Greenwald, John, James Castelli, and Madeleine Nash. "Am I my brother's keeper? A letter by Catholic bishops on U.S. capitalism whips up a storm of controversy", *Time*, Nov. 26, 1984.

Hamper, Ben. "I, Rivethead", *Mother Jones*, September 1986.

Harris, Marlys. "Hutton's hidden asset", *Manhattan, Inc.*, July 1986.

Hart, Kenneth D. "Emerging new patterns of volunteerism", *Canadian Business Review*, Spring 1987.

Hemeon, Jade. "U.S. revelations force Canadian regulators to sharpen their watch", *Financial Post*, June 14, 1986.

Henry, Gordon M. "Dark clouds over Wall Street", *Time*, May 26, 1986.

Hitchings, Brad. "Feeling charitable? Find out where the money goes", *Business Week*, Nov. 17, 1986.

Hopkins, Thomas. "The case against lawyers", *Report on Business Magazine*, April 1986.

Hunter, Jennifer. "Insider penalties stiffer in new B.C. securities law", *Globe and Mail*, Jan. 29, 1987.

Inwood, Margaret. "Ethical investors opt for principles over profits", *Globe and Mail*, Jan. 2, 1987.

Janssen, Richard F. "The kingdom and power of J.P. Morgan", *Business Week*, Jan. 9, 1984.

Johnson, William. "For Washington mandarins prestige, not pay, the lure", *Globe and Mail*, May 19, 1986.

————. "Wealthy men get wealthier after tenure in Washington", *Globe and Mail*, May 20, 1986.

Kanner, Bernice. "What price ethics? The morality of the Eighties", *New York*, July 14, 1986.

Keating, Michael. "Where there's smoke — polluters beware: cleaning up the environment is an Ontario priority", *Globe and Mail*, Aug. 9, 1986.

Kempton, Murray. "A sad heart at the supermarket", *New York Review of Books*, Feb. 26, 1987.

Kirkland Jr., Richard J. "Britain's own Boesky case", *Fortune*, Feb. 16, 1987.

Kleinfield, N.R. "The whistleblowers' morning after", *Washington Post*, Nov. 9, 1986.

Koepp, Stephen, Gisela Bolte, and Frederick Ungeheuer. "Bracing for more bombshells", *Time*, Dec. 8, 1986.

Kornheiser, Tony. "Jeffrey Levitt and the frontiers of greed", *Washington Post Magazine*, Oct. 26, 1986.

Kurtz, Howard. "Reagan's people: issues of propriety", *Washington Post*, Apr. 27, 1986.

———. "Of ethics and enforcement: violators allegedly unpunished", *Washington Post*, Sept. 30, 1986.

LaBier, Douglas. "Madness stalks the ladder climbers", *Fortune*, Sept. 1, 1986.

Laderman, Jeffrey M. "A humbled Winans goes to the confessional", *Business Week*, Oct. 6, 1986.

Laderman, Jeffrey M., and Christopher Farrell. "Are the 'arbs' too cozy with insiders?" *Business Week*, June 16, 1986.

Lapham, Lewis H , Michael Novak, Walter B. Wriston, Robert Lekachman, and Peter Steinfels. "Is there virtue in profit?", *Harper's*, December 1986.

Leacock, Stephen. *Other People's Money*, Toronto, Royal Trust Co., 1947.

Lees, David. "Besieging the banks", *Canadian Business*, September 1986.

———. "Club lead", *Toronto Life*, December 1986.

———. "Filthy riches", *Canadian Business*, December 1986.

Lewis, Geoff. "Is IBM's real secret a genius for monopoly?", *Business Week*, Nov. 17, 1986.

Lieberman, Jethro K. "The land of the fleeced, the home of the knave", *Business Week*, July 26, 1976.

Little, Bruce, and Christopher Waddell. "Estey harsh on auditors in report", *Globe and Mail*, Oct. 25, 1986.

Loomis, Carol J. "The Rockefellers: end of a dynasty?", *Fortune*, Aug. 4, 1986.

Louis, Arthur M. "The unwinnable war on insider trading", *Fortune*, July 13, 1981.

Love, John F. *McDonald's: Behind the Arches*, New York: Bantam Books, 1986.

Lydenberg, Steven D., Alice Tepper Marlin, Sean O'Brien Strub, and the Council on Economic Priorities. *Rating America's Corporate Conscience: A Provocative Guide to the Companies Behind the Products You Buy Every Day*, Reading, Mass.: Addison-Wesley Publishing, 1986.

Mactaggert, R. Terrence, Dr. Donald W. Kelly, Peter Broadmore,

‍

Dr. Lee E. Preston, and The Niagara Institute. *Royal Commission on Corporate Concentration, Study No. 21: Corporate Social Performance in Canada*, Ottawa: Supply and Services Canada, 1977.

Magnet, Myron. "The decline and fall of business ethics", *Fortune*, Dec. 8, 1986.

Makin, Kirk. "$1 million fine sought over false ads", *Globe and Mail*, June 10, 1983.

———. "Diamond ads bring record penalty, Simpsons-Sears is fined $1 million", *Globe and Mail*, July 1, 1983.

———. "Open season: more and more Canadians breaking the laws they want changed", *Globe and Mail*, Dec. 6, 1986.

Manchester, William. *The Glory and the Dream*, Boston: Little, Brown, 1974.

Mathias, Philip. "Sindona: his epitaph should read 'The greatest thief in the history of the world'", *Financial Post*, Apr. 12, 1986.

Maynard, Rona. "Tightwads Ltd.", *Report on Business Magazine*, April 1987.

———. "Power sharing", *Toronto*, May 1987.

McMonagle, Duncan. "Jail tobaco executives, group urges", *Globe and Mail*, Mar. 11, 1987.

McQueen, Rod. "The bailout of Bruce McLaughlin", *Canadian Business*, May 1984.

———. "The outsider", *Canadian Business*, August 1985.

———. "Crisis, what crisis?", *Toronto Life*, April 1986.

Melcher, Richard A., Mark Maremont, and Rose Brady. "How Guinness suddenly fell from grace", *Business Week*, Feb. 9, 1987.

Mintz, Morton. *At Any Cost: Corporate Greed, Women and the Dalkon Shield*, New York: Pantheon Books, 1985.

———. "Merige reprimands A.H. Robins officer", *Washington Post*, June 7, 1986.

———. "Robins tripled dividend during difficult years", *Washington Post*, Aug. 15, 1986.

Murray, Alan. "New book rates consumer firms on social issues", *Wall Street Journal*, Jan. 16, 1982.

Murray, Alex. *Great Financial Disasters*, London: Arthur Barker, 1985.

Nash, Laura L. "Ethics without the sermon", *Harvard Business Review*, November-December 1981.

Newman, Peter C. *Flame of Power: Intimate Portraits of Canada's Greatest Businessmen*, Toronto: Longmans, Green, 1959.

————. *Bronfman Dynasty: The Rothschilds of the New World*, Toronto: McClelland and Stewart, 1978.

————. *The Establishment Man: A Portrait of Power*, Toronto: McClelland and Stewart, 1982.

Nickel, Herman. "The corporation haters", *Fortune*, June 16, 1980.

Noah, Timothy. "The business ethics debate", *Newsweek*, May 25, 1987.

Norris, William C. *New Frontiers for Business Leadership*, Minneapolis: Dorn Books, 1983.

Nussbaum, Bruce, and Judith H. Dobrzynski. "The battle for corporate control", *Business Week*, May 18, 1987.

Nussbaum, Bruce, Kathleen Failla, Christopher S. Elkund, Alex Beam, James R. Norman, Kathleen Deveny, et al. "The end of corporate loyalty?", *Business Week*, Aug. 4, 1986.

O'Farrell, Stephen. "The business of art", *Metropolitan Toronto Business Journal*, July-August 1985.

Oldenburg, Don. "Profiting above the bottom line", *Washington Post*, July 25, 1986.

Otten, Alan L. "Ethics on the job: companies alert employees to potential dilemmas", *Wall Street Journal*, July 14, 1986.

Painton, Frederick, Don Kirk, and Ellen Wallace. "Red flows the Rhine", *Time*, Nov. 24, 1986.

Partridge, John, and Murray Campbell. "'Marvellous scheme' netted car, cash", *Globe and Mail*, Apr. 19, 1986.

Payne, Seth. "Paying a pretty penny for air-safety problems", *Business Week*, Sept. 8, 1986.

Payne, Seth, Dave Griffiths, and Lois Therrien. "Insider trading: the limits of self-policing", *Business Week*, June 23, 1986.

Philipps, Peter. "When a broker takes a client for a ride", *Business Week*, Feb. 25, 1985.

Potts, Mark. "1st Jersey Agrees to pay $10 million settlement", *Washington Post*, Jan. 17, 1987.

Powell, Bill. "The new dealmakers", *Newsweek*, May 26, 1986.

Power, Christopher, and Vicky Cahan. "Shareholders aren't just rolling over anymore", *Business Week*, Apr. 27, 1987.

Prokesch, Steven. "Remaking the American CEO", *New York Times*, Jan. 25, 1987.

Quirk, Rory. "Journal of a moral bankrupt", *Washington Post*, Sept. 28, 1986.

Randolph, Eleanor. "Foster home", *Manhattan, Inc.*, January 1987.

Read, Deborah. "Canada's top investor", *Financial Times of Canada*, Mar. 10, 1986.

Rehder, Robert. "The creative MBA: a new proposal for balancing the science and the art of management", *Business Horizons*, November-December 1983.

Root, Laurie. "The desertmakers", *Forbes*, Oct. 27, 1986.

Roseman, Ellen. "Shoppers favor firms with a heart", *Globe and Mail*, Feb. 24, 1987.

Ross, Alexander. "Toward the pure portfolio: the search for ethical investments in a wicked, wicked world", *Canadian Business*, May 1986.

————. "Family benefits: making the workplace a good place for parents", *Canadian Business*, April 1987.

Ross, Irwin. "How lawless are big companies?", *Fortune*, Dec. 1, 1980.

Ross, Val. "The arrogance of Inco", *Canadian Business*, May 1979.

Russell, George, Gisela Bolte, Michael Riley, and Frederick Ungeheuer. "Going after the crooks", *Time*, Dec. 1, 1986.

Russell, George, Gisela Bolte, and Frederick Ungeheuer. "The fall of a Wall Street superstar", *Time*, Nov. 24, 1986.

Salter, Michael. "Insider trading, Canadian style", *Report on Business Magazine*, May 1987.

Saporito, Bill. "Cutting costs without cutting people", *Fortune*, May 25, 1987.

Sassen, Jane. "Who's paying for Bob Brennan's American Dream?", *Business Week*, Nov. 18, 1985.

Schafer, Arthur. "Morals in the rat race", *Globe and Mail*, Feb. 27, 1987.

Seligman, Daniel. "The system keeps on succeeding", *Fortune*, Sept. 15, 1986.

Sferrazza, Carl Anthony. "First ladies amid the fray", *Washington Post*, Dec. 28, 1986.

Shames, Laurence. "Devil's work", *Esquire*, July 1982.

Shapiro, Walter, Barrett Seaman, Laurence J. Barrett, et al. "What's wrong: hypocrisy, betrayal and greed unsettle the nation's soul", *Time*, May 25, 1987.

Sherman, Stratford P. "Travail at Drexel Burnham", *Fortune*, Dec. 22, 1986.

Shortell, Ann. "The auditors", *Canadian Business*, New York: November 1986.

Shulman, Morton. *The Billion Dollar Windfall*, New York: William Morrow, 1970.

Simpson, Janice C. "United Way turns to small business as support wanes at some big firms", *Wall Street Journal*, Jan. 8, 1987.

Slocum, Dennis. "Some say TSE's bark is worse than its bite", *Globe and Mail*, June 21, 1986.

Smith, Adam. "Wall Street's outrageous fortunes", *Esquire*, April 1987.

Smith, Lee. "The unsentimental corporate giver", *Fortune*, Sept. 21, 1981.

Solman, Paul. "The lore of money", *Manhattan, Inc.*, October 1986.

Stein, Harry. "On becoming Mr. Ethics", *Esquire*, June 1980.

————. "Between good and evil", *Esquire*, July 1981.

————. "The fuel of success", *Esquire*, August 1981.

————. "Easy money, easy virtue", *Esquire*, September 1981.

————. "The struggle not to sell out", *Esquire*, September 1985.

Stern, Richard L. "The golden boy", *Forbes*, July 16, 1984.

————. "Bye-bye Bob Brennan", *Forbes*, Dec. 29, 1986.

Stern, Richard L., and Matthew Schifrin. "Crime wave", *Forbes*, June 29, 1987.

Story, Jane. "Seeking socially sound profits", *Now*, Feb. 26-Mar. 4, 1987.

Stroud, Carsten. "Do what's fair", *Canadian Business*, April 1987.

Stubbing, Richard. "Uncompetitive bidders", *Washington Post*, Aug. 31, 1986.

Tasini, Jonathan. "The clamor to make punishment fit the corporate crime", *Business Week*, Feb. 10, 1986.

————. "Playing with pension funds: what's the limit?", *Business Week*, Nov. 17, 1986.

Tell, Lawrence J. "Making punishment fit white-collar crime", *Business Week*, June 15, 1987.

Toffler, Barbara Ley. *Tough Choices: Managers Talk Ethics*, New York: John Wiley and Sons, 1986.

Toole, David, and Ann Shortell. "Why the boss steals", *Maclean's*, June 30, 1986.

Tuleja, Tad. *Beyond the Bottom Line: How Business Leaders are Turning Principles into Profits*, New York: Facts on File Publications, 1985.

Tully, Shawn. "The lifestyle of Rich, the infamous", *Fortune*, Dec. 22, 1986.

Valentine, Paul W. "Levitt sentenced to 30 years for theft from S&L", *Washington Post*, July 3, 1986.

Vasoff, James D. "From bicycle heaven to shareholder hell", *CA magazine*, March 1987.

Vogel, David. "The study of social issues in management: a critical appraisal", *California Management Review*, Winter 1986.

Wallace, G. David, Stan Crock, et al. "The heat's on banks that shortchange customers", *Business Week*, Oct. 14, 1985.

Waters, James A. "Catch 20.5: corporate morality as an organizational phenomenon", *Organizational Dynamics*, Spring 1978.

Waters, James A., and Frederick Bird. "The moral dimension of organizational culture", *Journal of Business Ethics*, 1986.

Waters, James A., Frederick Bird, and Peter D. Chant. "Everyday moral issues experienced by managers", *Journal of Business Ethics*, 1986.

Waters, James A., and Peter D. Chant. "Internal control of managerial integrity: beyond accounting systems", *California Management Review*, 1982.

Weiner, Andrew. "Dollars to donors: Revenue Canada helps those who help charities", *Financial Post Moneywise Magazine*, March 1987.

Wellemeyer, Marilyn. "The joys of closeup philanthropy", *Fortune*, Sept. 1, 1986.

Welles, Chris. "Why the E.F. Hutton scandal may be far from over", *Business Week*, Feb. 24, 1986.

———. "What's behind Bob Brennan's sudden exit at First Jersey", *Business Week*, Aug. 18, 1986.

———. "A big crack in the 'Chinese wall'", *Business Week*, Mar. 2, 1987.

Welles, Chris, and Gary Weiss. "A man who made a career of tempting fate", *Business Week*, Dec. 1, 1986.

Wilentz, Amy, and David Beckwith. "Through the wringer: a Senate panel questions Rehnquist on race and his past", *Time*, Aug. 11, 1986.

Williams, Monci Jo. "How to cash in on do-good pitches", *Fortune*, June 9, 1986.

———. "What's legal—and what's not", *Fortune*, Dec. 22, 1986.

Wilson, Deborah. "See movers, shakers up on their toes", *Globe and Mail*, Oct. 16, 1986.

———. "Biggest PR bang for buck", *Globe and Mail*, Oct. 31, 1986.

Winsor, Hugh. "Controlling the damage: Mulroney's greatest challenge", *Globe and Mail*, Jan. 24, 1987.

Witten, Mark. "Revolt of the minority shareholders", *Toronto Life*, December 1980.

Woodcock, George. *100 Great Canadians*, Edmonton: Hurtig Publishers, 1980.

Worthy, Fred S. "Wall Street's spreading scandal", *Fortune*, Dec. 22, 1986.

Zaslow, Jeffrey. "Market mover: rumors Reagan died can swing prices", *Wall Street Journal*, Oct. 3, 1986.

Zwarun, Suzanne. "The Peter principle, *Canadian Business*, May 1986.

INDEX